Fix What You Can

Fix
What
You
Can

Schizophrenia
and a
Lawmaker's Fight
for Her Son

Mindy Greiling

UNIVERSITY OF MINNESOTA PRESS
MINNEAPOLIS • LONDON

A companion study guide for this book is available at z.umn.edu/mg_guide.

Published by the University of Minnesota Press
111 Third Avenue South, Suite 290
Minneapolis, MN 55401-2520
http://www.upress.umn.edu

Printed in the United States of America on acid-free paper

The University of Minnesota is an equal-opportunity educator and employer.

25 24 23 22 21 20   10 9 8 7 6 5 4 3 2 1

Library of Congress Cataloging-in-Publication Data
Greiling, Mindy, author.
Fix what you can : schizophrenia and a lawmaker's fight for her son / Mindy Greiling.
Minneapolis : University of Minnesota Press, [2020] | Summary: "An illuminating
    and frank account of caring for a person with a mental illness, told by a parent and
    advocate."
Identifiers: LCCN 2020020385 (print) | ISBN 978-1-5179-0959-8 (pb)
Subjects: LCSH: Greiling, Mindy. | Schizophrenia—Minnnesota—Biography. |
    Schizophrenia—Family relationships—Minnesota. | Schizophrenia—Mental health
    services—Minnesota. | Parents of mentally ill children—Minnesota—Biography. |
    Legislators—Minnesota—Biography.
Classification: LCC RC514 .G6954 2020 (print) | DDC 616.89/80092 [B]—dc23
LC record available at https://lccn.loc.gov/2020020385

To Jim

Contents

Our Story

When publicity first broke about our son Jim's mental illness, I was besieged by desperate families asking for advice. I could listen and empathize, but the truth was that I didn't know where to turn any more than they did. Over the next twenty years, my family and I worked tirelessly to help Jim navigate the tangled, often dysfunctional web of Minnesota's mental health system. It became clear early on that the resources needed to help Jim succeed just weren't there. We struggled to understand why the laws in place to care for people like him were so inadequate. As a state legislator, I was fortunate to be able to channel my frustration into action and to enact some of the changes the mental health system so desperately needs.

There is no better lobbyist than a lawmaker. For good reason, savvy advocates develop a glint in the eye when they learn a legislator has personal experience. Elected officials work hard to pass legislation that benefits others, but they work even harder when they see the need in their own lives. A lawmaker whose elderly parents reside in a nursing home, whose sibling has a developmental disability, or whose child dies from an opioid overdose is a formidable ally. The late Minnesota representative Gloria Segal, who, like me, had a son with mental illness, started to improve the Minnesota mental health system before I arrived at the Capitol. I'm proud to have continued her important work.

My story is centered in Minnesota but reflects larger issues in the treatment of mental health in communities across the country. In 2013, for example, State Senator Creigh Deeds focused a bright light on Virginia's mental health system after he was nearly killed by his untreated psychotic son, who then committed suicide. Every national legislative conference on mental illness that I have attended has been populated by inspired lawmakers who have personal experience with the problem.

I was driven to write this book as a way to help others and to further the conversation on mental illness. It would not have been possible without Jim's willing help. As he said once when we saw a troubled young man on the street, he feels deep sympathy for people who have just discovered they have a serious mental illness: they have so much to learn about the system. Jim was the first reader of most of these chapters and edited the whole manuscript twice. Schizophrenia and related severe mental illnesses are often misrepresented. His advice, approval, and support were essential and allowed me to continue. This is his story as much as mine, and I am indebted to him for helping me get it right.

Though I am now retired from the Minnesota legislature, I continue to advocate for new reforms to the mental health system. While I am often recognized for my legislative work, I am first and foremost a mother who tries her best. No one—and certainly not me—has pat answers to the challenges that accompany mental illness. Sharing my family's story has become the most important part of my advocacy. I know from experience that this kind of personal witness is what works best to move elected officials to act. In the following pages, I have changed the names of some individuals or used only their first names to protect their privacy.

This is my story. It is Jim's story too. Many parts overlap with everyone's story.

=

I doubt I would have written this book were it not for my good friend Judy Berglund, who invited me to join her writing group shortly before I left the legislature. This incredible group nurtured my fledgling interest in writing and helped my storytelling grow. In addition to Judy, this group consisted of Lucinda Cummings, Leif Johnson, Phyllis Kahn, Pete Magee, Ann Nerland, Douglas Victoria, and Krista Westendorp.

For reading, editing, and commenting on the manuscript and cheering me on, I thank daughter Angela Greiling Keane, David Greiling (two readings), Barbara Greiling, Ann Greiling, husband Roger Greiling (who always has my back), Jean Brookins, Charlene Roemhildt, Dr. Megan (Gunnar) Dahlberg, Mary McLeod, Claire Jordan, Reed Jordan, and Sue Abderholden, executive director of the National Alliance on Mental Illness Minnesota (NAMI–MN).

Hugs to granddaughter Taylor Keane, who always said she believed in me.

Special thanks to quintessential people-connector daughter Angela for introducing me to these people who were crucial to getting the story published: mensch Paul Von Drasek, Jane Isay, Meg Waite Clayton, and Terry Golway. I also owe thanks to William Kent Krueger. All these generous people love books and relish finding the right homes for them.

The encouragement of friends and relatives too numerous to list also kept me going. Thank you all.

Thanks to the Loft Literary Center, the epicenter of writing in the Twin Cities. My manuscript editors were wonderful Loft teachers, and my writing group formed and meets there. Mary Carroll Moore taught me how to write a book, and Kate Hopper enhanced the story and taught me how to express my feelings.

Thanks to the deservedly lauded University of Minnesota Press for publishing this story, and especially to Kristian Tvedten, my brilliant editor. He polished the manuscript until it glistened and made it universal. Copy editor extraordinaire Kathy Delfosse made it perfect.

Finally, thanks to Dr. Megan (Gunnar) Dahlberg, who opened doors and connected me to Josh Mervis, the talented University of Minnesota researcher, teacher, and PhD candidate who wrote the study guide that accompanies this book. This guide is available at z.umn.edu/mg_guide.

Prologue

Drive into that car parked over there.

A white Honda Accord is parked in front of a two-story 1940s clapboard house. The house is still, like the warm spring night, and shrouded in dark shadows.

Just turn the wheel to the left and head straight for it.

"I can't. I need my wheels," the tall young man replies, driving on. "Might total them both."

What's more important—a sucker like you getting to your pathetic job or saving the human race? Crash into that Chevrolet!

The station wagon swerves but passes that car too. It's an hour after midnight, the desperate time.

"Please," the young man pleads, the older man's voice reverberating in his ears. "I can't do it."

Stop being such a fucking screwup—like you always are—and ram the next car, for Christ's sake. Do something right for a change, asshole. That Toyota, the one sitting at the stop sign.

"But there's people in it."

Do it now or the universe will be lost, no eternal bliss for anyone. You'll burn in hell forever. Without your soul mate. You'll never see Hestia again. This is your last chance.

The old wagon picks up velocity, careens into the oncoming lane of traffic, and blasts through the stop sign. Headlights reflect off two pairs of terrified eyes just before the wagon crashes into the Toyota, full force, head on. The sound of breaking glass shatters the night, metal crunches, and a burnt-chemical smell permeates the humid night air.

Then silence.

Part I

1
The Call

May 8, 2000

Soon I would have time to straighten out the mess in our house. Letters and messages from my constituents, piles of reports I should have read, newspapers, and campaign materials cluttered almost every room in our home and even the garage. And I needed to get Jim sorted out. We hadn't heard from our twenty-two-year-old son for days. A condition of his returning to college in Montana the previous winter had been that he call home regularly. My shoulders ached from the constant tension of worrying about him. Thankfully, it was the last day of the legislative session.

I was packing up the papers I needed, preparing to leave for the Capitol in St. Paul, when the phone rang—Montana area code, but not Jim's number.

"This is your son's landlady." Her voice was brusque, and she pushed on without waiting for my response. "Do you know what's happened?"

Sunshine pouring in the kitchen window suddenly seemed blinding. Was Jim dead? Had he overdosed? Those were the only reasons I could think of at that moment to explain why his landlady would be calling. He had been diagnosed with schizophrenia the previous summer, but we were all relieved when the treatment he received in Minnesota let him resume his education at the University of Montana. With Dr. David Brown, a college psychologist, supporting him in Missoula, we hoped he would pull through. We were worried though, because—against his Minnesota doctor's advice—after Jim's civil commitment expired in December, he had stopped taking the antipsychotic medication that had stabilized him. Civil commitment was one of many new topics I had taken crash courses in during the past months. It's a legal process that ensured Jim would accept treatment and take his medicine despite his illness, which prevented him from understanding that he needed the help. He hadn't relapsed without the medication, as the doctor had expected, so he was able to return to school. My husband Roger and I had dared hope Jim would be one of the lucky ones. We hoped he would only suffer one psychotic episode and would then skate on to health. But he should have called by now to arrange for us to meet his train when he came home for the summer. I had been trying to bury my worry in my legislative work, but now all my angst blasted to the surface.

"We haven't heard from him lately. What's going on?"

"He was in court this morning. Came from the jail." The landlady's tone was filled with disdain. "I was there the whole time. Bail was set at $2,000. Your son was arraigned for breaking and entering, felony burglary."

Felony burglary? My stomach clenched, nearly stopping my breath. I sat down, raising a hand to my chest, where I could feel my heart pounding. "What happened?"

"He broke into one of my other apartments." She sniffed. "Looked like he used his kitchen chair to bash in a window, because the chair was sitting outside the window in a mess of glass." I thought, How desperate must our Jim have been to do something like that? I heard the crash, saw drops of my son's blood dripping, coating the glass in speckles of red. "Someone saw the broken glass and your son lying on a couch in the apartment they knew wasn't his and called the police."

"That doesn't sound like something he would do," I said, with little conviction. The summer before, Jim had used psychedelic mushrooms and marijuana before his psychotic break. Maybe he had begun feeling worse and had resorted to self-medicating with illegal drugs. I'd learned that for people with mental illness, that was a common practice when they felt wretched. My body trembled.

"He was discombobulated in court. He had a strange look on his face the whole time that creeped me out," the landlady continued. "He'll be in jail until sentencing and I don't want him to return to his apartment. Ever." Her voice went up several notches. "I'm frightened for my tenants."

"I'll talk with my husband," I said. Roger had left an hour earlier for work at one of the grocery stores where he did marketing research. I started making a second cup of coffee, using twice as many beans as for my earlier cup. I spilled some grounds on the counter, and when I wiped them up, I noticed my hands were shaking. "One of us will come to Montana tomorrow." I thought fast, imagining the long drive and the chaos awaiting me. "Can I stay at his apartment a night or two and collect some of his things?"

"I'll leave a key under the mat." She was quiet for a minute, as if she understood my feelings, and then added forcefully, "You have until the end of the month to get all his things out."

A breeze blew the smell of damp earth through the windows. Despite the overcast May sky, robins that had recently returned to Minnesota were chirping. Minutes before, I'd been reveling in hearing their familiar melody again, but now it grated on me like an incessant racket.

When I reached the Capitol a half hour later, I skipped my usual stop in my office and went straight to the House floor, making it to my seat just in time. I was in my fourth two-year term, but I had chosen to sit in a section mostly populated by junior members in order to mentor them. The enormous chamber is framed by spectacular historical paintings. Most days I was able to recenter myself simply by leaning back and gazing at the paintings and the ornate skylighted ceiling. Today my mind was spinning.

Just before the speaker called us to order, I heard a popular legislator who sat directly in front of me brag to his seatmate, "When we debate the crime bill, you'll hear my libertarian constituents cheering me on from up north." This legislator often tried to badger me into voting his district instead of mine, but today I didn't want him heckling me about crime and punishment.

As soon as the opening prayer and the Pledge of Allegiance ended, I dashed to the adjoining room, poured myself a cup of weak government coffee, and claimed one of the small desks where an old-fashioned black dial telephone sat. Seated at the desk with my back to the room, I called Dr. Brown.

"Jim cried a lot at our last appointment," the psychologist reported over the phone. The doctor paused and then heaved a long sigh. "He's been missing classes and says he's talking a lot with a man he met in town. I've seen this guy, and he has issues too." Dr. Brown, too, was shocked that Jim was in jail and promised to check on him and call me back.

After I hung up the phone, I turned to face the room full of legislators. I engaged in a bit of small talk with a colleague who was setting out boxes of birthday doughnuts on a large oak table. Soon I returned to my desk on the floor to pass the time. In less than half an hour, I was paged to take a call.

"I've read the police report," Dr. Brown said. "Sounds as if Jim's in bad shape. In and out of reality. I'm sorry. I thought he could make it a few more days. He hasn't been this bad for very long."

"You made your best judgment call," I said reassuringly, my voice belying the anger boring through my gut. "How could we blame you, when Roger and I are the ones who let him go back to Montana?" Idiots that we were, we'd wished away our son's mental illness. After the Minnesota doctor had given the green light to Jim's return to Montana, we hadn't even debated the idea.

"I thought he could handle it too," the psychologist said. "And he almost did. Up until very recently, he was doing well in his classes and was even tutoring another student in calculus." This was amazing news, more like the Jim from middle school who got straight As and had nice friends, Jim before he got depressed, starting dabbling in illicit drugs, and found new friends.

"What did the police report say?"

"When the officer who arrived at the scene asked, 'What's going on here, son?' Jim replied, 'I'm talking to a voice.' The officer said Jim was very cooperative as he escorted him to the jail."

Behind me, other legislators were coming into the room, talking in small groups. I lowered my voice. "I hate it that mental illness is so often dealt with in the judiciary system, instead of with health care."

"Unfortunately, that's very much the case. What you need right now is a good attorney," Dr. Brown advised. "In this state you can't trust a public defender."

"I know," I said, my voice turning husky. I knew from meeting legislators at conferences that the state of Montana would probably consider defending criminals a waste of resources. After I hung up, I looked around and greeted a few people. The boxes of birthday doughnuts still sat on the heavy oak table in the center of the room.

My next call was to Roger. I have always appreciated Roger's steadiness. I had picked him—and a predictable, even-keeled marriage—instead of the musician or the poet I'd been dating, both of them more exciting. I had known even back in 1970 that I needed a reliable life partner who wouldn't get overly excited when things went wrong. My family included a couple of volatile door bangers, not counting my Grandma Teddy. Dear Jesus, I needed Roger's ballast today.

I pictured him being paged in a grocery aisle full of boxes of crackers, notebook in hand. He was often mistaken for a grocer: his tieless permanent-press shirt, gray slacks, stomach paunch, and the work he did made him look like a store manager. When shoppers asked him where to find things, he amiably told them rather than bothering to explain.

"Why were we so quick to believe Jim was cured?" I lamented after I explained what had happened. I was somewhat comforted by repeating the story to Roger.

"Well, he's safe in jail for now," he said in a maddeningly calm tone. "Call one of the attorneys the psychologist suggested and I'll arrange to have enough cash in the account." In addition to being the steadying force in our marriage, Roger was its money man.

"One of us has to go to Montana," I said, "but the other one has to visit Angela."

Our daughter Angela lived in Washington, D.C., where she had easily nabbed her first reporting job after a plum internship there. We had been planning for weeks to fly to meet her boyfriend, Matt, who we correctly suspected would become her fiancé. Angela was twenty-four, two years older than Jim. Photos she sent of Matt showed a trim, fetching young mechanical engineer with muscular arms, military-short brown hair, and a friendly, toothy smile. I'd been counting the days until we could say hello in person and give our daughter a big congratulatory hug.

"We already missed one visit to D.C. because of Jim," I continued. "We don't want her to come to resent him. And since I'm the one who has been dealing with his medical people, I guess it has to be me who goes to Montana and you who goes to D.C." This decision broke my heart. Angela was sentimental about many things, certainly including her family. I knew that my not meeting Matt this first time would hurt her.

Roger agreed, almost too quickly, I thought. I had always been the alpha parent and Roger the breadwinner, so it was natural for him to expect me to handle Jim's problems. But now they were too challenging for one parent alone—a fact Roger didn't seem to recognize yet.

Jail. I couldn't get my head around the fact that the sweet boy we raised was actually in jail. I would have to drive twelve hundred miles to Montana by myself, go to the jail to see Jim, meet with the attorney, and go to court, where I would see our son standing before a judge. I suspected the drive back would be the most frightening of all. People who disrupted flights could get in trouble, Dr. Brown had warned, so I would have to drive Jim home, even if he was psychotic.

I resented the fact that Roger had the easier assignment. I was concerned that he wouldn't do as good a job as I would have. He wouldn't gush to Angela in a private moment about Matt. He wasn't a touchy-feely person. He would shake Matt's hand and hug his daughter with one arm, lightly patting her on the back with the other. I would have to wait before I could assess the look in my future son-in-law's eyes when he gazed at my striking blonde daughter. Roger wouldn't notice such things.

After I hung up from Roger, I engaged an attorney and then sank into one of the chairs in the retiring room. The doughnuts were almost gone, and the lingering sugary smell made me nauseous. Televisions in two corners of the room blared the chamber floor debate from the next room, but I was oblivious, unaware that the judiciary bill was up until the popular legislator from northern Minnesota sat at my table.

"I bet you're going to vote for this bill," he immediately accused. He had a pleasant voice, one that could leave you unsure whether he was joking or angry. "You and all the other suburban legislators think you need to be tough on crime, and you won't be happy until everyone's in jail." I stared at him, as my eyes filled with tears and my face melted like wax on a cheap candle. Before I could censor myself, I brayed, "My son's in jail."

2
Alarm Bells

A couple of years before, Jim had been subdued when I dropped him off in northern Wisconsin for his sophomore year at Northland College. It had taken more than three hours to drive there from our home near St. Paul. Jim stood six feet four inches tall and was handsome, with dark eyebrows, a cleft chin, blue eyes that girls loved, and thick, wavy, light-brown hair. His strong, twenty-year-old body was well proportioned, with muscular legs from years of hiking, backpacking, and mountain biking.

He and three friends had rented a grand Victorian house near the college campus. He was sharing a large upstairs room with a fellow who had told me the previous summer that Jim was the best friend he'd ever had. Jim typically had just one good friend at a time, an unsettling contrast to his older sister's swarm of friends. In high school, she had been captain of three sports teams and the student school board representative.

One of Jim's housemates, a strapping blond boy about his size, arrived shortly after we did. Wearing tan bibbed overalls and a flannel shirt, he was typical of Jim's friends: hardy, anything but preppy, and not forthcoming with adults.

"Hey," the boy smiled at Jim, his look portending more than I could grasp.

"Hey, man," Jim greeted him. "Good summer?"

"Yeah, lots of action," he said, glancing at me. "You?"

"I had to work but got in a small trip to Montana with a couple of guys. Not enough time in the mountains to get healthy, but it helped." Jim said that when he felt down, mountain air healed him. He was attuned to his body and often sought ways to try to feel better. He confessed to me a couple of years after this conversation that once when he had looked in the mirror when he was eleven, he'd thought, "Something's wrong." That was four years before he started using drugs and ten years before he was diagnosed with mental illness.

It was ironic that Jim had become an inveterate camper: he had dropped out of Cub Scouts in sixth grade, after his first camping weekend with Roger, when it rained nonstop. Roger admitted he'd been bored huddling in their small tent, so I suspected his attitude hadn't helped Jim's outlook. Four years later he had only agreed to go on a YMCA backpacking trip under duress.

Jim finally introduced me to his housemate. I left shortly afterward, giving my son a quick hug and telling him to keep in touch. Jim used to be a mama's boy who clung to my hand long past when most kids did. He still didn't quite have his life together. If he went too long without calling, I felt a touch of anxiety for his well-being. I never felt that way about his sister.

As I closed the door, I heard, "Come on, Jim. The party tonight will be cool. Lots of women and booze."

"I'm tired. Another time."

"Really?" The blond boy sounded as incredulous as I felt.

Jim had always preferred small groups. Even as a small boy, he had never liked large birthday parties or crowds, but this seemed excessive even for him. During the long drive home, as I flipped through radio channels, I pondered why a young man like Jim—in the heyday of his youth—would choose to spend his first night back on campus alone. The coffee I was drinking soured in my stomach.

One of our son's ninth-grade teachers had warned us at a parent–teacher conference that when the class discussed drugs, Jim and a friend had exchanged looks that clearly revealed they were already using. The serious teacher regarded Roger and me with fierce disappointment when we just sat there blankly. My mind was reeling, but before I could process this information, our time was up. We had to move on to the next table, where another teacher was waiting. As we went, other parents hailed me, their newly minted state representative—driving concern from the center of my mind. None of Jim's other teachers mentioned anything amiss. Most amiably lauded our son or even discussed a bit of politics. In the hubbub of our lives, Roger and I never discussed the serious teacher's warning, which I have always regretted. What if we had done something then?

A couple of years later, we were forced to admit we had to do something. Jim was sentenced to two separate bouts of community service. Roger and I felt the first episode was little more than an adolescent prank. He and a friend had soaked a tennis ball with gasoline and set it on fire. When a neighbor called the police, the boys ran, compounding their stupidity. The neighbor, from past experience, was already wary of Jim's friend. The police told Roger and me that we should be too. "Your son's in bad company," the officer at the station had warned. The next year, Jim and two friends had damaged a classmate's front door. The boy had refused to come out of his house to take his punishment for horning in on someone's girlfriend. After the first incident, I took Jim to a summer resort for a week of intensive parenting. The following year, during his sophomore summer, we sent him to a YMCA camp where he would be far away from those friends and the drug scene. He grumbled about going but ended up loving it. He went happily his final two high school summers. It was after the senior year trip that Roger and I had first noticed that Jim was abnormally quieter than the other rowdy returning campers. It made us uneasy.

=

Four months after I had dropped Jim off at Northland College and he'd chosen to spend that first night alone, he came home for the winter holidays. He didn't have much to say. His semester grades were middling, like his high school grades.

"How do you like your environmental studies major?" I asked, as I sliced vegetables for our dinner salad.

"I'm thinking of switching next year to computer programing," he said, reaching for a piece of carrot. The lights from our Christmas tree cast a green-and-red glow on his shirt.

"That sounds like a great fit for you," I said, thinking of his penchant for small groups and solitude. "Why don't you talk to David next door while you're home? He's a computer programmer. Or Adam's dad?"

"Nah, I'm just thinking about it."

"Remember how Angela got interested in being a reporter after she shadowed one?"

"Mom, knock it off."

Angela had been working on a Girl Scout badge requirement in elementary school when she observed the reporter. Jim was a Cub Scout dropout, I thought uneasily. His future seemed invisible to me.

Jim and I remained close, but he liked to talk to me on his own terms. After he had started using drugs in middle school, he walled off that part of his life. Now, apparently, he felt the same way about my prying into his nebulous future.

After the vacation ended and Jim returned to school, I put these thoughts aside. I threw myself into calling my volunteer committee together to plan for our next reelection campaign. Suburban seats like mine were hard-won. The campaign filled almost every spare moment.

In the spring, Jim called to say there had been a fire at their house. Someone needed to come. I drew the short straw again since the legislature had adjourned. As I drove up, thoughts of the time Jim and his friend had set the tennis ball on fire flitted through my mind. I told myself it wasn't relevant, but my taut muscles said different.

When I arrived, I saw Jim in the backyard smoking, slumped against his stuffed backpack. He looked lost, just as he'd looked when Angela, whom he adored, started preschool. "When's Iya coming home?" he would ask repeatedly, using the name he called her. There were few kids in our neighborhood, so they relied on each other.

Charred windows were visible on the back of the house. Jim's possessions spilled over the grass—his drum set, the ti plant he had brought from home last fall. Thinking of that hopeful day made me feel hollow.

When Jim saw me, he tossed away his butt, hefted the pack, and started purposefully toward the car.

"We weren't home when it happened," he said. "Our band was at an international festival." As we started driving, I smelled the reek of smoke baked into his things, the way little Jim used to smell after playing with a campfire. Our family had taken several happy trips to a resort in northern Minnesota when the kids were small, and there'd been many bonfires. "A neighbor saw smoke coming out a window and called the fire department." Jim winced. "Lucky thing or it'd be gone."

"I didn't know you were doing gigs." I thought of his band that had practiced rock music in our garage. Even though neighbors had once called the police about the racket, I loved having them there. It was a rare chance to meet some of his high school friends. Girls had gone wild when they played in the talent show. "What started the fire?"

"The fire department is still trying to figure that out. I have a vague image of seeing incense burning when we left." He added hastily, "It wasn't mine."

"Be glad for your thorough father," I said with a smile. "You have rental insurance." I wondered if they had been using drugs, covering up the smell with the incense. I realized I was clenching the steering wheel and deliberately relaxed my hands.

"Really? Cool." The first smile of the day spread across his face, reminding me of his little-boy sparkle.

"Hungry? We can talk about where you're going to stay over lunch. We need to get you settled before I leave." The warm spring days were long and my energy was high, so I planned to drive back that night.

"I can't stay here. I've had so much stress over this," he said, his tense voice matching his words. "I need to come home."

"There's only two more weeks for God's sake," I said, perplexed. "You can't forfeit the whole semester." I looked at him more closely but saw no sign he was faking to avoid finals. I remembered the time in sixth grade when he had warmed a thermometer on a heating pad, claiming to be too ill for school.

"Mom, please," he begged in a wavering voice that alarmed me. Jim usually took things more in stride. He was certainly not a crier.

"Greilings aren't quitters," I said, settling the matter but not my growing alarm. Roger and I had both been strictly raised to be responsible citizens and had tried to raise our children the same way. I couldn't recall Roger ever missing a day of work, and I felt the same way about my legislative work. Angela had had perfect attendance in high school.

Jim gave up his protest about coming home. We moved the things he needed into a friend's dorm room and I took the rest. As I drove off, I saw Jim in the rearview mirror looking forlorn. His face hovered in my mind the rest of the way home and kept me awake that night—I tossed and turned a long while before I could fall asleep, prompting Roger to change beds.

One of Jim's roommates later told me Jim had stayed in bed every day of those last two weeks of school. He skipped classes except when there was a final. In one class, the teacher had rescheduled the test date, but since he wasn't there for the announcement, he missed the exam. He begged the teacher to let him make it up, but she refused and gave him an F.

"The fucking bitch," Jim said with surprising hostility when he called. He'd always been our easygoing, mellow child. When Angela fussed about the color of a Christmas present if they had received the same thing in different colors, he would offer to trade.

"Do you think it's because Jim's smoking pot?" I wondered to Roger, after I shared my concerns. He was reading a newspaper on the deck.

"Possibly, but who didn't imbibe in college?" He looked up from his paper and smiled, probably recalling his beer-drinking days in Wisconsin, where he could drink at eighteen.

"I think it's more than that, but I don't really know what's going on." I kept standing near him, waiting. Usually I appreciated Roger's calming, matter-of-fact nature, but today I thought Jim's actions required more.

My husband is not one to share his feelings, but that doesn't mean he isn't sentimental about family. On one of our early dates, he had painstakingly shown me the contents of his wallet, including a photo of his Methodist parents seated in front of three serious-looking sons. Roger was oldest and tallest and the only one with red hair. He was also proud of his ticket stub from the Ice Bowl, the 1967 NFL championship game played in minus-thirteen-degree weather. He was from Green Bay so was bred as a devoted Packer fan. He still carries that tattered stub in his wallet.

When I could see Roger wasn't going to offer more about Jim, I slid open the deck door and returned to the house. I was too restless to finish the report I'd been reading, so I headed out the front door for a walk. The rhythm of my steps and the passing scenery helped soothe me.

When Jim returned home for the summer, he informed us that he and two friends were transferring to a college in Montana. When I started to protest, he said they had already been accepted.

=

The following fall, after Jim and I crossed the state line into Montana, he insisted on driving the rest of the way. "I've been looking forward to driving in this state." He smiled, ramping the car up to one hundred miles an hour.

"Slow down." I gasped, wondering what in the world he was thinking. "Do you want to get us killed?"

"Mom, you can drive as fast as you want in Montana. There's no speed limit."

"Jim! Pull over this minute. You're scaring me." My hand clenched the door handle and I braced my feet for impact.

He looked at me scornfully, laughing like a maniac squeezing a small critter, and kept going without easing off the gas.

"Just because there's no speed limit doesn't mean you get to go this fast," I yelled in gulps over the wind whipping through our open windows. "This is dangerous!" Had he smoked a joint in the bathroom at our last pit stop? This was not normal behavior for Jim. Was he high? I was petrified of his driving but even more so of how bizarrely he was acting. He slowed down a bit for a short while, but soon he was going just as fast.

Before we knew it, snow-capped mountains that had been visible in the distance for hours loomed directly in front of us. When we neared Missoula, Jim wove in and out of traffic, missing cars and a semitrailer truck by mere inches. Honks retaliated. My legs and hands continued shaking long after we finally reached our destination. For once I was glad to sit and wait for Jim to smoke two cigarettes in the gas station parking lot after I refueled our tank. I pushed the harrowing drive out of my mind and thought of my own happy college days.

I hoped that Jim would be happy here in Missoula. We found a cheap motel, unloaded our suitcases, and went for pizza. That night in our room, Jim took a shower before bed. I noticed that after his hair had dried it was still oily.

"Are you running low on shampoo?" I asked.

"Shampoo's full of chemicals," he lectured. "I don't use it. Water's the natural way."

Jim had gotten more environmentally conscious since he started college, but this seemed extreme. His hair got darker and greasier over the next few days. How long had this been going on? Jim had never been fussy about his possessions, but he had always been a bit vain about his appearance. He took pride in his personal cleanliness. Small stabs of anxiety shot through me, but again I put them out of my head. We had too much to do to dwell on it.

We found Jim an apartment the next day. I wished he'd accepted the invitation to live with his Wisconsin college mates who were also transferring here, but he insisted he wanted to live alone. Deep down, I was beginning to know that something was really amiss with our son. But maybe it was just his introversion?

Jim is an introvert like me. Roger and Angela are the extroverts in our family. When we stayed at the resort when Angela and Jim were small, Roger wanted the cabin directly in front of the main communal campfire where he could strike up conversations, usually about sports. I wanted the most private one at the far end where I could unwind by quietly reading books. Like me, Jim preferred peace and quiet, unless there was a campfire. I remember him with sand-covered bare feet, animatedly roasting marshmallows and poking sticks into the flames.

While we were buying his supplies, I was struck by how long it took Jim to decide what to buy. He stood for minutes staring blankly at the shelf of detergent. He took so long selecting everything that I didn't have time to help him put things away before I left. I felt guilty and uneasy leaving him standing amid boxes piled as high as his shoulders and shopping bags from various stores flooding the floor at his feet. The lost look in his eyes lingered heavily in my mind all the way home to the Minnesota prairie.

He called a couple weeks later. "I can't stand my apartment."

"Why not?" I continued stirring the cheese soup I was making for supper.

"The women next door are always talking about me."

"How do you know?"

"Thin walls," he said. "I can hear them through the walls. And they don't say nice things."

Cold fingers tightened around my spine. Thoughts of my Grandma Teddy, who heard voices, flickered through my mind.

"You said before that the women were nice. Don't they have better things to do than talk about you all the time?"

"They come into my place too."

"How can you tell?" I asked. My hand froze on the spoon. "How do they get in?"

"Things are missing," he said, his tone indignant. "They must have a spare key."

I felt as if someone were injecting ice water into my veins. I felt it spreading throughout my body. "What's missing?" I turned off the stove and sat down.

"Well, they move things around more than take them, I guess. Things are in different places when I come home. So that's why I'm calling," he added urgently. "To tell you I'm moving."

"Moving! What about the lease?"

"The landlord's letting me out of it. After I told him about the women, he was very nice about it."

I bet he was. Once he heard Jim prattling on like a crazy person he would have wanted to be rid of him fast. I stared blankly out the window.

"I told him so he can warn the next people what his other tenants are up to," Jim ran on. "I've found a new place, and my friends are helping me move Saturday. Everything's taken care of, so you don't need to worry."

"Jim," I moaned. "It's such a nice place. Are you sure this is necessary?"

"It's over, Mom."

After I hung up the phone, I measured out coffee and reached for Jim's favorite Santa Bear mug. I wrapped my cold fingers around the warm mug and went out on our deck, where I eased into a lounge chair. I breathed in the fragrant scent of acorns and dry oak leaves in the backyard.

This was not marijuana. This sounded like mental illness. Like my grandmother. I had thought I could face the idea of my son using drugs, but thinking of Jim having crazy ideas like hers made my bowels turn. Tears sprang to my eyes.

=

Mary Rittenhouse was my grandmother's name. We called her Grandma Teddy. She had lived in the duplex across the street from my family in Rochester, Minnesota. A tall woman for her day, Grandma had symmetrical, sculpted features and curly black hair. When she went to her job at a women's clothing store, she wore jewelry, rouge that made her cheeks flame, fancy shoes with heels, and elegant suits. When she entered a room, you knew it. My sister Joan and I were proud to be her granddaughters.

But because of her mental illness, we couldn't always be sure what she would do. Grandma believed she had to do what the radio told her to. Sometimes she argued with what she thought she heard, but in the end she usually did it—like the time the radio told her she couldn't eat the meal she had just fixed for company. Grandma told the rest of us to go ahead and enjoy it though, even if she couldn't.

My Uncle Freddie, who had lived with her while he was in college, moved out after he got married. That's when the radio started talking to Grandma in earnest. She became suspicious of the renters who lived in the upstairs apartment, a young married couple expecting a child.

One summer night, when the mosquitoes were plentiful, my uncle and his new wife showed up at our back door. This was strange because they always used our front door. Daddy rolled down the living room shades, even though it was still light out. My sister and I sat down and made ourselves as small as possible. We weren't going to miss this. Joan was a lean and scrappy ten-year-old with freckles and straight brown hair cut like the Dutch boy on the paint can. A year younger, I was her spitting image but with longer, lighter hair that was braided.

"Mom actually told her renters, 'This old lady is going to kill you?'" Uncle Freddie asked my dad. "She really said that?"

"The girls," Mommy cut Daddy a look, motioning to Joan and me.

"They're going to know anyway," Daddy said impatiently, lighting a cigarette. "Mom believes the radio when it tells her the renters are killing babies up in that apartment. She thinks she has to put a stop to it before their baby is born."

"She must be delusional," Aunt Rosemary put in. She was a nurse.

"The wife's afraid to stay there now," Uncle Freddie said, standing in Daddy's smoke, "so we need to get Mom into a hospital."

My heart thumped wildly. Afraid of Grandma Teddy? The radio did tell her things, but that was nothing. She would never hurt a fly.

"She's been throwing good food out every day too," Mommy added. "Says someone's trying to poison her."

"She wouldn't poison you or me or the girls," Uncle Freddie said. "But what if she tries to poison the renters?"

I felt my throat constricting. Why were they talking about Grandma like that?

3

Bum

December 1998–June 1999

Storybook snowflakes settled on our coat shoulders as Roger and I walked from the car to the train depot to pick up Jim for winter break. After his first semester in Montana, I was anxious to lay eyes on him. We had hardly heard from him since his paranoid-sounding call in the fall before he changed apartments. Employing a tactic that was becoming familiar, Roger and I had tried to put him out of our minds. I had been busy with my campaign. Still, I thought about him more than I wanted to, especially in quiet times. We rarely spoke about him, however. No news was good news. Now there was a welcome pause after the election and before the legislative session began the next month.

I hurried down the platform ahead of Roger, scanning the crowd of students pouring out of the train. Rosy-cheeked young men and women hugged each other and called goodbyes before turning to waiting families and friends. I stepped around a bedraggled man, searching for Jim. I wrinkled my nose at the whiff of his body odor.

Then I saw a grin peeking from beneath the man's rough reddish beard.

"Mom?" he said.

"Jim?" I stopped. The grin widened and became familiar. "Jim!" I shouted and gave him a bear hug. I pressed my face into his shoulder, breathing my son's ripe body. I noticed the dingy yellow stars in the shape of the Big Dipper across his chest—Jim's all-time-favorite Alaska sweatshirt.

Roger caught up, pushing around excited students. My husband looked conservative, clean-cut, out of place beside his son. As Roger reached out to shake his hand, he looked over Jim's shoulder and gave me a look.

20

Long locks of greasy brown hair snaked from beneath Jim's woolen cap, the one he had learned to knit on his backpacking trip in Alaska his senior year. The huge mountain pack on his back, now grimy like his sweatshirt, was also from that trip.

I hung one arm around Jim's shoulder on the way to the car. The snow was coming down more heavily, flecking Jim's hair and beard, suddenly making him look old at twenty-one. "I'm so glad to see you." I reached across my stomach to pat his arm with my other hand. Jim smiled as if he were happy to be back in Minnesota but said nothing.

At home, after I brushed the snow from my coat and hung it up, I went to our bedroom to put away my purse. Jim followed me in and sat on the side of the bed. I looked at him with surprise. This was more Angela behavior.

"What is it, Jim?" I set down my purse on the dresser and sat down beside him. Heavy snow was still coming down outside.

"No one at school likes me," he moaned, covering his face with his hands. Our reflection in the dresser mirror showed a concerned mother with furrowed brow comforting a disheveled son who looked greatly troubled.

"People always like you," I rejoined.

"No, they don't." He broke into jagged sobs.

I was shocked. I didn't remember Jim crying like this since he was in elementary school. I put my arms around my rugged son and rocked him as if he were five. I was surprised when he didn't pull away.

"What about your two friends who transferred with you?" I asked when he was subdued. "You were such good friends at Northland."

"They have new friends at Missoula, and one has a girlfriend he's with all the time." He sat in a slouch with his feet on the floor.

I tried to smile at him but in the mirror my mouth looked pinched. My heart quickened. I was getting panicky, afraid that I would have to admit that something was very wrong. Yes, Jim preferred to spend time with just one friend at a time, but he'd never been without several friends. No wonder he was upset. Being all alone in a new state with no one to have his back was harsh. I started twisting a strand of hair from the back of my head, as I often did when I was reading, tired, or tense—a trait I had inherited from my mother. "You must have some new friends."

"No, Mom, I don't. And people always talk trash about me. One day when I came out of class, two girls were standing by my bike. I heard one say, 'He thinks he's such hot stuff, with that expensive bike.'" Jim had used high school graduation gifts to purchase his bike, whereas Angela and his cousins had bought old cars.

The cold fingers touched my spine again. "Do your friends know you're having a hard time?"

"They come to my apartment sometimes." He resumed sobbing, shoulders heaving. The bed moved as if it were filled with water, taking us out to sea. "They don't know what to do either."

Jim's classmates' voices supposedly talking about his bike; the neighbors he said were talking about him through the wall. Eerie echoes of the voices Grandma Teddy had heard floated through the air. Even in my thick wool sweater, I shivered. Was Jim going to be like her?

Jim's voice brought me back to the bedroom. "I need to see a doctor," he croaked.

=

Roger and I were glad that our family doctor prescribed Zoloft (sertraline), an antidepressant, for Jim before he returned to Missoula and that Jim sought out a campus psychologist. We were relieved that he was still taking it when he returned home for the summer and that he scheduled an appointment with a psychologist in Minnesota. Jim was handling this.

But worry crept into our lives again after I found psychedelic mushrooms in his room. I knew that mixing prescribed and illicit drugs wasn't good. At first I didn't know what the mushrooms were, but a drug counselor I knew identified them. The following week when I was planting flowers in front of the house, Jim came out and asked to use my car. He was talking fast and his eyes looked unfocused, his pupils large. He seemed high. I refused.

Jim pursed his lips. The skin around them turned bluish white. With astonishing speed, he kicked the tray of pansies I was planting into the middle of the street. I shuddered violently as goose bumps sprouted on my arms and legs. I'd never seen Jim so furious. He stomped off down the street without looking back.

I rescued most of the flowers, looking up and down the cul-de-sac to see if any of our neighbors had witnessed this shame. I was grateful none were in sight.

One morning a couple of days later, after I had watered the rescued purple-and-yellow pansies that were now hanging in a basket outside the front door, Jim's psychologist called. Neither Roger nor I had yet talked to any health professional about Jim's depression. I wiped sweat from my brow as my words poured out. "My husband and I have wished we could talk to someone, but we thought Jim's doctor visits—and especially ones with psychologists—were private."

"You're right, my visits with Jim are confidential," he hemmed, "but there are times when we do need to communicate."

I changed hands holding the phone and wiped the first sweaty hand on my shorts.

"It's probably nothing, but I'm required to let you know about a threat Jim made during our last appointment."

I swallowed and heard him swallowing too.

"There are a very few people with mental illness who follow through on delusional thoughts, so the law specifies that medical people must report such threatening thoughts to the person they're directed at."

I took a sharp breath.

"In this case," he said softly, "you."

I released the air and shut my eyes, blotting out the sunshine. The fear that I had been trying to keep in a box leaped out and began a violent dance in my chest. "Actually, he told me the same thing last night," I said carefully, willing my voice not to crack. "He said he should shoot me in the face because I'm the Antichrist. My face looks evil, especially my eyes. He seemed so serious he unnerved me."

It scared me even more to hear this psychologist repeat the threat, just as a thirdhand compliment feels more genuine than one delivered in person.

"Instead of depression," the psychologist said, "Jim may have bi-polar disorder. That could cause his brain to have these thoughts."

My breaths became shallow and my vision blurred. I could imagine no circle of hell that would be worse than fearing one's own son would kill you. I was glad there were no guns in our house.

"What do you recommend?"

"Jim's agreed to a family meeting."

"Anything." I let my breath out. After I told the psychologist about the mushrooms and the kicked flowers, he scheduled a meeting for two days later.

The doctor's office was on the other side of town from where we lived. Roger, Jim, and I drove there together and sat silently side by side in the waiting room, like students waiting to see the principal.

The psychologist was a calm middle-aged man, much as I had pictured him over the phone. I had been shocked that I didn't sob into the phone when we first talked, but now I cried softly throughout most of the appointment as this stranger who used to be Jim repeated his threats against me. Roger sat silently with his arms crossed and legs tightly wound.

"Something needs to be done about her evilness," Jim said earnestly halfway into the appointment. He was addressing the psychologist. "So I can get my real mom back." He glared at me, causing me to reach for another tissue. Mucus was building up in my nose, making it hard for me to breathe. I shivered. This couldn't be happening. This must be some other family sitting here.

"Remember we discussed you may have bipolar disorder, Jim," the psychologist replied. "Let's get you an appointment with a psychiatrist. Maybe a medication in addition to the antidepressant will help."

"I won't take any more meds," Jim sneered, backing away as if he had been slapped. "And I don't need a shrink."

The man handed Jim a card anyway, for an appointment that was a shocking six weeks away. "Tuck this in your pocket," he said. "You might change your mind."

Is this all? I thought. He isn't going to make Jim do anything? It seemed pointless to complain about the appointment being so far away, given Jim's opposition to going at all.

"Bipolar disorder is worse than depression," I said to Roger, after we had returned home and Jim had left. I followed my husband into his basement corner. "But still better than schizophrenia, like Grandma Teddy had."

"I guess so," he said uncertainly, picking at a hangnail. I noticed that his eyes now looked a little red too.

"No one is really helping us," I sighed, sitting down beside him on the couch. I wiped one last tear from my cheek before I blew my nose. "I feel like we're on a rudderless boat in rapids."

"You know more than I do," he replied. "There's no mental illness in my family."

There it was. Did he think this was my fault? Bad genes? Bad mother?

"I minored in psychology in college because of Grandma Teddy," I said, "but the textbooks said mental illness wasn't inherited." A controversial study using monkeys at the University of Wisconsin in the 1960s had concluded that kids develop mental illnesses because of bad mothering. I had stayed home with our children, trying to be the best mother I could. This theory had long since been debunked, but I was already finding that many still believed it.

"You're a wonderful mother and you know it," Roger said, reaching over to pat my shoulder. I knew he was right, but even so another tear spilled down my cheek.

The next week, the psychologist called again. "Jim threatened you at our last visit. I advise you to call the police if he ever becomes violent."

"The police?" I shrieked. "Why not you or some other *medical* person?"

"I'm afraid that's the system," the psychologist replied in a besieged voice.

"What kind of violence?" I asked.

"Like the flower kicking." He cleared his throat. "Or anything else. The police can get him into the ER. It's the fastest way to get anyone into the mental health system."

Thankfully, for the time being, we were spared knowing how the mental health system would overwhelm our family in the years to come.

4

Psych Ward Silence

June–July 1999

Roger and I began tensing up when Jim was around. We watched him out of the corners of our eyes. I tried to concentrate on reading books about bipolar disorder, but I startled whenever he entered the room. Many days he and I were home alone while Roger was at work.

Jim rarely talked, but when he looked at me, the angry, fearful look in his eyes told me he was seeing the Antichrist. Once after a prolonged glare, he stomped down the hall to his bedroom and slammed the door so hard the house shook. Later I saw a large hole in his wall where the doorknob had punched through.

I was relieved every time he went to work. I couldn't imagine how he functioned at the restaurant, preparing food, but didn't ask because I was happy to get him out of the house. As I drove him there, Jim spit forcefully out the open car window—two or three times per block—trying to purge the air. He glared at me in between spits, causing me to shiver. One of his high school friends told me this wasn't the Jim he had known in school.

I found myself praying for a violent incident so I could call the police on my own son, as the psychologist had advised. It happened on the Fourth of July, a cool, sunny day. Idyllic weather for a picnic, as used to be our family's tradition. Intermittent fireworks rat-a-tatted nearby.

Jim came home around nine in the morning—he'd been gone all night a lot lately—and headed for the shower. While the water was running, I ransacked his backpack, the one on which I had sewn his precious Alaska and Grateful Dead patches before he left for college three years before.

Just as I expected, I pulled out a baggie full of loose drugs: weed and mushrooms that I now recognized.

"Look at this!" I whispered to Roger, who was coming up the stairs from the basement. "Is this the chance the psychologist talked about?" I pointed to the garbage disposal.

He gave me an alarmed look. "I guess."

I hurriedly dumped the contents of the baggie into the sink, ran water, and turned on the disposal. When Jim came out of the bathroom, a damp white T-shirt clinging to his wet chest, I said in a low, quiet voice, "Drugs are unacceptable in this house."

"Where's my stuff?" he demanded, rushing to his backpack and pawing through it like an angry bear. He hurled out a dirty T-shirt, empty cigarette packs, a stubby pencil, and crumpled scraps of paper.

"Down the disposal," I challenged, my voice shaking. Please God, have this turn out all right.

"You bitch. You fucking bitch." He kicked the cat's litter box as if it were a soccer ball, sending gales of litter everywhere. Transformed into a maelstrom of fury, he raced down the stairs to the basement. Roger and I followed.

"Calm down," Roger said, walking slowly up to Jim, who was standing near the laundry room wall. I smelled the stink of our son's tobacco breath.

"Where the fuck does she get off going through my personal stuff?" Jim asked Roger. Without waiting for a response, he punched a hole in the drywall as if it were cardboard. "I've always wanted to do that." He smirked before turning and running back up the stairs.

I gasped, feeling as if it had been me he had punched instead of the wall.

Jim stalked out the front door, paused on the steps long enough to yank my basket of defenseless pansies off the house, bracket and all. He hurled it with all the force he could muster onto the concrete steps. It shattered. Dirt and wounded flowers flew everywhere.

Even with a million panicky thoughts in my head, I wondered again what the neighbors would think if they saw him. What kind of parents were we to have a son like this? But now we needed help. With my heart in my throat, I made the 911 call.

A seasoned officer with snowy white hair arrived quickly. I jumbled out the situation to him as Roger, he, and I stood in our living room. "He went that way," I concluded, pointing to the end of our cul-de-sac. "He turned left at the corner."

The officer looked from Roger to me and shook his head. "I don't know why they tell families to call us," he said ruefully. "There's nothing we can do unless a person's practically assaulting someone. The law says he needs to be an imminent danger to himself or others. This damage to your private home—where you allow him to live—doesn't qualify, unless he's willing to cooperate."

"You mean he could tear down the house but has to practically kill someone the minute you arrive before you can help?" I asked incredulously. "Or are you suggesting we throw our very ill son out onto the street?"

"That's about it," he said quietly. With a sympathetic smile and shrug, he turned to depart.

"Don't leave. I'm calling the station." I ran up the stairs to the kitchen phone.

Luckily, I reached someone to rant to as the officer waited docilely with Roger in the living room. I heard Roger quietly explaining how Jim had been behaving, that he wasn't usually like this.

The person at the station heard me out and asked me to put the officer on the phone. After much discussion, they decided to call a county crisis team.

"A crisis team!" I exclaimed. "Why didn't you say so in the first place?"

Two women arrived in a plain car, and the officer joined them looking for Jim while Roger and I waited anxiously. I lay down on the couch beside him.

"I don't think I can do this," I said to my husband. He was riffling through a newspaper that I doubted he was even seeing. He continued turning pages. I noticed the paper was a week old.

Roger was a slow reader. Years earlier he had had to cancel his beloved *Sports Illustrated* subscription and had told his mother to stop giving us the *Reader's Digest,* which I rarely read anyway. He had insisted on keeping back issues of the magazines until he finally read them all. He still fell behind with the daily newspapers, but he felt compelled to read each one in order, so there was always a stack on his desk. He seemed to cope better with life if it had already happened.

"Remember how Jim used to love the Fourth of July?"

After most fireworks became illegal in Minnesota, I had driven him to Wisconsin to buy them. Nine-year-old Jim bounced beside me as we crossed the border and he spotted fireworks signs. At night he had been in his element as he presented a sound-and-light show in front of our house. Many neighbors were out doing the same, lighting up the street with smoke and color.

"Angela never cared for fireworks the way Jim did," I said, sitting up to look at Roger. "I shouldn't have taken him to Wisconsin and taught him it was okay to disobey the law. Do you think that influenced him to buy illegal drugs?"

"I think you're thinking too much," Roger replied, smiling sadly.

Minutes later, a woman from the crisis team called. "We've found him. He was still in the neighborhood," she said calmly. "He's willing to go to the hospital with us. He agrees he's hearing voices."

Voices. The word sliced through my heart. I immediately thought of Grandma Teddy.

=

"Don't eat anything at Grandma's," Mommy told me, "unless Daddy's there."

I didn't listen. The next morning, as a gentle breeze cut into the summer heat, wafting the sweet smell of wash drying in our backyard, I headed across the street to Grandma's.

She was bent over her large kitchen sink, rinsing berries. Damp curls framed her smiling face and the apron she'd embroidered covered her red housedress. She had taught Joan and me to make French knots the winter before.

"The radio says it's going to be cloudy, but no rain," Grandma said. We took our Blue Willow china bowls, filled with raspberries, to her dining room table. Mauve peonies from her garden adorned the center of the lace-covered table. Being careful not to spill, I heaped sugar and a generous pouring of cream on my berries. It didn't sound scary when the radio told Grandma about the weather.

"I had to throw out the chicken I fried last night," Grandma said, taking a large spoonful of raspberries. "It was poisoned."

I kept my smile from being crooked and took another spoonful. Grandma would never poison me. I ate all the sweet berries and scraped with my spoon to get every last drop of cream before I went home.

It was the end of August. Mommy said it was time to go shopping for school clothes. She let Joan and me dawdle as we made our selections instead of hurrying us along as she usually did. When we got home, I told Mommy, "I'm going to take the red plaid dress I'm going to wear the first day of school over to show Grandma."

"You don't need to go over there," Mommy said from the stove. She had pork chops sizzling in a cast-iron pan.

"Why?"

Mommy studied the meat as if there were a hair on it. "Grandma isn't there anymore."

"Where is she?" I asked in alarm. Grandma had lived across the street from us since I was born, but I knew something wasn't right, especially after Uncle Freddie and Aunt Rosemary's visit.

"You know Grandma's been sick." She turned over a pork chop and salted and peppered the other side. "She's going to the hospital."

"She's not sick," I protested, switching a hand against my thigh. "She didn't want to go, did she?"

"No, the sheriff came and took her in his car."

"While we were shopping," I cried.

"You girls put away your things," Mommy commanded. "Daddy will be home soon."

At dinner that night, Daddy said, "That sheriff should've just plain told Grandma the radio doesn't talk to her." He salted his pork chop. He never tasted his food first to see how much salt Mommy had already put on. "If he made her listen to reason, she wouldn't have had to go." His good eye looked sunken, like the glass eye he got after a teenage hunting accident.

No one disputed with him.

After supper, Joan and I went outside and sat on our front steps. When Daddy had painted them the summer before, Grandma brought over lemonade. Across the street, her flower beds curled around the base of her white clapboard house. The lilac bushes stood sentry on the west side of her yard, the same as always, but the house looked smaller now that we knew she was no longer inside.

"Mommy tricked us," Joan said, her brow furrowed. "That's why we got to shop so long."

"She even let us get ice cream cones on the way home," I added.

"I didn't want to watch the sheriff take her away though," Joan said, scratching a mosquito bite. "She might have thought we were in on it."

"I hope she gets well soon," I said. "I want to show her my new clothes and tell her about school. And who will I watch *Fury* with?" We didn't have a TV, but Grandma had gotten one two years before.

The next week, Uncle Freddie gave away his dog, Robbie, who stayed with Grandma, making Joan and me wonder just how long Grandma was going to be away. The next time we heard about Robbie, he was dead. Uncle Freddie said he'd been poisoned, probably by someone who didn't like his barking in his new yard. We were sad, but Robbie was gone for good anyway so we didn't cry much.

Grandma wasn't poisoned after all, but maybe she wished she was, because she seemed to be gone for good too.

After she had been gone for nearly a month, the mailman walked slowly up our front sidewalk, his leather mailbag squeaking at his side and dampness circling both armpits of his light-blue shirt. I was sitting barefoot on the front steps. He stopped and looked at a letter in his hand. "Mary Rittenhouse isn't across the street anymore?" he asked. His glasses were slightly steamed.

"No." I stood. On the step, I was taller than he was. "She isn't." I wanted to shout it.

"Here's some mail for her," he said, pushing up the glasses that were sliding down his shiny nose. "I'm supposed to leave it here."

"Okay." I stepped into the grass. The concrete sidewalk was too hot. Now the mailman was taller. My bare toes splayed in the wet grass. I extended my hand and took the official-looking white envelope. The postman plodded back down our walk.

Grandma's house across the street was locked. School had started the week before and I'd worn my new red plaid dress, which I hadn't gotten to show Grandma. I couldn't run over after school to tell her things, but Joan and I didn't cry at night anymore either. No one talked about Grandma.

I looked at the letter. Her address had been crossed off with pencil and ours written on instead. In the corner, in the same penciled hand-writing, it said, "Crazy."

==

"Your son's done a no-no, so he got a nice, strong something and will be out for quite a while." The woman answering the psych ward phone the next morning sounded almost gleeful. "There's no point in your visiting."

A squirrel jumped to a different limb of the large oak tree in our backyard, shaking the leaves into a storm of green. I felt light-headed. Was Jim really going to be like Grandma? I turned away from the kitchen window, trying to focus on the hospital woman's words. I cleared my throat. "What does . . . ?"

"Anyway," she broke in, "I just checked his chart and I shouldn't be talking to you."

"I'm his mother."

"And he's an adult." A pause. Her voice softened. "You could try visiting tomorrow."

I felt like she had punched me in the stomach, knocking out all my air. I was too stunned to argue. That Jim was twenty-one meant nothing in his current state. Strangers at the hospital were ripping my son away from me just when he was defenseless against a mind that had gone haywire. I walked to the top of the stairs and called down to Roger, who was watching a baseball game in the basement.

"No one at the hospital will talk to me about Jim because he's an adult."

I heard him mute the television, and there was a short silence while he thought. "I don't know what we can do about it," he finally replied, and then I heard the television again.

I knew by this point in our marriage that this was my husband's way of dealing with things he didn't believe could be changed, but this defeatist attitude—given Jim's situation—made me angry.

I knew Roger wasn't going to try to call the hospital back himself.

The kids' education and medical needs had been my realm since they were born. Roger did all our finances. I had been a teacher when we got married, and it bothered him when I used my red pen in our checkbook. He was the numbers guy. Poor psych ward communication didn't fit in that kind of logic. I went back to the family room, sank into a chair, and held my head in my hands, wondering what to do next. I felt like I was in this alone.

I was never one to take things lying down or to assume that the way things were always had to be. During my days on the school board, some people had wrung their hands about the legislature and its edicts, but I was inspired to run for state representative. I was glad now that I was at the Capitol. I vowed to look into this ridiculous situation—after I had regrouped.

I spent the afternoon talking on the phone to my mother and to a close friend who had been my college roommate. My friend didn't have children, so she was like an aunt to Angela and Jim. I often turned to female family or friends for commiseration, but I knew Roger would join me if I came up with a plan.

The hospital was near the Capitol, so the next day, between meetings, I hurried over. I shivered as an orderly unlocked the doors that let me into the psych ward. Sitting near a window veined with reinforcing metal, Jim was staring vacantly across the large room. I didn't know if I should go over to him or first check in with the staff busy behind a high desk. Before I decided, a woman in a suit who was holding a clipboard motioned to Jim. He rose and followed her out.

I had only an hour before my next appointment. When the legislature was not in session, I had my assistant pack my schedule on the days I came to the office. My damp blouse armpits felt cold as I realized the gulf that now lay between me and my son.

"Looking for Jim Greiling?" A nurse was suddenly standing next to me. She was wearing scrubs and the bows of black-framed glasses disappeared into her long blond hair.

"Yes, but he just went off with that woman." I pointed to the exiting back of the woman in the suit.

"Oh, that's his doctor," she informed me in a chipper tone. "Haven't you talked with her yet?"

"I haven't talked to anyone. Someone told me over the phone yesterday that the staff can't talk to me since Jim's an adult." She raised her eyebrows, the cue I needed to press on. "Our only contact was Jim's psychologist, but now he doesn't know anything either."

"You can know whatever you need to know if Jim signs a release," she replied matter-of-factly. "Want me to ask him when he comes back?"

"Yes, thanks," I said, as gratefully as if she were returning a lost toddler.

"Hey, Jim," she greeted my son when he returned shortly. "Don't you want to sign this paper so your mom can talk to your psychiatrist since they're both here?" She casually placed the form and a pen on a square table near him.

"Sure." Jim scribbled his name on the page without hesitation.

"Why couldn't the desk person have done that earlier?" I asked.

"They get busy," the nurse replied, gathering up the paper and pen. "And it's easier not to bother." She said she'd tell the doctor I wanted to talk with her and then disappeared.

I wish I had a dollar for every time I would have to repeat that scene in the coming years.

Jim was perched on a chair next to the same window. He stared out, then back at me. I waited, wondering how to begin. "I was having the best summer of my life," he finally accused me in a slow, hostile voice, "until you screwed me over. Why'd you call the police?"

I took a gulp of air. "To keep you safe. To get you medical care."

"I'm not sick." He pursed his lips and blew air at me, as if he were exhaling cigarette smoke. Then he spit into a nearby wastebasket. His ways of purging me. "They're torturing me here."

"No, they're not, honey."

He glared at me. "You're not my real mom, are you?"

I blinked back tears. You aren't my real son either, I shouted in my head.

"I should have married my soul mate. Then none of this would've happened," Jim loudly interrupted my silent shouting. "And I'd be the new devil." He stared balefully at me for a long second and then stomped off.

My throat swelled shut and I gasped to breathe. This was the first I'd heard of any of this. Even Grandma Teddy never came up with shit like this—shit that my son now believed was true.

I waited to talk to the doctor, now that I had my release form. But she was busy, of course. I feared if I waited any longer, I would dissolve into another crying puddle. She caught up to me in the hallway as I was walking out, already late for my appointments.

"I'm sorry, I don't really have time to talk to you right now," she said, her voice harried. "But you should know. Your son has schizophrenia. I'm sorry." And she hurried off. My world changed orbits forever. Is this going to be his life, our lives? I hardly felt the beating sun on my way back to the car.

That night, I dreamed I saw a cloaked figure walking slowly toward me. When it raised a pale hand and pulled back its hood, I saw it was Jim. Grandma Teddy's eyes stared out of his face.

===

On a crisp fall day, the family went to visit Grandma Teddy at the state hospital. We hadn't seen her since school started, almost two months before. The perfume of dry leaves blew in the open car windows.

Daddy was driving. "Don't say anything to Grandma about us having her TV at our house," he said, without turning his head. Joan and I were in the back seat.

"Don't say anything about Robbie," Mommy added, turning to look at Joan and me. She was wearing a summer dress because it was still warm.

"Don't say her renters moved," Daddy warned sternly, looking at us through the rearview mirror. "Don't even mention them. And for God's sake, don't say her house is up for sale."

Joan and I tried to think of things we could talk about, so we wouldn't blurt out wrong things to fill silence. Mommy and Daddy had already instructed us about what we could and, mostly, couldn't say to the neighbors. Most of them knew Grandma was at the state hospital, but we weren't supposed to say exactly why.

We drove by a large cemetery. Mommy said our great-grandparents were buried there. It seemed like Grandma Teddy was dead too. We passed tennis courts. People in white shorts were running after balls, carefree as the wind, as we used to be when we ran across the street to Grandma's.

Several light-brown brick buildings came into view. "That's it," Mommy said, pointing at the complex. The buildings were surrounded by expanses of lush green grass and towering shade trees. Acorns rattled down from the oaks. The door was heavy, like my feet felt, when we went inside.

While we waited for Grandma, Daddy coughed. The noise reverberated around the bland room, where tan tiles covered the lower two-thirds of the walls. A limp spider plant, riddled with dry foliage, cascaded over a plant divider. Grandma must not have been in this room, or she would have tended to that plant.

Grandma entered the waiting room with a flourish in a stream of sunshine radiating from a large window. She had on her bright-red house dress; her pink cheeks and red lipstick announced she was ready for company. She also had on her delighted smile. Joan and I rushed to her embrace. It felt good. She smelled like the perfume she always wore.

"Here're my girls. Do you miss me?" Grandma cooed. "Don't worry. I'll be home soon." She looked with disdain at the desk lady and said, "Let's go outside."

Once there, we headed for a lawn swing, where a worn-out, ageless woman sat huddled into herself.

"Move," Grandma told her. "We need this swing." I was glad Grandma was still her commanding self. "These here are my granddaughters, and this is my son Robert." She left Mommy out.

The lady got off the swing without a sound and scuttled off. The seat felt warm on my bare legs. Joan gently pumped the swing.

"We can talk better here," Grandma said, looking around. "They hear everything inside. The radio told me I have to be careful."

"The radio doesn't talk to you, Mom," Daddy said, with the exasperation he showed whenever she brought it up.

"You don't know anything about it, Robert," she retorted. "I don't belong here. I'm coming home with you."

Joan stopped rocking the swing.

"You have to get better first," Daddy growled.

"I like my teacher this year," I interjected. "He's a man, the only man teacher in the whole school."

"That's nice," Grandma said with a brief smile at me, before turning back to Daddy. "I need to get back home."

Then she addressed Mommy. "Jeanette, this is all your doing, isn't it?" Grandma glared at her. "You and Rosemary want me out of the way."

"No," Mommy said, then tried to change the subject. "I hear you cook in the hospital kitchen."

Joan pumped the swing again.

"I'd rather cook in my own kitchen," Grandma said boldly. "Let's go to the car right now." She put her hand on Joan's arm to stop the swing and got up.

"Now, Mom," Daddy said, also rising. "It's time for us to go."

I was surprised when Grandma followed Daddy back into the building. She didn't hug us as tightly this time. Her smile was gone, like the sun that was no longer shining through the window. I wished I could do something, intervene, let her come with us. I wanted her home again, even if we had to give back the TV, but I followed Daddy toward the door.

I turned back to look at Grandma before I went out. She was pulling dry strands from the plant on the divider. I guessed she couldn't do anything else, now that she was inside, because they were listening.

5
Sharing the News

July 1999

When I called Angela the next day to let her know Jim's new diagnosis of schizophrenia, I tried to tamp down my hysteria. In her first year out of college, she should have been able to bask in her young life without this burden. When she asked about Jim, I first told her about a call I'd had that afternoon from one of his friends in Missoula.

"Something's very wrong with Jim," he had told me. "He wouldn't leave his apartment or do anything with us. When some of us went over, he cried a lot." The young man paused, then added, "I'm sorry. We should have done something or let someone know, but we didn't know what to do or who to call."

I had assured him he *was* doing something: he was calling now. I informed him about Jim's diagnosis, and I told my daughter now.

"Schizophrenia." Angela's voice was unemotional, flat. Too much to take in—for all of us.

I took a drink of iced tea to soothe my dry throat. "Like Great-Grandma. But there are so many more medicines and services now." I felt as if I was trying to convince myself that Jim's illness wouldn't be as bad as hers or that it might even go away. We talked only a short while longer, discussing Jim's current behavior, not his diagnosis.

Jim's college friend had ended our conversation by offering to buy some of Jim's things from his apartment. His assumption that Jim wouldn't be able to return hit me like a rock. When I thought of our son not finishing college, abandoning the path Roger and I had always assumed both our children would take, my chest tightened. When I thought of the horror of Jim being like my grandmother, whose life had all but ended when she was committed, I felt as if a python were squeezing the life out of me.

Angela was nine when Grandma Teddy died; Jim seven. They had visited her several times at the state hospital, where she remained for more than twenty years. My father visited faithfully every other week, and I dutifully went with him until I left for college. Joan mostly dropped out from visiting, and my mother stopped going after the time she upset Grandma. It wrenched our hearts when Grandma begged to come home.

The hospital moved Grandma to an apartment in the late 1960s when the national push was starting for the deinstitutionalization of people we then called mental patients. I was in college at the time, and I could tell it wasn't working when I received letters from her telling me people were trying to poison her, letters that made it hard to concentrate on my studies. I fantasized about moving in with my grandmother when I graduated, rescuing her. I imagined us cooking together, talking. She returned to the hospital after being booted out of her apartment for yelling at people about the poisoning. I struggled to understand how anyone expected her to do well all by herself with no support. Grandma's story was all too common: closing state hospitals saved money, but socialization and care within the community never came.

After my parents moved and were no longer living across the street from her house, Grandma was able to come for visits. By then she had been at the hospital for ten years and had made peace with her daughters-in-law. Later Grandma often traveled the ninety miles with my parents to visit Roger and me in the Twin Cities. She savored being with family and was a loving great-grandmother, as she had been a grandma to Joan and me. I can still picture her reading to Angela as baby Jim pulled himself up her leg to look at the pictures.

When Grandma moved from the hospital to a nursing home three years before she died, she took her pills when they were dispensed like all the other people there. She served on the governing board, recited "The Night before Christmas" by heart at holiday programs, and was written up in the local newspaper for being a "hot shot" at a new video game called *Pac-Man*. The reporter described her as having a "quiet, pleasant personality." When I read that, I ached, wishing that she had gotten this kind of support much earlier so she could have stayed in our lives. I vowed to fight to do better with Jim.

The next time I talked to Angela, she said the first person she had told about her brother's schizophrenia was Paul Wellstone. She covered the U.S. senator from Minnesota as part of her job as a Washington correspondent for two midwestern newspapers. "He knew just what to say," Angela said. Paul had had a brother with mental illness and was a hero in the mental health community. It calmed me to know our daughter had such a wonderful confidant in D.C. Later, I was glad to be in a press conference with him at the Minnesota Capitol about mental health parity, but I was always sorry we never had an in-depth conversation about his brother or Jim or the mental health system before he died in a plane crash three years later.

Angela wrote a column for her Minnesota newspaper, the *Rochester Post-Bulletin,* highlighting our family's openness about Jim's illness. Our story about the difficulty of getting early treatment for Jim and my legislation had been featured on the front pages of the Minneapolis and St. Paul newspapers and in *Newsweek.* Jim was interviewed by a radio station, and our whole family was featured in a National Alliance on Mental Illness (NAMI) educational video that is still being used in their classes today. Angela's column detailed the types of responses she received when she told people about Jim. Serious looks with nods of concern and nary a mention of the topic ever again, real concern but a lack of understanding about mental illness and the system, or genuine understanding because the listener had also been affected, a not uncommon response. Roger's and my experiences were the same.

Besides family and my closest friends, the first people I told about Jim fit into Angela's third group: people with experience who would deeply understand. JoAnn Zwack served on the state board for NAMI, and her husband Joe was its president. A couple of years earlier, they had invited me to speak at a candlelight vigil on the Capitol steps for people with mental illness. No other legislators attended. I shared the story of my grandmother's illness with the handful of sober, sad people who huddled in the darkness clutching candles. Joe spoke too, sharing that their son Kyle was in prison because of his mental illness. Later, after we mental health advocates raised more awareness of mental illness, I was glad to have opportunities to speak at mental health rallies inside the Capitol where the rotunda was packed with boisterous supporters.

I sought out the Zwacks at a local Democratic Party picnic in a park near our home. Jim was still doing poorly in the hospital. We huddled in the shade of a pavilion with many familiar people. As we wiped sweat from our faces, Joe and JoAnn directed us to the NAMI website and encouraged Roger and me to take their family classes. They also recommended a group called the Minnesota Bio Brain Association.

I adjusted my stance to avoid the strong rays of the lowering sun. As we talked in a seemingly matter-of-fact way, we were surrounded by people who were unaware of the serious nature of our discussion. The conversation felt surreal, as if I were gathering information for a constituent family, as I had many times, rather than for my own. Asking for myself was another matter. I felt vulnerable.

"After you get situated, dear," JoAnn concluded, touching my shoulder gently, "we'll talk." I detected an unmistakable glint in her eye that I interpreted as her happiness at the prospect of a sitting legislator gaining firsthand experience.

But how could I gather experience when doctors were still saying it was possible that Jim's illness was temporary, that it was just the result of drug use? Only later did they explain that it is common for people experiencing a first episode to clear up after taking an antipsychotic medication. Patients could even remain stable after discontinuing them—until they crashed again, but worse.

At home after the picnic, I read online into the night, gasping jagged breaths. Seeing or hearing things that aren't there, people reading your thoughts, inability to recognize your illness. Everything I read confirmed our son's diagnosis.

The next night, Roger and I went to a long-planned dinner with a group of friends, many from our church. Roger had called the church to add Jim to the prayer list, something we had never done before for anyone. He had also already shared the news with several of the people who would be there. They would know. I worried I wouldn't be able to hold it together when I saw these good people. It's always harder to put on a strong face for the people who know you best.

When Roger and I arrived, several people were already seated on both sides of a long table. The man I sat across from had been Jim's high school band teacher. He was one of the few teachers who had been able to motivate our son. A chill used to run down my spine whenever I watched Jim on the stage, playing the drums with perfect rhythm and just the right amount of nonchalance. This teacher had escorted Jim's large band to New York City for a competition. Jim had returned bubbling with enthusiasm and had presented Roger and me with a statuette of the Empire State Building. Could that have been just three years before?

I was relieved to find that I was able to exchange a bit of small talk with the teacher and others near me. No one mentioned Jim. I lost it, however, when another good friend arrived. She greeted Roger and me compassionately, saying, "I understand you've been in hell."

I took a large drink of water, stalling for time as I tried to unlock my throat. I finally croaked, "We're still there." I set down my glass so hard some water splashed out. Huge shaking sobs started forming deep in my gut. I tried to swallow them down as I had the water, but they boiled over and kept coming. I couldn't bear looking at the wide-eyed, shocked faces staring at me with deep sympathy. Roger shifted in his chair beside me and tried to deflect the attention with small talk. I could tell he wanted me to pull myself together so we could go on with the evening. I couldn't, so finally I told Roger we had to leave.

Even in my state, when he started the car I found it appropriate that the radio was blaring AC/DC's "Highway to Hell." I was glad the windows were rolled up to keep in the air-conditioning. Otherwise the whole freeway could probably have heard me, even over the music, as Roger drove us home, with his jaw slightly jutting.

Roger didn't cry. I have never seen him cry about Jim's mental illness—or much else for that matter, not even at his dad's funeral. The only time I can recall seeing him cry was shortly after Jim was born. Angela was barely two. We parents were exhausted. Roger had tried to be helpful by making the bed one morning, which was always my job. But I was planning to change the sheets that day, so I morphed into a shrew, yelling that he had only made it harder for me to pull off the sheets. Roger hastened from the room, but not before I saw his crushed face and leaking tears. I'm ashamed every time I recall that stupid, mean incident.

When we reached home, I felt as tired as I had that day I had made Roger cry. Now his dry eyes made me feel worse, made me feel alone. I went straight to bed and cried myself to sleep, thinking of our kind, considerate son who had brought us the souvenir from New York City. I felt as if that son had died.

6

Frustration Inspires Legislation

A few days later, a friend arranged for Mary Schulte, the coexecutive director of the Minnesota Bio Brain Association, to come to our home to further our education about mental illness. Reflecting its name, the organization strongly held that mental illness is a biological brain disease, no one's fault. Mary was an earnest, fine-boned woman with wavy brown hair. As we sat in our living room and the sun grew dimmer, she calmly shared her family's experience with her daughter's mental illness. After she covered many basics we ought to know, she stressed that we should be sure to take care of ourselves. Easier said than done, I thought. How could I relax when our son thought he should be the new devil?

At the end of our time together, Mary cleared her throat and brought up one last topic. "Many people in the mental health community want to sweep the possibility of violence under the rug," she said gently, "but you should be aware that it sometimes happens when people are very ill. Our daughter is small, but when she's in crisis it's all my husband and I can do to get her to the hospital. It's rare, but people shouldn't be blindsided."

I stopped twisting a lock of hair and shifted my weight on the couch. I took a deep breath. I wanted to tell her how afraid I was becoming of Jim, how nervous we were about his coming home from the hospital. But my voice caught in my throat.

After Mary left, her last words kept repeating in my mind, making my stomach churn.

Soon after Mary's visit, I began sharing our family's story more broadly and was invited to speak at many mental health gatherings. My sudden popularity was indicative of the desert that existed among legislators working on mental illness.

One group I spoke to was the Minnesota Psychiatric Society. I told them of Jim's psychiatrist abruptly breaking the news about Jim's schizophrenia and then hurrying off. During the discussion that followed my talk, they vowed do better. I felt a calmness talking to such a sympathetic audience. Perhaps this was going to be my calling.

As I drove to work the next day, I tapped my fingers on the steering wheel in time to Beethoven, trying to calm my thoughts. They had been racing all night, ever since Roger and I found out the hospital was discharging Jim to a chemical dependency program. He wasn't ready.

The only thing that lightened my heart was having something real to do that day. I was meeting with the legislative staff attorney who covered privacy statutes. Soon after I entered my office, the attorney arrived and laid her papers on my table. Her law book was marked with multiple sticky notes. I had worked with her before. She was typical of nonpartisan House staff: buttoned-down, intelligent, and delightful. They were experts whose only agenda was to do their job well.

"I want a bill to make psych wards do better with medical information releases," I began, briefly explaining what had happened when Jim began his psych ward stint. "It seems like just plain old common sense to me."

"Many laws are common sense written down," she said with a laugh. I liked her even more.

"And many are based on a legislator's personal experiences or those of their constituents." I smiled.

"At times, certainly." She smiled back.

"I want the statute for people with mental illness to read the same as for people with other illnesses," I said. "I could talk to doctors and nurses just fine when my dad was in the hospital."

"Actually, Representative Greiling, the release of information statutes already are the same for all types of illnesses. It's just that medical people enforce them more strictly when mental illness is involved."

"You're kidding!" I sat back in my chair, staring at her. How did I not know this? Now that I thought about it, no medical professional had ever spoken rudely to me, as the psych ward staff person who answered the phone had done. For other illnesses, medical staff were caring and gentle, seeing the virtue of family members being informed so they could help.

"If the law were used uniformly all the time, families would have more trouble communicating about all illnesses," she added.

"How can we do this then?" I ran my fingers through my hair. "I certainly don't want to ruin family communication for other illness too."

"Here's a possibility." She pulled up closer to the table and turned to a page in one of her massive law books. "We could spell out specifically what hospitals have to do. Require them to offer releases right away and to keep trying if patients initially refuse. We could also require that they inform families about releases and how they can help encourage patients to sign."

"Works for me."

I also asked for legislation to raise the age for when parents could be involved in their children's mental health care without a release. I had heard about the urgent need for this from a police officer who worked with youth. We proposed changing that age from sixteen to seventeen. It was unthinkable that that hadn't been the law all along.

I almost wanted to hug the attorney when she left. Instead, I gave her the warmest handshake possible. I knew her bill draft reflecting what we had discussed would arrive on my desk in short order, ready for introduction when the session started.

I turned the radio volume up on the way home, trying to block out my conversation of the night before with Jim in the psych ward.

"See that man over there?" Jim had asked as soon as we were seated in the dayroom. He pointed across the room at a male nurse. "He's my dad."

"Does he look like Dad to you?" I had asked. The man was slim and fairly young with blond hair. "He doesn't to me."

"No, but he's my real dad." I decided to let that pass.

"What did you have for supper tonight?" I asked, striving for a safe topic, as I used to do with Grandma Teddy when I ran interference when she and my dad had argued about her voices.

"I don't remember."

I studied my son. He hadn't shaved since before he left for the hospital. His hair was oily. He didn't smell at all like what I always told my children was my favorite smell in all the world: fresh air plus kid. I couldn't see the little boy with loosely curled brown hair who used to have to wear suspenders to keep his pants up. I couldn't see the boy who sat on my lap, pressed close, counting every object on every page of his favorite counting book.

"He's bound to do something with numbers when he grows up," I had told Roger one such night long ago, after I had tucked little Jim into bed.

"Well, he wouldn't be the first Greiling to do that," Roger had laughed. Many Greiling men were engineers, and Roger's father ran a financial business.

"Macaroni."

"What?" I asked. I realized I'd been daydreaming, finding comfort in my memories. My son's voice brought me back to the psych ward.

"Macaroni is what I had for supper." Jim's small smile showed a glimmer of the cute little boy he once was.

"I'll probably never see Dad and you again," he announced when I left, "but it's probably for the best."

A visceral ache seeped into every crevice of my body.

=

In the fall, Roger and I signed up for NAMI's Family-to-Family classes, which were taught by trained family members. Angela took the same class. For twelve weeks, after work in downtown D.C., she traveled many miles to Leesburg, Virginia, to learn about her brother.

The first evening that Roger and I walked into the classroom in a nearby community center, I spotted Mary McLeod, a petite blonde lobbyist I knew from the Capitol. She flinched, apparently feeling as I did about seeing someone from her professional life there. At the Capitol I tried to retreat into my shell, walling myself off from having to acknowledge the pain going on at home. I introduced Roger and Mary, and we all shared that we had sons with schizophrenia.

Over the course of the next several weeks—facilitated by the excellent participatory curriculum—we became friends for the long haul, the type of cut-to-the-chase friends people need when they or a family member has a lifelong debilitating mental illness—or any illness, for that matter. One of my most understanding friends, Stephanie DeBenedet, has multiple sclerosis and uses a wheelchair; her father had undiagnosed bipolar disorder. She totally gets it on both levels. Stephanie and her husband Jim started a dinner group with two other couples and us, where they asked about our Jim from time to time. Roger's and my friends from church did the same.

Many friends were a comfort. Roger's tended to accompany him to ball games, where they might or might not check in about Jim. But they were with him. My friends were usually more hands-on. Many asked about Jim regularly and really listened. Two cried with me, which I appreciated, and another ended every conversation with, "Everything's going to be all right."

One friend, Kathy Juenemann, scrapbooked with me. I was glad on the days she showed up with her box of photographs, saving me from the melancholy I felt when looking at pictures of our family in happier times. We each claimed half of our long dining room table, and the kitchen counter behind us was filled with scrapbooking supplies and tools. We turned up the music. I relaxed as the former elementary-school-teacher in me kicked in, cutting photos and using paper shapes to create attractive pages.

"I remember that day," Kathy said, pointing to a photo I was cropping of a debonair Jim. He was leaning back in a deck chair on the day of his high school graduation party. Jim was seated beside one of his garage-band mates, grinning broadly into the camera. In another photo taken that day, his arm rested easily over my shoulders.

"We knew he was into drugs by then," I replied. "But when I called the school they were no help. Who would have thought he'd be so sick just three years later?"

Jim was going to court next week to be considered for civil commitment.

"Hmm," Kathy murmured knowingly as she pressed a photo onto her page. She used to be a teacher too. I would be glad in future years to help initiate school funding to help students who had drug and mental illness issues.

"Jim's court-appointed attorney believes he shouldn't be civilly committed," I said. "But that's the only way to make sure he takes his psych meds." Nausea washed over me every time I thought of the hearing. I'd cut a photo from the previous Christmas—of Angela, Jim, and Roger's mother—into a heart. I laid down my scissors and brushed the scraps into the wastebasket. It was hard not to notice that Jim's smile and full cheeks from his graduation party had morphed into a forced, tight smile and gaunt, sallow cheeks.

"What does he propose?" Kathy asked in her cynical way. "Let Jim keep getting sicker until he hurts you?"

"He actually called our home to plead Jim's case." I raised my eyebrows at my friend before I pressed tape onto the back of the photo. "He said he wants to keep Jim out of the mental health system. Doesn't think he belongs there."

"What a guy." Kathy laughed. "Does he want to live with unmedicated Jim?"

"I hate this whole idea of police and civil commitments." I thought of my hammering heart on the Fourth of July, the day I called the police after Jim exploded when I put his drugs down the disposal. That had probably been easier than having to testify against our own son, as our attorney said we must do at the hearing if we wanted to get him help. "Whatever happened to just medical people?" I tapped the heart photo into place on my album page.

"Novel idea."

"I'm working on legislation to improve hospital information releases," I said, "and after that I just might tackle civil commitment."

7

Allies in Empathy and Action

September 1999

I arrived at a stately St. Paul mansion a month later to hear a story another legislator suggested might help with the civil commitment legislation. I had learned a bit of the tragic story from a newspaper article from two years before and agreed it would be riveting testimony to show the need for earlier care for people in the grip of psychosis.

I was glad to have something to work on to take my mind off Jim. He had only lasted one day in the chemical dependency program the hospital had dismissed him to. His mental illness had been nowhere near in check. Unlike the young man in the story I was about to hear, Jim had been ordered by the court to accept treatment. After he scared the staff in the chemical dependency program, he was transferred to another hospital and then to the longer-term facility where he currently resided. During all this, I took heart only when I worked on legislation—something I could actually affect.

The mansion's concrete front steps were steep. Shadows enveloped me as I entered a cool, dark entryway. In the dark-paneled dining room, Eileen Stack, the homeowner, greeted me warmly. It was her story I had come to hear.

"Would you like a glass of wine?" asked her friend, who had come for moral support. She took a sip of hers. "You might like one before you hear it."

"No thanks." I wanted to listen attentively in my best legislative mode. I had changed into more professional attire before I came. I felt official and hoped to stay that way. Slipping into my emotional-mom role wouldn't serve any of us well.

We sat down. The two women took generous sips from their glasses. Fortification. I hoped I wouldn't regret my hasty decision.

"I'm a nurse so I knew our son was sinking into mental illness," Eileen began, in a quiet, dignified voice, "but Tom and I couldn't convince him to keep taking his medication." The article I'd read about her son, Will, said he had gone to the same YMCA camp as Jim, the wilderness experience Jim had so loved during his high school summers.

"I was at work," Eileen continued. "I knew Will wasn't doing well, so I called to check in with Tom, but he didn't return my calls. I figured he and Will must be out doing errands."

"You were worried," I encouraged. Eileen's salt-and-pepper hair added to her distinguished look. I related to her plaguing worry when she couldn't reach her ill son.

"With good reason." Her lower lip quivered and she stilled it with her hand. She and her husband had tried many times without success to get help for Will's increasingly erratic behavior. "We pieced it together later. When Tom was working in the basement, Will came downstairs. The blood trail the police found the next day told the rest of the tale."

I heard the refrigerator start up, a familiar hum. Such a benign sound should have made this home feel safe, but it didn't.

"Will picked up a heavy hammer and hit his father over the head." She took another healthy sip of the wine. "Tom stayed conscious, but as he crawled up the stairs, Will continued pummeling him with heavy blows. They got as far as the dining room."

A sound came from the back of my throat. I thought of Grandma Teddy saying she had to kill her tenants, of Jim saying he should kill me for looking so evil.

"Will's still refusing meds in prison," she said weakly. Her son would serve many years before being paroled. "He has the right to refuse there too, unless he meets the same civil commitment standard he didn't meet before he killed his dad." She looked deeply into my eyes, wringing a Kleenex, as if she were conveying a warning. "Yes, I want to help you change the law." Her volume built. "I'll testify, tell my story, anything that will help."

I wasn't worried about the rarely used tools in our home, but when I returned that evening, I took Jim's camping knife from his top drawer and hid it. Our kitchen knives were in a drawer getting dull, not in a butcher block on top of the counter. I was glad. We didn't know yet when Jim would be released or where he would go. He was still civilly committed and had to take his meds. Earlier in the fall, when Roger and I had visited and Jim was still in full-blown delusional mode, the psychiatrist had advised us not to take him home, possibly ever.

I was surprised at how grateful I had felt about that.

After meeting with Eileen, my hands trembled as I set the table for supper. Roger asked me what was wrong. I wanted to tell him Eileen's story. I wanted him to reassure me that Jim would never do something like that. I would tell him later, but not that night—the lump in my throat was too large. When I sat across from my husband, eating the supper I'd prepared, I imagined him or me lying dead on the kitchen floor. I could never let that happen. But I also knew I couldn't control what Jim's delusional thoughts would have to say about us.

8
Angela Visits

Angela hadn't seen Jim since he'd been diagnosed nearly two months before, but I had kept her updated. Thank goodness Jim was better now. She wouldn't have to see him thinking I was the Antichrist. I knew Jim's illness was hard for her. Not only was she concerned about her brother, but she was also worried he might harm us. There had been a lot in the news about a mentally ill teenager in Oregon who had killed his parents the previous year. When Angela came to Minnesota for work, she went with Roger and me to visit Jim.

I turned to look at my daughter in the back seat. Her long blond hair was newly blunt cut and pushed behind her ears. She looked younger than her twenty-three years. Despite being raised in Minnesota, Angela was a Packers fan, a Cheesehead (her father's influence). He was driving as Angela and I talked on our way to Anoka-Metro Regional Treatment Center, the secure hospital where Jim was now being treated. Roger and I had first visited him there the week before. He was missing the fall semester in Missoula.

"Jim said if he has to be at Anoka, he doesn't want to live," I said. My bare arms felt a chill as Roger turned up the air-conditioning. The trees along the streets were wilting in the sticky heat. Roger kept his eyes on the road, ostentatiously listening to a ball game, but I'm pretty sure he was riveted to our conversation as well.

"Sounds pretty depressed," Angela said. "But if he keeps taking his meds he could have a good life." Like us, she had learned in the NAMI class that mental illness was very treatable. And like me, she was trying to put a good face on the situation.

"Yes, I keep telling him that." I'd assured Jim that his setback was temporary. He'd soon be back at college. "When we try to leave, he often begs us to stay longer," I said, "so be prepared. He says he only feels alive when someone's there." When Jim begged, he reminded me of Grandma Teddy wanting to come home, triggering my guilt about both of them.

We arrived at the hospital complex, parked, and stepped into the blistering afternoon. Roger pushed open the heavy door to Jim's building. A receptionist ensconced in a Plexiglas cage silently slid a clipboard through a window. She glanced at our signatures, grabbed a large chain of jangling keys, and pawed through them. After she clanked open the door between us, she led us down a windowless hallway with a tiled floor and through another locked door. I had noticed right away when we first visited that the wall tiles were identical to the ones in Grandma Teddy's old hospital building. I found that jarring. They conjured up the old smells of disinfectant.

Angela walked between Roger and me wearing a grim expression. Her neck was flushed, so she was undoubtedly more anxious than she was letting on. The air was stale, as if we were in a cave. Occasionally we passed doors that probably led to offices, but no sound escaped to enlighten us.

When we first spotted Jim in the dayroom, his head was down and he was squeezed against the farthest end of a couch. He was wearing a gray jersey sweatshirt and blue jeans. He'd grown painfully thin, unlike the sophomore I had dropped off at college a year before, who was beginning to fill out into manhood.

He blended in with other listless patients who sat motionless, eyes glassy. I noticed one young man walking three steps forward and then three steps backward—again and again in the same spot. His arms swung stiffly, and his hair was cut in a Mohawk. He looked harmless enough compared with some of the patients who laughed roughly as they played cards.

The staff was in a station off to the side, also behind glass. A staff woman stared at us. I wondered whether it was pity or contempt I saw in her eyes. On our last visit, a friendly nurse who confided that she was also a family member warned us that some staff regarded patients and families with repugnance. I remembered the desk woman who had curled her lips when we visited Grandma Teddy. The thought that we hadn't come very far in the mental health system since then dropped through my body like a stone.

Jim's hair was still wet from his shower. It looked as if he had taken more care with his clothes too. They smelled freshly laundered. Last time we'd visited, he had reeked of unwashed sweat, something I noticed was not uncommon among the patients. And his teeth didn't look fuzzy when he gave us a small smile.

Angela stepped forward first. "Jim," she said, reaching in for a stiff hug. "How are you?"

"Been better." He rationed a fleeting smile as he looked up at her from lowered head. "How're you doing?"

"Okay," Angela said in a thin voice, "but worried about you."

"Yeah, well, my life's over," he said, somewhat angrily, but then he seemed to think better of it. "Want to go outside? I can go to the courtyard now that I'm on a higher level." Roger and I had received a letter in the mail describing the various levels, rewards for good behavior. Patients could advance to leaving the ward for meals in the dining room, visits to the library, or prized time in the courtyard, where they could smoke.

Roger and I greeted Jim quietly but let this visit be Angela's. The three of us trooped behind Jim, who knew his way through the catacomb of hallways. Bright sunshine greeted us as we emerged from the old building into a grass-covered courtyard surrounded by a shiny new building. The outside air hung hazy with cigarette smoke.

"Want to go around the walking path?" Jim asked hospitably.

"Why don't you and Angela go?" I suggested. "She's only here until Monday. Dad and I can sit here on this wall."

Angela shot me an annoyed look but reluctantly joined Jim on the path. Roger and I sat down and savored watching our tall children bending toward each other chatting as they used to.

Even though they had traveled in different circles in high school, Jim and Angela had maintained a friendship. When Jim was cut from tryouts for the high school ski team, Angela was hotly indignant, saying everyone knew he was one of the best skiers in the school. Because of his social anxiety, Jim had fallen each time he skied down a hill during the trials, even easy ones. Not that I knew any of that from him. He just came home that day—silent, arms nearly dragging on the floor—and went to his bedroom and quietly closed the door. It was after that that I noticed Jim was high a lot. I called the school to see if there was a drug counselor, but I was advised to go through our health insurance. I never did. It seemed like too big a step to take.

Jim had traveled with me each time I took Angela to college in Missouri. They talked on the way, he helped unload her possessions, and they hugged goodbye. And she called him to come home from college for the surprise fiftieth birthday party she and Roger planned for me. As recently as that, just a year before, Jim had been in his right mind.

Angela and Jim veered near a volleyball game loudly in progress in a sandpit. Young men smacked a white ball, as "damns" and "fucks" flew back and forth like the ball. Were they showing off for Angela? A couple of staffers watched from the side, talking quietly to each other, smoking.

They took ten minutes to circle the yard. We watched hungrily.

"Jim's so much better with Angela here," Roger said. He wiped sweat from his brow with his handkerchief.

"Yes, and the meds are finally kicking in." I leaned back, putting my hands on the wall. "Also, he can't use weed or mushrooms here. That surely helps. Maybe we'll get through this."

I wished we could hear our children's conversation. Once, Angela laughed a little, and I was heartened. It was good for Jim to see her.

We stood up as they approached, and we all made small talk for a few minutes, then went back into the cool, darkened building. Jim didn't put up his usual resistance when it was time to leave, perhaps not wanting Angela to see him beg.

"Thanks for coming," he said, looking at his sister with a smile that didn't reach his eyes, eyes that followed her out of the room, as she returned to living her life, while he was left behind.

Melancholy crashed through me as we walked down the hallway past those same tan tiles. They made my insides twist with despair.

My fragile front had dissolved by the time we got to the door, but I hid it from my daughter. All of a sudden I didn't believe a word I had said to Jim when Roger and I had first visited. We had promised that his setback was temporary, that he would go back to college. How could I continue to try to console him when I myself had so little hope?

9
Advice from a Prisoner

Despite my pessimism, Jim improved and was discharged from Anoka to another chemical dependency facility and then to our home. He was quieter than usual but otherwise seemed like the old Jim. But after he'd been with us a week, he announced that he didn't plan to keep taking the meds once his commitment expired.

Having recently been appointed to the board of the National Alliance on Mental Illness Minnesota (NAMI–MN), I asked friends there for help. Joe and JoAnn Zwack arranged for Jim and me to visit their son, Kyle, in prison. They hoped Jim would see the connection between not taking medication and ending up there.

"Kyle was an engineering student before he got paranoid," JoAnn told me. "But now he rots in prison." Kyle had started traveling around the country on a motorcycle. The police in Texas got involved after a friend there, who knew he had a gun, became worried about him. The officers and Kyle had exchanged shots and engaged in a chase during which he had crossed a state line. He ended up with two prison sentences.

I had read that although people with mental illnesses were no longer confined for years in state hospitals, as they had been in my grandmother's day, they were still equally often kept under lock and key, now in prisons and jails.

Jim drove my car on our way to the prison. "Isn't that where we picked apples?" he asked, pointing at a billboard. He was talking loudly because the windows were open. It was fall, and apples and pumpkins abounded at roadside stands.

"Good times, right?" I replied. I pictured Angela and Jim as kids romping in rows of the red fruit, Roger lugging our bushel basket.

"Kyle's parents tried to help him but couldn't," I said, steering the conversation back to the reason for our visit. I had already briefed Jim on Kyle's story. "Aren't you glad Dad and I got help for you?"

"Yeah, now I guess I am," he said, looking at me briefly with a mellow smile. "You might've saved my life."

When Jim had ceased to believe I was the Antichrist, it was like having the weight of the world lifted from my shoulders. Hearing this further vindication made my heart swell. For once I felt giddy with appreciation for pharmaceutical companies. I took a deep, appreciative breath of fragrant fall air and hoped to heaven that Jim would connect Kyle's fate to what his own could be, that our visit would hit its mark.

The prison wasn't visible until we turned down the entry road. It was a plain building surrounded by a fence topped with gleaming razor wire.

"Thankfully Kyle's parents got him extradited to Minnesota from Texas. The prisons there are rough," I said as we pulled into the parking lot.

Inside, Jim set off the metal detector twice and had to remove his belt and then his shoes. He handled the inconvenience with a shrug and a smile. No one would have guessed that this sweet-smelling, clean-cut young visitor had the same disease as Kyle.

Jim had filled out some from his meds, which increased his appetite. He wore a black, fuzzy sweatshirt and smiled pleasantly. His brown hair was neatly cut, and when our hands were stamped, I noticed his nails were clean. In a passageway, when our wrists were scanned with ultraviolet light to detect the stamp, Jim smiled again. He was enjoying this experience rather than being sobered by it. I hoped it was the technology that interested him, and not some misplaced macho image of prison life.

We waited for Kyle, sitting on hard plastic chairs bolted together in long rows. Two uniformed guards with pistols were seated on a dais behind a high protective counter. Their stern eyes swept the room. Clusters of people sat on chairs like ours, each group talking quietly with a tan-uniformed young male prisoner.

Kyle emerged. We recognized him from photos. He was a pleasant-looking man in his late thirties, of medium height with neat, dark-brown hair and beard. He scanned the room, picked us out as the only unpaired visitors. He walked over with a hurried gait, looking down except to peek up at us a couple of times.

"We're allowed to shake hands before we all sit down," he said helpfully, extending his hand to me first. His grip was firm.

"So, this is young Greiling," he said after we were settled. He looked paternally at Jim with a broad smile. They were about fifteen years apart.

"How're you doing?" Jim asked. "Sucks you have to be here. Wow, high security."

"Jim set off the alarm twice," I said.

"You don't see anyone breaking out of here," Kyle chuckled. "Beats the Texas prison though." He shook his head, remembering. "Rats contaminated our food. We had to eat it anyway if we wanted to eat."

"Wow," Jim said again, sympathetically.

"Hard to get meds too. Night and day here." He lowered his voice. "Not that it's any picnic. That prisoner over there?" He pointed discreetly from his thigh. "He's a murderer."

Jim stared at the man. I shifted in the plastic seat. A guard glanced our way.

"And remember the man who buried the woman alive?" Kyle said softly, looking serious. "He's here."

My mouth felt dry. Kyle was doing his best to help Jim see the virtue of staying out of prison. I hoped his words were having the same effect on Jim as they were on me.

"How long are you in for?" Jim asked. Behind him, a group of visitors stood to say goodbye. Their prisoner looked wistful.

"Fifteen years. I'm finishing my Texas time here," he said matter-of-factly. "Then I have the federal sentence at another prison."

Jim and I would later visit Kyle at a lower-security facility that was in Grandma Teddy's old state hospital. It had been repurposed into a prison, tan tiles and all. It seemed as though the system hadn't progressed whatsoever. Kyle turned and looked into Jim's eyes. "That's why you should take your meds, Jim. If you don't, you could end up here. You'll be like an engine that locks up without oil." Spoken like the engineer he wanted to be.

"I don't think I need them," Jim said. Then he allowed, "It would've been good if you'd taken some."

On the way home, Jim was quiet. I was disappointed he hadn't connected his situation to Kyle's. I guessed I shouldn't have been surprised. When he was in the psych ward, he had pointed out another patient and said, "That guy's crazy." Jim could recognize illness in others, but not in himself. I knew about anosognosia, a biological, medical inability to be aware of one's mental illness.

I broke the silence. "It's really sad Kyle didn't get help. Now he has to rot in prison, as his mother says."

"I can't imagine being in his shoes and keeping my sanity," Jim empathized. "Can we stop and get some apples?"

"Sure, at the next turnoff. What a great analogy Kyle made." I kept on doggedly. "Comparing not taking meds to an engine without oil. Right?"

"I'm not like him, Mom. I had a pot-induced episode. Medication helped me get over it. I'm well now. I'm going to do things naturally." He smiled at me, with wide-eyed innocence. "I don't need meds."

My God, he hadn't learned a thing from the entire visit.

=

After his commitment ended in December, Jim kept his promise. Against the advice of his psychiatrist, he refused to take any more psych meds. Miraculously, he didn't crash as everyone expected, so his psychiatrist said it was all right for him to return to the University of Montana for the second semester. The doctor told us some people only have one psychotic episode and then recover.

Before he left, Jim attended a reception our newly elected governor held for legislators and their families. He put on a suit and tie and went with Roger and me to the governor's mansion on St. Paul's stateliest street. Governor Jesse Ventura's election as a third-party candidate had rocked Minnesota. I smiled as the chief executive and Jim talked amiably near a table of fancy appetizers. It turned out they both love wilderness areas and discussed them with animation. The governor had no idea Jim had been ill.

10

The Third Rail

"Civil commitment is the third rail in the mental health system," said Mary Schulte, the woman from the Minnesota Bio Brain Association whom Roger and I had met the previous summer. We had kept in contact, and she was now helping me with new legislation. Mary was perched on a chair in my office, preparing me for our meeting with the Mental Health Legislative Network, the umbrella organization for mental health advocates.

As usual, I was heartened to be working on legislation—transferring my fear about Jim's illness into power—but I was nervous about this meeting. We were counting on the groups that represented families and mental health professionals to support the legislation. Surely they would see the need to make earlier care more available. We also wanted to at least touch base with the other groups in the Network. Families and providers saw the problem up close and knew that often the people who didn't get help committed suicide or ended up homeless or in the judicial system. The groups representing people with mental illness, such as the Mental Health Association and the Consumer Survivor Network, worried about coercive treatment and pointed to past abuses of power.

"We need the opponents to see we are seeking more need-based criteria," I said. "This is only for the really sick people, ones for whom timely help can make all the difference."

"No one wants to bring it up," Mary said. "Even those who agree with us." Talking about changing civil commitment laws destroyed the otherwise harmonious relationships among the various mental health advocacy groups.

"I see civil commitment as a way to save lives," I countered. "Like Jim's."

Mary shifted in her chair. "Unfortunately, not everyone at the meeting will think in those terms. Especially Bill Conley, the lobbyist for the Mental Health Association. He's the big gun." Her voice was flutelike. She picked up the paperweight, hefting it in her small hand. "The Mental Health Association focuses on the people who have mental illnesses. Not their families much. Some people who've been locked up in hospitals against their will harbor raw wounds afterward." I thought of Grandma Teddy, begging to come home. "The biggest problem is that the Mental Health Association doesn't see civil commitment as health care. They see it as taking away people's civil rights."

"Well, the National Alliance on Mental Illness was started by families of people with serious mental illnesses," I said, calling on my recently gained knowledge, "so they should be strong supporters, right?"

"NAMI *should* support our legislation." As Mary had said last summer, she was a family member too. She taught NAMI educational classes. "Their executive director will be cautious though, because he usually defers to Bill's leadership, as most Mental Health Legislative Network organizations do. Bill's the most knowledgeable and connected lobbyist."

"I'm now on the NAMI board. That should help."

Mary nodded, then looked at her notes. We ran down the list of other lobbyists who would arrive shortly. She predicted which organizations would be supportive, which would play it cool, and which would join Bill. She was prescient on all counts.

From Mary's descriptions, I was able to identify all the players when they filed into my office an hour later. After everyone was seated, Bill, a solidly built man with a wide nose and pleasant face, smiled charmingly and asked, "What's your son's name?"

"Jim."

"Why don't you tell us what happened with Jim?" He leaned forward, hands tented in front of him. "We have a little background, but there's nothing like hearing your story firsthand."

I studied him for a minute, trying not to feel patronized. I could tell he was here to talk me out of this legislation, and I wouldn't let that happen. "Jim was pretty normal until this summer," I began. "He dabbled in drugs when he was a teenager, but we didn't give it much thought. Marijuana is today's alcohol, right? We didn't suspect mental illness." I robotically recounted the chain of events surrounding Jim's hospitalization, from the preceding spring onward. I'd already told this tale many times. It seemed to be a familiar story to my listeners too.

"Six weeks!" Bill exclaimed on cue when I recounted that Jim's psychiatrist appointment had been scheduled weeks out. His neck and face reddened. "That's the problem right there." All heads nodded but Mary's and mine, the two mothers in the room. "If we had a better mental health system with psychiatrists who would see people in a timely manner, we wouldn't be talking about civil commitments."

"Even if Jim could have gotten in that very day, he refused to go," I pointed out. "Jim said he didn't need any help, and he still doesn't accept that he has a mental illness."

"Jim's case is classic," the NAMI executive director broke in. "Our son, who has schizophrenia, started out like that too."

"Why don't we talk about the many problems with the mental health system? Civil commitments aren't a silver bullet." Bill spoke for the group, untenting his hands.

"I'm more than happy to work on other problems too," I said, uncrossing my legs and smoothing my skirt. "You can tell me what those are, but no matter how great the mental health system is, what good is it if people like Jim think they don't need it?"

"When untreated people do dangerous things, the news stigmatizes everyone." Mary added her soft voice to mine. She convinced no one either. The NAMI executive director went quiet.

"What we need is funding for what we know works," Bill concluded. "That's what would really help people with mental illness." He listed a few of those things, such as more short-term crisis care in the community, more psychiatrists, suicide prevention, police training, and peer helpers.

"If the Network drafts a comprehensive bill covering those things, including funding, I'll work hard for that too," I promised. "I'll author it." They said they would.

"It's what I expected," Mary whispered, last out the door, touching my arm. "It won't be easy."

I retrieved my lunch from the break room and read the mail at my desk. None of it held my interest. I kept hearing Bill's deep voice, denying Jim a right to a safer life. At 1 p.m., Senator Don Betzold walked across the street from the Capitol to my office. He had agreed to be the Senate author for this legislation. He had skipped the morning meeting with Mary and the Network organizations because he already knew that cast. Don was a civil commitment defense attorney, and I was glad I'd be working with him because he was an expert on the statutes.

Our afternoon meeting was with Minnesota Supreme Court Justice Sandra Gardebring. About my age, she was a versatile and talented woman who had been handed many challenging government assignments and had recently chaired a judicial task force that looked into civil commitment laws. I had long admired her and respected her decisions, knowing her to be fair and diligent. Don had also served on the task force, as had representatives of all that morning's groups.

"We want to change the commitment standard so that it's based on a person's needs instead of the danger they pose," I told her. "That's a criminal standard—not a health care one. And it blocks many people from getting treatment."

Sandra listened intently. "The task force heard from many families who share your view," she said, her large bright eyes radiating understanding and intelligence. "Some of their testimony still haunts me, but our group didn't agree to many changes." Research staff informed me afterward that the small law changes that resulted from this work were ineffectual and were rarely if ever used by civil commitment attorneys, including Don.

Don stayed silent. I didn't know if he had stepped on the third rail and taken an active role on the committee supporting families like mine or not.

"I'm not surprised, after meeting some of the participants this morning," I said.

"But that was one point in time," she stressed, with a wise smile at both of us. "I believe you're on the right track with this legislation."

Her words meant the world to me. They, not Bill's, rang in my ears for the rest of the day.

=

The week before the session began, the NAMI lobbyist came to my office with a pen and a sheaf of papers in green bill jackets.

"The Network drafted the comprehensive bill for mental health system reform that includes the things we discussed at the meeting last month," he said with a weak smile. "We very much want to get your signature."

"Excellent," I said heartily. "February 1 is coming up fast."

"We'd be honored if you'd be the second author," he said, thrusting the jackets and pen at me. I immediately saw another legislator's name on the line reserved for the chief author, the one who would shepherd the bill along, present it in committees and on the House floor.

The person the bill would be known for, who would get all the credit, good or bad—the person who should have been me.

I was deeply stung. I didn't ask him to sit down. My gut felt as it had when I'd learned my first teenage love was giving rides to another girl on his motorcycle. "This is an important bill that I'm honored to sign," I said, trying not to miss a beat.

I took the pen and signed my name on the second spot of each of the four bills. "I agree that changing the civil commitment statute alone won't fix everything," I said. *That would have been easier to demonstrate if I had been chief author on both bills,* I thought to myself.

But I understood the snub. Bill didn't want to work with me on this proposal when he was fighting me on the other one. He would have been smarter, however, to tie up my time making me the chief author. Now I was freer to focus on civil commitment.

I smiled at the lobbyist as I handed back the bills. He nodded, without smiling, and left fast.

=

"There must be a purpose to all that happened to my family," Eileen Stack said resolutely, taking off her coat in my office a month later.

I hadn't seen her in person since she had told me her tragic story the fall before. Her energetic, sweeping movements told me she was hyped for our press conference in one hour.

"My New Year's resolution is to start speaking out about the mental health system too," I agreed. "We can't keep hiding our stories, like my family did with my grandmother's schizophrenia." I smiled at how easily that last line slipped off my tongue.

"I'm determined to do what I promised," Eileen said. "Hard as that may be." Her voice missed a note, reminding me of the glass of wine she had sipped for courage that evening when she told me about her son hammering her husband to death. Today she was going to tell that story again.

"Unfortunately, stories like yours are needed if we're going to be able to cut into our opposition. Who would think getting earlier treatment for people who don't know they're sick would be so hard?" I searched through the pile of files on my desk for the one containing today's press release. I still felt a pang of hurt in my chest as I added, "Another legislator is carrying the Mental Health Legislative Network's bill for system-wide reform." I would have to work twice as hard to pass our bill, because the other one would probably be portrayed as an alternative.

"Getting help for people like our sons is essential if they're going to be able to benefit from the rest of the system," she replied.

"Yes. Also, families probably don't realize just how much company there is in having a member with mental illness," I added. I thumbed through the file I had found. "If they think they're alone, they're less apt to speak out. It's clear to me that mental illness is the last horizon in the civil rights movement. We should be talking more about discrimination against being able to get mental health care and services instead of stigma. It's an easy out for those who should be providing care to say the person doesn't want it."

My legislative assistant interrupted us by ushering in our third press conference participant, Mary Zdanowicz, a dark-haired, serious-looking woman wearing a business suit who looked like the attorney she was. She had just flown in from Virginia that morning. I had been communicating with her for weeks about reforming Minnesota's civil commitment laws. She returned my calls and emails faster than anyone in Minnesota.

"Mary Zdanowicz is the executive director for the Treatment Advocacy Center," I told Eileen, touching each woman lightly on the shoulder.

"We formed last year as an offshoot of NAMI," Mary supplied, as she shook Eileen's hand. "We help states create laws so people with serious mental illness get the treatment they need."

After coordinating our pitch order, we walked to the pressroom downstairs. We were joined by my Democratic Caucus press person, the young man who had handled the logistics.

I was used to multiple newspeople crowding into press conferences, a stock tactic for publicizing legislation. The number of TV cameras was often a measure of the success of an event. When we reached the hallway just outside the press room, I slowed my pace and stopped talking. I could see through the window that there were only two reporters. No TV cameras.

My staffer shot me a guilty glance. Part of his job was to round up participants. Eileen's story sounded juicy and our topic was controversial. Were the press writing off this legislation as dead on arrival? Didn't they know how many families were affected? Or were they buying into the secrecy of mental illness? I felt this slight deep in my belly as I thought of Jim staring vacantly in the psych ward.

Thankfully, the other participants were oblivious to the significance of the poor turnout. They were pleased with the presence of both a major newspaper and a radio station.

The radio reporter, Eric Eskola, was a colorful man who always wore a wool scarf around his neck when the weather was cool and who usually asked the best questions at press conferences. "Good morning, Representative Greiling," he greeted me cheerfully.

The room was warm. I felt sweat starting on my back. I nodded, smiled, then moved to the podium, motioning the others to follow me. I gave my opening spiel and introduced the two women. I was proud of Eileen as she eloquently told her story.

"Our son Will was threatening people with a knife, but the police said they couldn't do anything about it." She swallowed hard. "I remember yelling at them, 'He's putting other people in danger.' We decided to try to get him committed instead. His psychiatrist agreed, but the psychiatrist at the county hearing disagreed. He said, 'Will is too bright and functional, so there's no reason to commit him,' as if that had anything to do with his being sick. Later, when I came home," she wound up her story, "the dog was tied, the garage door was open, and the van was gone." A tear leaked down her cheek. "I walked through the house and then . . ." She paused a long minute, her lip quavering. "And then I discovered my husband's body." She heaved a long sigh and finished with stronger cadence, "We really have to change some laws so this doesn't happen to another family. There needs to be an easier route."

Mary Zdanowicz wrapped up our presentation, saying legislation like ours was being introduced across the country. The radio reporter asked her what counterarguments opponents made and then asked, "What groups are supporting this?"

"The National Alliance on Mental Illness, Minnesota Bio Brain Association, Minnesota Medical Association, Minnesota Psychiatric Society, League of Women Voters, and others. Our list is growing," I said. I was glad that NAMI was now a full-fledged partner with a highly supportive board. Some groups had come forward on their own to sign on, and I had solicited others. I gathered my papers from the podium. "I hear from people who tell me their stories almost every day."

"Planning to pass it this year, Representative Greiling?"

"I've asked for a hearing and have bipartisan cosponsors. We're hopeful for passage this year, but we're in it for the long haul."

"Thanks for coming," I said to Eric, after the other reporter, who never wrote a word, dashed away.

"Thanks for the press conference," he replied, with his boyish grin. "It's a good story." I felt like hugging him. He replayed a good deal of the testimony in his radio coverage later in the day.

I was disappointed with the lack of interest from the press, but I didn't take it personally. By this point in my legislative career, I had enjoyed my share of media coverage on a variety of other topics. I had a sign taped to my door that read, "It's better to live fifteen years as a tiger than a hundred years as a chicken." I had spoken out on government ethics, education policies and suburban school funding, high school sports rules, school energy-saving contracts, chemical spraying for mosquitoes, unchecked caucus leadership power, and University of Minnesota regent selection. I had authored a constitutional amendment to abolish the state treasurer office, an amendment that passed into law. All these things had gotten me press—but I didn't care half as much about any of them as I did about this legislation. I swallowed my disappointment and looked at our setback as evidence of the huge amount of work we had ahead of us.

=

By the time I dropped Jim off in Montana for the second semester, Roger and I had started to believe he might be one of those people Jim's psychiatrist had talked about: the ones who suffered only one psychotic episode. He still hadn't crashed, even though he was no longer taking any medication. We put his illness out of our minds. We wanted him to have the chance to return to his budding life in the mountains he so loved.

When our plane landed, snow covered the evergreens that stood tall on the mountains surrounding the Missoula valley. Jim was quiet, but he registered for classes and purchased his books. We met with Dr. Brown, the campus psychologist Jim had seen the year before. Dr. Brown put Jim in touch with a psychiatrist in a nearby office who would see Jim monthly and stand ready to prescribe psych meds if the need should arise. Finally, as a concrete way to celebrate his regained good health, Jim and I scrubbed every inch of his apartment.

I was elated when Jim contacted one of his friends, who had also transferred from Northland, to go skiing. Since he had been diagnosed, Jim had had very little contact with his friends. Word had gotten out about his troubles. He'd had to quit his restaurant job in Minnesota, and he was too subdued to reach out when he was better. That Jim was alone with his illness was a heartache for me, and I could only imagine how it made him feel.

While Jim and his friend were skiing, a service man came to fix the gas range in Jim's apartment. I felt proud to be his mother, reading in my normal son's clean, cozy living room.

=

When I returned to Minnesota, I continued to push hard for the civil commitment legislation. Other families might not be as lucky as we were.

One warm morning in March, I felt mellow as I drove to work. I greeted several earlier risers as I walked to my office and talked briefly with my assistant. When I scooped up my mail I spotted an important caucus memo. It was distributed to legislators each year just before the session, describing bill proposals legislators should know about.

I went into my office, threw down my belongings, and ripped open the briefing. The memo was several pages long. I scanned each page but couldn't find anything about the bill. I hung up my coat, straightened my desk, and checked again. Nada. Zilch. Zippo. I checked for the proposal from the Mental Health Legislative Network. They'd been dissed too. If that hadn't been the case, I would have suspected Bill and his connections of sabotaging our bill.

Our caucus staff researchers, who were experts in assigned areas, wrote this memo. They sometimes ran their text by the legislators who were committee chairs. Only legislators in the majority party could chair committees, however, and we were in the minority. Our staff would have to guess which bills would get hearings. Still, they should know which bills would be high profile, the ones legislators should know about.

My mellowness vanished. Torrid anger ignited within me. Since there was nothing in this memo about mental illness, our staff obviously hadn't deemed it important. I charged past my assistant, down the hall to the office of the staff researcher who had written this section. He was a young man known for his stellar work. He was always on top of everything, so it had not occurred to me to ask him to include my proposal. When I stomped in, he was seated behind his desk, which nearly filled his office. He looked up, startled at my expression, and laid down his pen.

"My mental health legislation isn't here," I charged, stabbing the memo with my finger. "I've been working on it for weeks. It's been in the media, and the entire mental health community is talking about it."

His eyes opened wide. "I'm sorry, Representative Greiling." He didn't say he didn't know about my bill.

"I wasn't expecting a glowing review," I spewed, waving the briefing wildly. "I know the bill is controversial, so I fully expected cons along with the pros, but fucking nothing at all?"

He stared at me, pushing back his chair, putting more distance between us. "And what about the Network's proposal?" I fumed. "That's not here either. Is mental illness invisible?"

I half expected I might upend his desk in my fury, so I whirled around and stormed out. I headed down the hall in the opposite direction, toward the leadership corner, heels clicking rapidly. No stopping me now. The office of our head caucus staffer was there.

Mike Charboneau had shown up at my office when he'd first heard about Jim. I'd thought he was one of the many people stopping by to confide about their experience with mental illness.

"You too?" I had choked, overcome at his kindness.

"No," he smiled. "I just came to support you." I hugged him.

This morning, Mike was haplessly in his office, reading the newspaper. He was respectfully formal with all the legislators and was never without a tie. He called each "representative" or "senator"—even those who asked to be on a first-name basis—contributing to his survival during leadership changes. I accosted him with the same vitriol I had used on the other poor staffer. He stood to meet me.

"Members use this briefing to gauge the gravitas of bills," I said, waving the now-wrinkled packet. "There's nothing here about my legislation, or any other mental health legislation for that matter. Am I invisible around here? Is mental illness invisible?"

A veteran of legislator tirades, Mike was unflappable. "Representative Greiling, I hear you. I'll look into this."

"I'm communicating with families all around the state, and they're contacting their legislators, so this is a serious omission. Legislators need to know about my bill."

"I'll talk to Research." He smiled knowingly.

I knew his word was his bond.

"So typical of how we treat mental illness," I said, winding down, rolling the memo into a scroll.

This was the first time I had ever acted this way at work, although I'd witnessed other legislators employ this tactic. For me it wasn't a tactic. It was organic. I had surprised myself, but I was glad I'd done it. Unlike in other more normal workplaces, at the legislature the loud, squeaky wheel often got the oil.

I walked back to my office, my heart pumping more slowly. My assistant looked up from her computer. She had borne witness to my clomping up and down the hall and had wisely held her peace.

I went into my office, closed the door, and sat on a chair facing the window. I saw dirty snow and wished it were spring so I could let in fresh air. My mind was reeling. It was as if the psychologist was sending us home again with no help for Jim in sight, the police officer was in our living room refusing to take him to the hospital, and the hospital was declining to talk to me. I was mad Grandma Teddy had left, and I was furious that Jim might have an illness like hers.

A couple of months later, on the last day of the legislative session, any doubt about Jim having a mental illness was dispelled when I got the call that he was in jail in Montana. The civil commitment bill had not gotten a hearing.

11
One of Them

May 9–September 2000

Halfway into Montana I turned up a mountain pass. Bright sunshine had been helping keep me awake, but now the sky was darkening. I had caught a couple hours of sleep at a wayside stop in North Dakota, but not enough to make up for the lack of sleep the night before at the Capitol when we had worked through the night to finish the session's work, the night I had blurted out to another legislator that my son was in jail. I had dashed out as soon as we adjourned, skipping the retirement speeches I always enjoyed.

Now I felt as if I had stepped out of the wardrobe into frozen Narnia. The warm spring sunshine abruptly transformed into a full-blown blizzard, and I strained to see through driving snowflakes. I joined a long line of bumper-to-bumper cars filing slowly up the mountain. I flipped radio stations to see if I could find a weather channel, but I'd lost the signal. A small, foreign-looking car was stalled on the side of the road beside me, and a semitrailer truck had jackknifed into the ditch.

I was used to harsh winters in Minnesota, but this sudden storm had caught me by surprise. My tires spun, grappling for traction. I couldn't believe this was happening. I felt like I had the summer before when, out of the blue, mental illness had smacked our family in the face.

When I crested the mountaintop, the sun was shining again. The radio came back on in a loud blare. A family in shorts and T-shirts were filling up their car at a Mobil station. The boy and girl were laughing and scraping snow off their warm, dripping vehicle and throwing chunks at each other—a happy family, like ours used to be.

I was beginning to realize that we weren't going to be an all-American family any more. I could no longer pick up a newspaper, read about a tragedy, and be safe, knowing we had once again been missed. I thought I'd left mental illness behind when Grandma Teddy died, but now, deep in my stomach, I felt that familiar brew of loss, anger, and guilt.

When I reached Missoula, Jim's key was under his mat as the landlady had promised. As I stooped to get it, a young couple who were holding hands walked by. The woman called out, "Are you his mom?"

I nodded.

"He bikes all the time. From early morning until after dark," she said, with a sympathetic smile. "Just bikes and bikes. Always by himself. We're glad you're here." She sounded as if she had experience.

"I'm hoping to take him home to Minnesota."

As I inserted the key in Jim's lock, I thought about dropping him off for the second semester, less than four months earlier. We had cleaned his place from top to bottom, a calming, symbolic new beginning. I had been full of hope that my son had escaped schizophrenia. Now I was as alone as the woman said Jim always was.

When I opened the door, the skunky smell of marijuana accosted my nostrils. The small living room was relatively neat, but I saw crumbs of weed strewn over the couch and floor. The kitchen counter was lined with dirty dishes; pots and pans were piled high in the sink. The bedroom floor was littered with dirty clothes. You could have fooled me if the sheets had been changed since I left. I added my clothes to the floor and flung on my nightgown, brushed my teeth, and descended into the embrace of Jim's sheets. They smelled strongly of him, bringing some comfort.

In the morning, I turned on Jim's sound system. Out blared the Grateful Dead, his favorite band. Jerry Garcia had died during Jim's third mountain-hiking trip, as had my father, who would never know that his grandson had the same dreadful illness as his mother. I straightened a few things and washed the dishes, waiting for visiting hours.

The jail waiting room was loud and crowded. A kind woman with dyed orange-red hair filled me in on the ropes. Still, I was unprepared to see my son handcuffed and wearing an orange jumpsuit. He sat behind a pane of glass, the typical black telephones on each side. Haggard and unshaven, he smiled tightly at me.

"You have a good attorney, sweetheart," I said into my handset. "Dr. Brown recommended him."

He didn't answer. His eyes were unfocused, wild. I could see he wasn't tracking.

"You remember Dr. Brown visiting?"

"Things are confusing, Mom," he said slowly, as if he was drugged. I hoped that meant they had started him on psych meds in the jail.

I told him as simply as I could that I intended to bring him home after court tomorrow. I'd see him there.

I spent the rest of the day packing up his apartment, listening to the Grateful Dead, knowing Jim would never again be a student at the University of Montana.

A line of prisoners shuffled into the courtroom the next morning. Six young men in handcuffs, shackled at the ankles. My Jim was one of them. *My God!*

I sat on a hard chair in the spectator gallery along with a couple of people who looked like students. Jim was the only one with an attorney. Roger had transferred $5,000 into our account to pay him. What happened to other people with serious mental illness who ended up here without an attorney? I knew the answer. No one, probably including they themselves, would have a clue they were ill. Even if they did, the result would be the same: They would be labeled criminals. I was here to stop that from happening to our innocent, ill son.

After Jim's attorney spoke, the judge kindly said Jim could go with me to Minnesota, provided he got treatment. If he kept his nose clean for a year, his felony charge would be dismissed. I beamed at her.

No one at the jail could tell me whether Jim had been given any meds while he was there, and none were provided for the trip home. I hadn't found any at his apartment, which hadn't surprised me greatly. I had learned when I talked with Dr. Brown that last night at the Capitol that Jim had fired the psychiatrist soon after I departed in January.

On the way back to Minnesota, Jim and I stopped for the night near where I'd encountered the mountain blizzard. I was shaking with tiredness, so I immediately got ready for bed. On the bed next to mine, Jim crouched on his haunches, puffing a cigarette. His unsettling eyes glared at me, except when he glanced off to one side and smirked. It looked as if he was enjoying a private joke with someone only he could see.

I knew I should be watchful. I should protect myself in case Jim tried to hurt me, but all I could do was fall asleep.

The next morning, Jim grabbed the car keys out of my hand. He chortled, "I'm driving."

I knew he wouldn't respond to motherly commands. It would be fruitless to try to wrestle the keys from him. If I tried, I might enrage him. I didn't want to know how that might end, but I feared that at best it could result in my being left behind. I saw no option but to get in the passenger side and clutch my seat, as I had done when we first drove him here. How had I not seen then that he was ill?

As we careened around mountain bends, I thought about missing a curve. What if he drove us over on purpose to satisfy his delusion? It might be peaceful, I thought, but when I looked over the sheer cliff, I was afraid. All I could see was air.

=

Roger and I kept our promise to the Missoula judge to get Jim treatment in Minnesota. After a month in a care facility, he was home with us, and we weren't sure he was taking his meds. Short of watching him place the pills in his mouth and making sure he swallowed—which Jim wouldn't allow—there was nothing we could do.

At first Jim and I enjoyed good conversations, talking of hope for his future. When that wore thin, I suggested he call a friend. He didn't. None called him. I ached for my solitary son and tried to fill the gap. We shopped for new jeans. He accompanied me to the Capitol for a constituent reception, smiling amiably when I introduced him. He got a summer job with a county road crew. When I picked him up after work, he was sitting as far away from the other young workers as he could get, slumped over with his head on his knees. The other young men were talking and laughing. He quit after a week. I doubled my efforts to keep him occupied. We made pizza. We washed my car. I let him take it occasionally, but all he did was go to bars. My heart burned thinking of my son all alone in such a social place.

Roger traveled to Montana over Memorial Day weekend to retrieve Jim's things. While he was gone, Jim and I played a lot of cards, and he did a lot of smirking and glaring at me. Once he slammed his cards on the table so hard he made me jump. I felt cold and sweaty and was relieved when Roger returned.

A sure sign of spring has always been when I peel off my shoes and socks and go barefoot. This summer I started wearing my running shoes at all times, ready for action.

One day, after Roger left for work, I decided to clean our walk-in bedroom closet. I wanted to get it done before Jim woke up. Cleaning usually calmed me, but not this morning. While I washed dirt from the shoe rack—including the empty space for the shoes I was wearing— my thoughts turned to Eileen Stack's story. I'd heard similar stories at a meeting of the Forensic Network, a NAMI chapter made up of families with loved ones in prison, many of whom had murdered people. My heart beat faster as I thought about our family becoming one of those stories.

As Jim continued to sleep, I relaxed a little. Dust floated in the air, backlit by the open windows beyond the closet. Each shelf sparkled, smelling freshly of bleach. I vacuumed the carpet, getting winter furnace dust out of every corner. If only I could clean out Jim's mind. Thinking of him made my fingers clumsy. I dropped a belt, picked it up quickly, replaced it on its hook.

Don't be cornered, I'd read. Keep yourself between the person and the door, especially one not taking prescribed meds and using illicit drugs. Jim had been acting secretively about his backpack. He made sure to take it to his room immediately instead of throwing it on the floor by the front door. Roger and I feared that in addition to not taking his prescribed meds, he may have started using again. His meds didn't cover all his symptoms, especially anxiety and depression. But illicit drugs didn't help him for long. They only hastened his downward spiral. I knew by now that drug abuse occurred in more than half the people with mental illness.

I felt alone. How many people could ever understand being so afraid of one's own son? What could be worse than that? Fear compounded my grief over his illness.

I crept up to Jim's bedroom door and poked it open a crack. In slumber, my son looked like the affable teenager he so recently had been. His mouth was relaxed from its sneer, his glaring eyes shut, fists uncurled. I smiled.

The bed sheets rustled, startling me. I returned my gaze to his face.

"Why are you looking at me like that?" His eyes narrowed beneath his tousled hair.

"I wondered if you were ever getting up," I said, backing away, my small enjoyment ended.

Jim yawned and stretched, then suddenly flung off the bed covers. I recoiled further. He came swiftly toward me, his painfully thin body clad only in boxer shorts. He smelled rank. My heart beat faster. A trickle of sweat glided down my armpit. Then he squeezed past me and headed to the bathroom. I felt limp with relief. I grabbed the phone and hastened to the living room to sit near the front door. I wanted to be ready to call for help. My stomach soured.

After I heard the toilet flush, Jim sauntered into the room. "I need the car," he demanded.

"Not today," I said, thinking of other motorists. I tightened my grip on my phone. "Want some breakfast?"

He started toward me. I jumped up, dodged around him, and ran out the door. My pulse was pounding. When I reached the center of the front yard, I stopped. I blinked in the strong midday sunshine. All was quiet and peaceful. No other person was in sight. I waited awhile and then gingerly went back inside.

Jim was standing where I'd left him, looking bewildered. "What was that all about, Mom?" He sounded hurt, like the real Jim. Did he suspect I was terrified?

When he went to the kitchen to make himself a sandwich, I lugged the vacuum cleaner downstairs to its laundry room corner. It belonged across from the gaping hole Jim had punched in the wall the previous summer when I put his drugs down the disposal. When I had taken that drastic step, I had been hopeful that getting help for Jim would cure him, or at least make him better. Now we were back where we started, except worse.

I was as tired as I had ever been, even more tired than when Angela and Jim were new babies. I fell into bed each night exhausted.

In the morning my limbs felt leaden, as if I were moving through mud. I thought that maybe being dead would be a relief.

Leaning back in bed one night, Roger read a two-week-old newspaper as I stared at the same page of my book. Jim wasn't home yet. Would I always have this taut ball of fear in my stomach about him? I was both afraid *of* him and afraid *for* him at the same time. The cat pounced on my restless legs beneath the bedspread, making me jerk. Roger turned out the light and managed to nod off, but I remained awake. From the darkness outside, I heard a mosquito buzzing near the window screen.

Jim's key turned in the lock. I held my body still. He came up the stairs and strode down the hallway between our room and his. I stiffened when I heard him pause outside our door. I heard him turn into his room and rustle around, mumbling to himself; I listened until the house went quiet.

The next evening while I was preparing supper, Roger came up from the basement with a strange look on his face. Jim followed close on his heels, looking sheepish. I put down my mixing spoon.

"I thought I had to pull Dad's ear off," Jim said, speaking rapidly.

"He didn't pull very hard," Roger said, looking at me searchingly.

"I heard a crunching," Jim grimaced.

I braced my stomach muscles. The mounting tension was coming to a head. We could be calling the police tonight. That had panicked me last summer, but now I felt as if it could bring relief. I knew we couldn't call too soon, or the police would come and then leave.

"Why don't you set the table, Jim?" I suggested, as if he were a preschooler needing his attention diverted. He opened the silverware drawer.

After supper, I made popcorn and Jim and I started to watch a movie in Angela's old room.

"Stop crunching," Jim said crabbily.

I sucked the kernels in my mouth, then set my bowl aside.

Jim stood up abruptly, almost upsetting his bowl of popcorn. "Just a minute," he said. He dashed out of the room. I heard him thunder down the steps to the basement. Was he going to try harder with Roger's ear? I heard a loud crash of glass, as if Jim had taken a hammer to a basement window instead.

Calm flooded over me. It was time.

"It's your turn to call," I said to Roger when he came upstairs. I smiled wearily at him, as if I'd just birthed a baby. Roger returned the same smile. I surprised myself and chuckled a bit. Roger chuckled too. What was with *us?* I guess we had to laugh to stop ourselves from crying.

While Roger was talking calmly to 911, Jim slunk up the stairs. All the steam was out of him. "I broke a window. Sorry."

"Dad's calling for help. You need some, don't you, honey?"

"Yes," he said, contritely.

"Which window?"

"The laundry room."

"Hammer?"

"Vacuum cleaner."

"Wasn't it heavy?"

"Not really."

He followed me submissively outdoors. After we sat down on the front steps, I put my arm around his shoulder. At least for now his delusion wasn't making me the enemy. He was still my little boy. The sun was going down, but it was still fairly light.

How could we help Jim see the connection between what had happened tonight and the fact that he needed to take his medication? How did other families do this? Why couldn't we get more help? After Jim left a hospital or treatment program, they just left everything to us parents. Why wasn't there somewhere else to get help besides the police? What did families do who were from cultures that feared police?

I saw an officer driving up our street at a snail's pace. He stopped midway. He was afraid too. 'What's going on?" he hollered out his window.

"We have someone here who needs to go to the hospital," I shouted. "It's okay. He's calm now."

The relieved officer called an ambulance and Jim went docilely.

The next morning, I saw glass sprayed halfway across our backyard.

=

I tried the county crisis team the next time. I'd found out I could call them myself. After Jim returned from the hospital, he was gone many nights and soon sank back into the same shape he'd been in before.

The day I deemed Jim would qualify for the crisis team, I slipped out the front door with the phone in my hand. I judged that they would be able to come sooner than the police and without Jim having to be in such a crisis. I stationed myself under our red maple and dug a slip of paper out of my pocket. I'd been carrying the crisis team's scribbled number around for the last couple of days.

"My son needs to be hospitalized," I said to the woman who answered.

"Why don't you describe him?" Her voice sounded sterile.

I told her about his being in jail earlier in the spring, his breaking the window, and his recent hospitalization. "We think he's stopped taking his meds, because he's not eating or sleeping much. My husband and I are so worried."

I heard papers rustle. "What's he doing?"

"Just now he was yelling that I'm evil."

"I mean something physical."

"He gets out of control on a dime. Violence seems just around the corner. We'd rather not get to that point." I leaned a hand on the rough tree bark. "He has thoughts he should kill me."

"Has he harmed you?"

"No." I struggled for composure. "But I might not mind terribly being put out of this misery."

The woman's voice softened. "You don't want to say that."

"I think I do," I declared, "but I don't want to leave my son to deal with this so-called mental health system by himself. I can't deal with it, with my supposed-right mind."

"We could come out and talk with him," she offered, "but if he doesn't meet criteria and isn't willing, there'd be nothing we could do."

"He won't be willing. If you come out and then leave, in the state he's in," I said, "he'd be madder. And I'd be alone with him."

"From what you describe, we couldn't do anything. Sorry."

"I want you to record that I called and you didn't do anything," I barked. "In case anything happens." I knew this woman was just doing her job, following the stupid laws, but I needed to be mad at someone. My insides were steaming.

The next day, Jim hadn't appeared by midafternoon, so I checked in his room. It was dark and stank of sweat, unwashed clothes, and tobacco. Clothes and junk were strewn on every surface: empty cigarette packs, a cheap lighter, keys, bottles, food containers, billfold, coins, crumpled paper. I noticed his body's outline under his bed covers. When I called his name, he didn't respond. I thought he was asleep, but when my eyes adjusted, I was startled to see him staring straight at me. His hollow, vacant eyes looked ghostly, as if they'd seen the Holocaust.

They reminded me of a game my cousins and I played when we were kids. We would pretend one kid "went crazy." That kid would sit quietly, glaring intently at another kid, then rise from the chair and walk slowly, stiff-legged, toward the second kid.

"Stop. Let's not play this game anymore," someone would say. "You're scaring me." The one who was "crazy" kept coming, slowly reaching out monster arms until we all ran screaming to the grown-ups. Where were those grown-ups now?

"Jim?" I gasped. He still didn't respond, so I hurriedly shut the door. I hastened to the kitchen phone. The back of my neck prickled. This time I skipped the crisis team and called 911. "Please send someone. Our son is very ill."

Three police officers arrived. Jim didn't respond to their questions either. Except for his open eyes, he seemed comatose. They immediately called an ambulance. Jim was strapped to a stretcher and placed in the back. I was invited to ride in front, beside the driver.

"I tried to get the mental health crisis team to come yesterday," I said, half to myself.

"I know how that goes," the driver replied, shaking his head.

Roger joined me in the emergency room. I was grateful for his comforting presence. He was the only other person in the world who had the same stake in our son as I did. We sat together by Jim's bed. His eyes were closed, but in a few minutes his eyelids fluttered open.

He gazed around and his body stiffened. His eyes turned fiery. "I'm at the hospital, aren't I?"

"You're very sick," I said, looking uneasily around for medical people.

"Fuck!" Jim raised his upper body on one elbow. "Why'd you bring me here? I'm supposed to die."

"To get better, Jim," Roger said soothingly, trying to calm him.

Jim trained livid eyes on me. "You raped me, didn't you? My own mother."

"Of course not," I moaned. What must be going on in his poor head?

He slumped back down, looking as relieved as I felt. A nurse returned. Roger and I were ushered into a small private room, the kind our family had been offered when my dad died.

"He wasn't like this yesterday," Roger said after she left. His face was drawn, his eyes bloodshot. "Is this all there is to the mental health system?" he asked, sounding dazed.

"There isn't one," I said.

A young man in green scrubs came in and introduced himself as a physician. "Did you notice any empty containers?" He fingered the stethoscope around his neck. "Your son says he was trying to kill himself. He took pills. We need to know what they were."

We were dumbstruck. Roger went home to search, while I waited in the small room. When he returned, he handed three empty bottles to the doctor. Jim had taken all his psych meds and some over-the-counter medications.

Before any of this had begun to sink in, a nurse reported that Jim was asking for us. When we arrived in the exam room, a doctor was giving him a cursory admission physical. When he pushed up Jim's sleeve to take his blood pressure, he halted. "Whoa," he said, holding up Jim's arm. "What happened here?"

I winced when I saw a large, raw wound on Jim's forearm. I pressed Roger's arm.

"Candle wax," Jim said, then added quickly, "I did it accidentally."

The doctor scrutinized the burn, pressing around it. "Looks like more than dripping wax, son."

Jim squeezed his eyes shut. "I burned myself with my lighter."

"More than once, right?" The doctor began applying antiseptic.

Jim inhaled sharply when it touched the wound. "Yes."

Roger took a quick, shallow breath, as if he were the one feeling the sting.

"Didn't that hurt terribly?" I asked incredulously.

"A lot," he shuddered, "but I had to."

Since he was talking candidly, I continued. "Where'd you go, when you were gone those nights?"

"St. Paul."

"You didn't have the car."

"I walked. I had to keep walking." He looked at me sideways, with a miserable expression. "Otherwise I had to kill you."

The doctor stopped working and looked at me. Roger brushed his eyes.

"You poor thing," I said, heaving a ragged sigh.

Jim was apparently as petrified of killing me as I was of being killed. I had been so focused on fearing my own son, I'd neglected to be sympathetic to his terrors. Relief poured into my veins, as if I were being prepped for surgery. I felt as if I could fall into a deep sleep from which I would awake fully rested.

"I'm such a loser. I *had* to kill myself. I couldn't do what I was supposed to."

"No, Jim," I said. "You are strong."

"Why'd you obey the voices other times?" Roger asked, his face brighter.

"I saw awful weapons coming to torture me if I didn't." He cringed. "You haven't been to hell, so you aren't afraid. You would be if you knew what it's like, like I do."

I hugged Jim, my heart swelling. I kissed the top of his head, something I hadn't dared do for a very long while.

"I marvel at his strength," I repeated to Roger, as we drove home. "He resisted killing me, even when he had so many other terrible thoughts." I felt relaxed, as if I'd taken sips of wine.

"And he barely pulled my ear," Roger replied.

"I don't think I'll be afraid of him anymore," I said. "But now I'm even more terrified *for* him."

12
Early Intervention

One day that fall when I was at my office trying to catch up on constituent work, a handsome, puckish man with a neat mustache and longish gray hair combed back from his forehead popped his head into my office. I was intrigued by his dancing eyes and merry charisma, so I ushered him in. His name was John Milton, and he wanted to tell me about his stepson. It was a cloudy day, so I turned on the lamp.

Twenty years earlier, John had been a feisty young state senator. He had chaired the Health and Human Services Committee.

"My stepson and I got along well," he said, in his deep baritone. He was nearing the end of his story. "I tried to provide support, but in the end, I couldn't help him out of his mental illness." His eyes glistened behind his wire-rimmed glasses. "Just when I thought we were getting someplace, he killed himself."

My eyes prickled. I straightened the magazines on the table.

He recovered. "I've heard about your legislation and want to help." He smoothed his mustache with his thumb and pointer finger. "I was elected the same year as Senator Linda Berglin," he said with a smile, referring to the current powerful, long-tenured chair of the committee he'd once chaired. "We had a good relationship back then, and I'm confident I can be helpful."

"The Mental Health Association is our chief opponent," I said. "People tell me their lobbyist has her ear."

John laughed long and hard, a laugh that bolstered me. It was just what I needed right then when things weren't going well with Jim. We laughed often over the summer as we brainstormed in my office. No one walking by would have guessed our serious mission.

"Let's call the bill 'early intervention,'" John sagely advised, "instead of 'civil commitment.'" He stopped typing at my computer and leaned back in the desk chair, smoothing his hair.

We agreed it was better to focus on the need for care rather than on taking away rights.

We made lists of likely allies, and I went through the people I had already contacted. "The governor's mental health point person seems favorable," I said, "but the attorney general isn't sure. He said he once represented a friend in a civil commitment hearing and saw himself as rescuing his friend."

"Seems sensible," John said, "until you've lived it."

"I've told the head of psychiatry at the university, Dr. Charles Schulz, about a family the U had turned away when they came about their son's mental illness. The son was unwilling to be treated and was not deemed a danger. The mother said she cried all the way across campus, her husband at her side, with their very ill son loping ahead in his own world. The university had been their last hope."

"Jesus," John said.

"Dr. Schulz vowed to do better. He said doctors should at the very least tell people that they don't agree with the law. He went with me to the League of Women Voters office, where he told their legislative committee, 'Even if the system were lined with gold, it would be of no use to a person too ill to recognize he or she needs it.' We got their endorsement."

"Next, we'll meet with editorial writers." John's eyes twinkled. "I know some of those people. I'll come with you."

The Minneapolis and St. Paul newspapers were located in imposing buildings in their respective downtowns. Kate Stanley, at the Minneapolis *Star Tribune,* was particularly interested in hearing about our early-intervention legislation. She met John and me in a gigantic foyer and led us up the elevator to a windowless conference room. Kate was a tightly wound, effervescent, slim woman.

"I was one of the prime movers wanting to reform the mental health system by closing institutions," John said. "As you know, Kate, that was in the days of *One Flew over the Cuckoo's Nest.*" During those days of deinstitutionalization, patients like my grandma were often sent to apartments without any support, all in the name of freedom.

"I feel responsible to help fix what we did," John continued. "Many of those former state hospital patients—who aren't dead like my stepson—are homeless or in prison."

Kate swiveled in her chair to face me. She'd been listening intently but took no notes. "What're you proposing?"

I handed her the one-page summary John and I had prepared. It stated that 40 percent of the people with schizophrenia and bipolar disorder don't recognize their mental illness because of anosognosia; that the sickest people are the ones who receive the least care; that NAMI called psychosis "a fire in the brain" that needed to be put out before serious damage was done; that considerable money could be saved if people were healthy and could work.

"Unless the public takes notice," I said, "opponents will prevail like they did on Justice Gardebring's task force." I explained that the recent task force had recommended mainly useless changes to the civil commitment statutes because they had been up against the same opponents we were.

Both newspapers wrote positive editorials.

We continued amassing support during the fall. Some groups came forward on their own, such as the American Federation of State, County, and Municipal Employees (AFSCME), the labor union representing many mental health workers. Other groups needed to be persuaded to join us or, in the case of People Incorporated, one of the large mental health providers, to at least remain neutral.

In February a benefactor emerged. Martha Muska wasn't a woman to trifle with. Her son had done jail time after not getting proper care when he needed it.

"I'm going to fund a lobbyist," she announced with an effervescent grin over lunch. "You're a busy lady, and having a good person at the Capitol to keep track of this important bill would really help, wouldn't it?" She reached over and squeezed my hand.

"Definitely." I grinned and reached for my dessert, suddenly feeling hungry.

"Find a person with a little pizzazz, dear," she winked, signaling for more coffee. A waitress hurried over.

Martha contributed $25,000 to secure the lobbyist. A veteran lobbyist whose son had also died by suicide—a friend of John Milton's—recommended one: Christine White, a tall, industrious young woman who gave her heart to our legislation. Martha gave her stamp of approval, declaring that Christine did indeed have pizzazz. John and Christine became fixtures at the Capitol whenever our bill was in sight. They combed bill hearings each day and showed up each time the early-intervention bill was scheduled. They met in advance with each committee member who would vote on our bill at the hearing. My spirits rose whenever I encountered their smiling, confident faces in the Capitol. The names on our supporter list were hugely important, but it was a great relief to also have savvy allies in the thick of the action—where bills lived or quietly died. Maybe we had turned a corner.

13

Tasks Unlimited

2001–2002

After Jim's suicide attempt, we turned a corner at home too. Roger and I announced to Jim's doctors—as soon as he reached Anoka-Metro Regional Treatment Center for the second time—that he couldn't come home and that their social workers had better start making other plans. We weren't equipped to make sure our son took his meds. I suggested they look into a promising-sounding program one of Paul Wellstone's aides had recently acquainted me with, Tasks Unlimited. The organization is geared to people with serious mental illnesses, as we now had to admit Jim had, and provides supported employment, housing, and mental health services. Their jobs include mailroom and remodeling work and outdoor maintenance, but most clients work as janitors.

After weeks of despondency at Anoka (and of my fighting the insurance company for payments), Jim was discharged to Tasks. After the doctors had stabilized him, he once again looked like the up-and-coming college student he had so recently been. Then he announced he was going to do janitorial work for Tasks. This broke my heart. My father had been an untrained blue-collar worker. He had dropped out of high school when his father died during the Depression, and he was discriminated against because of his glass eye. I had always counseled our children to work hard and get an education, as he wished he'd done. Jim was so elated to be leaving Anoka that he didn't care. It was winter and he was twenty-three.

The first day Jim got to the Tasks training facility, he was told to pack a lunch and be ready for work. Tasks stationed mental health staff at their work sites, a brilliant idea. His progress was slow at first, but by the time days began to feel longer in Minnesota, we noticed our son's step was lighter. After five arduous months, he graduated.

With a little help from us, and with money Roger's mother gifted all her grandchildren that year, he bought a 1992 maroon Cadillac to celebrate. When he drove it into our driveway on a sunny May afternoon, his smile seemed to reach both oceans. We loved his having the car almost as much as he did: it saved us from driving him so many places.

After the training facility, Jim moved into a large, stately home in a nice St. Paul neighborhood. It was owned by Tasks, which rented it to Jim and five other men who also had mental illnesses. Tasks called it a lodge to distinguish it from a group home. In a group home, staff was present at all times, but at the lodge staff just stopped in periodically to meet with individuals and to hold group meetings. The men witnessed each other taking meds. Everyone worked and paid taxes. Most continued doing janitorial work after the training period, but Jim's new job was driving a van, shuttling Task's clients to and from jobs. Each man had his own bedroom and shared household duties, including cooking.

"Jim makes us pizza," enthused one man when I picked Jim up at the lodge shortly after he moved in.

When we were in the car, Jim said his lodge mates were impressed that he made everything from scratch. "I make the pizza crust with my special recipe. They like it when I toss it in the air like at the pizza parlors."

"That is something to be impressed about!" I said. I was living every day with happy exclamation points.

In the not-yet-distant dark days, I hadn't believed Jim would come this far. He now had a purpose and a rhythm to his life. Tasks also worked well with parents—something I didn't fully appreciate at the time because I hadn't yet encountered other mental health programs.

Roger and I were thrilled we didn't have to be Jim's main support. We could just be his parents.

Best of all, Jim now had friends, the lack of which he said had bothered him the most. Leaving college had severed his ties there, and his high school friends were mostly scattered. Two had checked in with him at first, but they soon lost contact. It was hard for them too.

Now when Jim visited us, he chomped at the bit to return to his friends at the lodge. They were people he could relate to and with whom he could complain about things like work, parents, anything— just like anyone else.

Roger and I began to relax deep in our bones.

In the fall Jim asked to host a dinner at our home for his lodge mates and Jenny Harmer. Jenny was the lodge coordinator, a young woman who went the extra mile and then some to assist the men. Recently she had started helping Jim register at Metropolitan State University in St. Paul so he could finish his degree. He told her he was interested in accounting, so she and Jim had visited the Tasks office and met with an accountant there.

"We'd love to have you host a dinner here for your lodge mates," I said to Jim quickly, before the offer could become a mirage.

"It has to all be organic," Jim said, "but my friends will want meat." He had recently become very health conscious and strove to eat only organic vegetarian foods. We were happy he did, because we were becoming more and more concerned about his weight gain. One side effect of his main psych med, clozapine, was to make him hungry.

On the day of the dinner, Jim came over to prepare. He set the table with a tablecloth and our good dishes and lined up his ingredients on the kitchen counter so he could prepare in an orderly fashion. Like me, he liked to be organized.

The young men were ten minutes early. The delectable aroma of savory juices from the organic beef roast wafted throughout the house when they filed in, bright-eyed and hungry. None were as heavy as Jim, I noticed, but some had what I called "medication bellies." Jenny arrived right on time. Our house felt cozy and warm, swelling my mother's heart.

Roger, in his most social mode, joined us in the living room, where Jim served grapes, crackers, and cheese. When Jim retreated to prepare the salad, I brought out glasses of juice.

"Is this nonalcoholic, Mrs. Greiling?" one man asked. He looked to be about ten years older than Jim.

"Juice," I said, so he reached for a glass. Not only was Tasks an amazing total package for meeting Jim's mental health needs, it appeared he would also have reinforcement to stay sober. Now that his meds were properly adjusted, however, Jim's need to self-medicate in order to feel better was at bay. I raised a mental toast with my juice glass. I couldn't stop smiling any more than Jim could the day he got his Cadillac.

When we went to the dining room table, one man said he used to work at an expensive restaurant but could never afford to eat there. "This meal is just as exquisite," he proclaimed, looking at Jim, who beamed back. Jim ended the meal with a dessert he had concocted: individual pavlova shells filled with organic whipped cream and fresh raspberries, blueberries, and strawberries, topped with shaved dark chocolate. Some asked for seconds.

"They enjoyed it," Jim said after everyone left. Like his father, he was rarely one to effuse, but I could see his pride in that simple statement.

"Your dinner was amazing, Jim," I said. "And I can see everyone likes you."

"Yeah."

I was glad Jim was healthy enough to see that people liked him, something he hadn't believed when he had been delusional.

Our new son surprised Roger and me by staying to help with the dishes. "Jenny told me I should," he said happily. "It's the Tasks way."

The Tasks way helped Jim get healthy enough to fully participate in Angela and Matt's wedding. When he was still at Anoka, he had been pleased when Matt had asked him to be one of his groomsmen. Not only did Jim fill that role nicely on the big day, he also accepted his sister's invitation to chauffeur the newlyweds to their hotel that night in his Cadillac.

Jim accepted another invitation, this one from Roger, to read at his mother's funeral the following month. "I was surprised he said yes," Roger said. "He did a nice job."

"Tasks has given us back our son," I replied.

14
Debating the Governor

March 2001

It wasn't even close to spring yet, but I skipped the tunnel that connects government buildings and hurried across the street from my office building to the Capitol. I walked up the many steps and opened the heavy door nearest the governor's office. The foyer was empty. It was often crowded with lobbyists and reporters waiting to enter the governor's reception room for press conferences and high-level meetings. I loved this room. Everything was enormous: glistening glass chandeliers, vast historical oil paintings, windows covered with heavy draperies and reaching nearly to the gilded ceiling, and a table that spanned most of one end of the room. Even the plants were huge.

Having an Independence Party governor and split-party majorities in the House and Senate made for more bipartisan work than usual. Governor Ventura was easy to spot across the huge room—a tall, muscular man whose shaved head made his mustache and cleft chin more pronounced. I smiled thinking of the chief executive and Jim talking amiably at the reception after he was first elected.

Today's meeting with the governor was about education, but I hoped for a moment with him to get his take on my early-intervention bill. The House Education Committee chair was talking with the governor when I arrived.

"It would be great if we could have better funding," I volleyed amiably when I joined them. The education commissioner was talking with other legislators, behind the governor. I heard them break into laughter.

"I'm sure you'd want that," the governor bantered, "but what I'd like to know is why public schools cost so much more than the privates." Not this old saw again, I thought, before he growled, "Of course, there's special education and kids who don't speak English."

"Governor, I said the same thing when I first ran," the chair said, putting a friendly hand on Ventura's shoulder, "but then I was educated about the different kinds of kids and the responsibilities we owe them." I surreptitiously touched the chair's arm in appreciation for his tactful help. Just then the commissioner called him over to her group to ask him something, so he excused himself.

"You answered your own question, Governor," I asserted. "Special education students and those learning English cost more."

"Privates don't get money for them," he said with his typical bombast. His jaw jutted forward. I heard more laughter in the other group and wished I'd been called over too.

"Private schools kick out problem kids," I said. "Public schools can't." My hands were sweating. I jammed them in the pockets of my navy blazer. If the governor of our state didn't think problem kids— many of them children with mental illness—were worth considering, how would they ever get the help they needed?

"Kids nowadays," the governor snarled, as if he had read my thoughts. He made wide circles with his hands, as if the problem could be managed simply. "They're all on pills and drugs—and I don't mean illegal drugs." For a moment I was startled. He sounded as if he'd been lobbied to support a recently introduced bill to prohibit psych meds for children.

"Some do need medication," I said more loudly. I pulled myself up to my full height. "They need our help too."

"What those kids need is the board." The volume of his gravelly voice rose. Several people looked our way.

"Mental illness can't be cured with punishment." This felt personal now, as if Roger and I weren't good parents.

He snorted. "I can't see why some people want death so badly, when I saw Navy Seals trying so hard to live."

I didn't hear the rest of his words. I just saw his squinted eyes above his contorting, mustached mouth. I thought of the ambulance ride the year before, of Jim's haunted eyes in his rail-thin body in the emergency room, of the doctor telling us our son wanted to die, of Roger's sad face when he returned with the empty bottles.

Governor Ventura was probably waiting for me to agree. He was used to people agreeing with him, wanting favors, wanting recognition. He was known for speaking his mind, and it was one reason he got elected. I couldn't fault him for that. I couldn't fault him for his ignorance either: the governor had no idea my son had schizophrenia. He didn't know the young man he had enjoyed talking with at his reception, exchanging enthusiastic comments about the wilderness, had hung onto life by a thread.

Supporters of the anti–psych med bill argued that school shooters were teenagers taking antidepressants. Jim had been hyped up from his first antidepressant when he broke my flowerpot and punched the holes in the wall, but my conclusion hadn't been to stop his meds. Instead, I thought he should have been monitored more closely by a medical professional. The meds weren't the issue; inadequate medical help was.

Before I could form my thoughts into any response and use this moment to say something that might help someone like Jim, the governor's chief of staff appeared and pulled his boss away. I stayed only a few more minutes, as long as my job required, without asking for support of my bill. Then I walked out of the huge room, across the empty foyer, down those long steps.

15

"This Bill Will Save Lives"

Unlike the press conference, the first committee hearing on the early-intervention bill was packed. A flood of people from across the state had been barraging legislators with letters, calls, and emails. They told heartbreaking personal stories about mental illness. I hoped this was having an impact.

One woman had written about her daughter breaking car windshields with a sledgehammer when she had needed relief from her schizophrenia. The current commitment standard didn't cover property damage. The dangerousness standard only applied to people—being a danger to oneself or others. Another woman's daughter, who had unaddressed mental illness, had been missing for years. The woman's representative was a Republican leader, a powerful ally since his party was in control, the one calling the shots.

I wore a calf-length red dress, a gray jacket, and multicolored earrings for the hearing. I had also put on a silver ring set with a large piece of black petrified wood. My father had purchased it for my mother before they were married, but she had never worn it. She thought it was too big and flashy. She gave it to me when I was elected to the legislature. I called it my power ring.

When my bill was called, I went to the table in front of the dozen legislators on the committee and introduced it. "This bill will save lives," I began. "Lives of family members of many people in this room. We aren't proposing just locking people up." I thought of Grandma Teddy and cleared my throat. "We are asking for brief community care to return people back to health." I was concise, because I wanted to leave time for testifiers. I started with the National Alliance on Mental Illness.

Before I finished calling my list of organizations and people who wanted to testify, the chair said, "Representative Greiling, we need to give equal time to the opponents."

I saw what he was up to. The other side only had three testifiers: the Mental Health Association, the Church of Scientology, and the American Civil Liberties Union. After them, the chair wanted to move on to the next bill.

"Mr. Chair, there are more people who want to testify for the bill," I said loudly after those opponents concluded. I motioned one to sit beside me. I knew there were even more waiting in the rows behind me, rustling in their chairs with impatience to be heard. The hearing room rustled with murmurs and coughs and was crowded with people desperate to get justice. As soon as one finished, the next leaped into the chair beside me, then another and another, so the chairman was forced to allow more testimony before calling a halt.

The bill passed on a divided vote, with the chair voting against it, but it was still a win. We supporters streamed into the hallway with wide smiles.

The next hearing, two weeks later, was more difficult because the Minnesota Hospital Association had joined the opposition. The bill still passed handily. It was the last hearing before the full House vote.

"Where does the Hospital Association get off, working to deny care to people who so desperately need it," John Milton griped afterward, "while saving themselves money."

We vowed to stay resilient.

=

The day finally came when the bill was to be heard on the House floor. It was late spring and tulips and daffodils were in full bloom on the Capitol lawn. I hadn't seen Jim for days but felt secure he was doing okay now that he was at Tasks. I also felt more confident that our bill might pass. We had lobbied legislators for weeks and had made some concessions at a meeting with opponents, changes that lessened the concerns of the Mental Health Association and their allies.

As I entered the House chamber, I spotted John and Christine sitting in the gallery directly across from me. I took strength from their presence. When it was time for the bill, I spoke first, naming each of our supporters. I started with the powerful labor union AFSCME, always a good ally to have.

"Our son Jim is doing better now," I continued. "He is grateful to us, his parents, for caring enough about him to not let him go. Even though we had to civilly commit him when he was confused about what was going on in his mind. He says we may have saved his life." Today was one of those rare occasions on the raucous House floor when you could have heard a pin drop. I stacked my papers with clammy hands and sat down.

My Republican cosponsor, Representative Bruce Anderson, gave eloquent testimony about his wife's two brothers whose schizophrenia had landed one in jail and set the other to roaming the country. "I challenge this body to tell my wife and me what we should do when her brothers show up at our home hungry and homeless," he said in an emotional voice. "One tried to light himself on fire using a stove burner while he was with us, but still we couldn't get him help."

A couple of legislators asked me hard questions, including about changes to the bill since the committee hearings. In the end, only two voted no. I felt light as a feather floating on a breeze, soaring with happiness. I left the chamber to celebrate with a choked-up John, Christine, and other advocates. At that moment, we all felt as if we'd wrestled mental illness to the ground.

There is an old adage in the legislature, however. When a controversial bill passes too easily in one chamber, watch out for the other. I soon heard scuttlebutt that the bill was in trouble in the Senate, and sure enough, when the Senate health and human services bill came out, it didn't include our provision, as the House omnibus bill had.

I stomped over to the Senate as soon as I heard. They were in session.

I knew advocacy was the final stage of grief, but grief cycles back and forth. As I had stormed around at the Capitol these past months, I knew that I was only in the second stage—anger. It fueled my fire. As I walked past marble columns, I was flanked by John and Christine, bolstering my courage as we marched. I had to leave them at the door because only senators, their staffs, and House members had floor privileges. I entered, breathing heavily.

I stood before the desk of Senator Linda Berglin, the powerful Health and Human Services Committee chair and author of its omnibus bill—the person John had said he could influence because they'd been pals back when he was in the Senate.

"Civil commitment reform isn't in your bill," I huffed.

"Is that what the *Tribune* was referring to in today's editorial?" she asked. Kate Stanley had written several glowing editorials on our bill since the first one. Today she had praised Senator Berglin's bill for including parts of the Mental Health Legislative Network's bill, the one for which I would have liked to be chief author to demonstrate that I supported broad mental health reform. Kate had compared the bill to a delicious Thanksgiving dinner. Except, she had written, "The cranberries are missing." She meant the civil commitment bill.

"Yes, and it passed easily in the House," I said. "It should have been given a chance for a vote in the Senate too."

"If it's in the House bill," she said crustily, without blinking an eye, "it's still alive."

I thanked her and beat it back to the hallway, trying to read what she had meant. Bills that passed either the House or Senate could be included in the final bill that was hammered out in a joint Senate–House conference committee, but if this esteemed chair wouldn't accept our provision into that bill, it wouldn't have a chance in hell. We stood and talked about what Linda had said. John told us she had ignored his note requesting that she come out of the chamber to talk.

Back at my office, I sat at my desk and stared at a vase of spring flowers. How many months had I been working on this legislation? It had been more than a year. Now there was nothing for it but to dog every meeting of the conference committee and lobby all the legislators serving on it as relentlessly as we could.

Our legions of supporters descended on them in person or by calls, mail, or email. The House conferees hung tough supporting our bill, but only one senator openly supported it. Over the days that followed, we were on edge. At times I was called to testify when questions arose. Our underdog bill became the darling of several veteran lobbyists. They helpfully kept John, Christine, and me informed if we missed part of a conference committee meeting. One night when I had to run to another hearing room, a lobbyist called after me, "Godspeed."

We were so weary by the time the final printed bill was passed around that it took us a while to find the right section. It was there. The word "imminent" was deleted every time it appeared before "danger to self or others." It meant people needing mental health care wouldn't have to be quite so sick before their family or friends could get them help. Property damage was also added to the list of things triggering care—another major achievement. The young woman who had hammered on windshields or people who punched through walls as Jim had could now get help earlier.

I felt mellow and warm inside. I was nowhere near the final grief stage yet on any day but this one, but today's success had given me a small, sweet taste. It was enough: enough to feel we had done something, enough for me to feel as if I was helping Jim and others like him. Our voices were beginning to be heard at the Capitol.

=

In the fall, I was fortunate to sit next to Senator Berglin when we flew to a mental health conference in Georgia. She took out her knitting.

"The Early Childhood Caucus would be a good model for a mental health caucus, don't you think?" I slid at her, after small talk. My heart was thumping. "Most legislators from both chambers and parties have joined that caucus, and little kids are getting a lot more notice."

"I'm a member too." Her needles clicked rapidly. The fine brown-and-purple yarn was gorgeous.

"I wish we had that much attention on mental health," I said. I'd planned this discussion from the moment I had realized we'd be sitting together. "The system needs mammoth improvement and change, but most legislators don't pay much attention to mental illness. I know I didn't until Jim got sick, even though my grandmother had schizophrenia."

"True." She looked at me while her fingers kept knitting.

"You and I could be the chairs, and we could each ask a Republican too, like the Early Childhood Caucus. I could ask the Republican who cosponsored the early-intervention bill. He says his wife would kill him if he didn't do something about mental illness, given her brothers." I shifted in my seat to face her. "Minnesota would be the first state in the country to have a mental health caucus."

She stopped knitting and turned toward me with a beautiful smile. "I think that's a good idea. I know who I'll ask too."

16
Mind over Fat

December 2000–April 2003

"Have you lost weight?" my mother asked Roger at Christmas.

"He looks smaller," Jim explained humbly, "in comparison to me."

My mother blanched and said no more. Neither did anyone else.

Since Jim had started on clozapine the year before, he had gained nearly one hundred pounds and had recently had to add blood pressure medication to his regimen. Doctors usually prescribe clozapine last even though it's considered the best antipsychotic. In addition to causing severe weight gain, it also requires frequent blood draws to monitor for agranulocytosis, a deadly condition that could wipe out a person's white blood cells.

In January, after all the holiday goodies, Jim looked even heavier when he arrived at our house from his lodge. He took off his snow-crusted shoes and lumbered to the kitchen, where he rifled the refrigerator and cupboards, searching for edibles—sugary coffee drinks, thick sandwiches, fried meat, cheese piled high on crackers, chips, cookies, ice cream, leftovers, anything. He barely finished eating before he started foraging again, as if he had recently emerged from hibernation.

"I'm just so hungry," he marveled.

When he dropped a piece of cheese on the floor and bent to pick it up, I heard a sound like a beaver's tail slapping the water. I turned to see that one of his thighs had erupted from his jeans. We laughed a little, but neither of us thought it was funny. The next time he came over, he was wearing sweat pants, garb he wouldn't normally be caught dead wearing in public.

"Let's go to the mall," I suggested. "You need clothes."

"Okay," he agreed, head down, ashamed.

When we pulled into the parking lot, dead stalks greeted us in beds where marigolds and petunias had burst forth the fall before. Inside the mall, the bustle of fall shoppers was replaced with sparse January traffic.

Jim was twenty-four. He and I hadn't shopped together for clothes since before he had learned to drive. We used to have fun arguing over his selections: I wanted preppy, but he preferred a more alternative style and usually prevailed.

With more energy than he'd displayed in months, Jim led us to American Eagle, his favorite store. With pop music crooning in the background, he swiftly picked out a couple of long-sleeved cotton shirts and some posh jeans. I was relieved when he selected large sizes. He disappeared into the changing room, and I unbuttoned my coat and settled on a chair outside.

"Can you get me a larger size?" he called after a bit, his muffled voice filtering through the dressing room door. He tossed a shirt over the partition.

"Sure." I grabbed it and hastened to the rack. I was distressed to find there was only one size larger. "Try this." I shoved the shirt over the door. "It's the largest they have," I added, hoping to short-circuit another request that would be embarrassing.

When he came out of the dressing room, he looked bewildered and shouldered his way past me out of the store.

Nothing fit at Eddie Bauer, the Gap, or any other store where he usually shopped. How could Jim have been so much smaller just last summer? Where do heavy people buy their clothes anyway?

"What about more adult stores?" I suggested. "You aren't exactly a teenager anymore."

He shrugged in mute agreement, minus the expectant smile from minutes before. We trudged to a few more stores, but none had his new size. As we slogged out of JCPenney's, I noticed their Big and Tall section. Why hadn't I thought of this before?

"That's for old guys, Mom."

"We could look."

He shook his head. We went home humiliated and defeated.

I suggested a walk. Jim and I had recently started walking on trails and around lakes. I used to have to scramble to keep up with him, but lately he went at a snail's pace. People passed us by on the asphalt path around Como Lake, a short distance from our house. Some appeared impatient at his huffing gait. I felt like putting my arm around my son to deflect those vibes, even though sometimes I felt impatient too. Jim's medicine was the elixir that allowed his mind to be well, but I damned the awful side effects that made his body so unhealthy. The old-fashioned meds that Grandma Teddy used to take weren't murder on her body or anyone else's I saw at the old Rochester State Hospital, but doctors said they didn't do as much to improve the mind.

At home, after Jim left, I made a cup of tea. I had intended to sit in the family room and read, always a centering activity for me, but I found myself thinking of the NAMI class Roger and I had taken.

"Raise your hand if you'd be willing to gain thirty pounds from psych meds," the NAMI teacher had asked. No one put up a hand.

The teacher then explained that antipsychotics slow metabolism and block the body's ability to feel full. "The unfortunate person feels ravenous all the time, but mental illness is full of hard trade-offs," she asserted. "It's better to have one's mind."

Roger joined me on the couch when he got home.

"I feel practically as bad about Jim's being fat as I do about his mental illness," I said. "Not really, but . . ."

"If someone didn't know he used to be slim, they wouldn't think about his weight," Roger replied in his infuriatingly reasonable way.

"But I know his handsome youth is prematurely ruined," I insisted. "How's he ever going to find a partner when he's so ungainly? Someone who could love him and help take care of him after we're gone?" I knew Roger would relate to this. He had had pipe dreams that Jenny might fill that role until I told him she had a boyfriend. "What about his health? His knees and back will give out. He's going to die prematurely. And he's still gaining."

"We should be glad he's on clozapine, despite the weight gain it causes," Roger said. "Think how he was before."

=

When I dashed by my office between committee hearings a few months later, my legislative assistant waved a pink slip at me. It was a message from Jenny marked *URGENT.* Jim had been at Tasks for two years. I couldn't imagine what could be urgent. We didn't get calls like that about Jim any more.

"Jim's blood draw results tanked this week. The lowest that white blood counts should go is fifteen hundred. Jim's is three hundred," Jenny said. "I'm going to have to stop his clozapine and get him to the hospital."

"Agranulocytosis," I murmured, feeling as if she'd said nuclear bombs were headed our way. "How long will he have to go without it?"

"He can never go on it again."

My breath practically stopped. My legs felt too weak for me to stand. I shivered. All the progress we'd made was going to go up in smoke. How far back would we go?

I hung up the phone and ate a sandwich from my office refrigerator. I was beginning to learn to take care of my basic needs, not only before I dived into my shell and rushed off to committee, but now before I let myself think any more about this. I knew that when I did, nothing else would matter.

Jim smiled brightly when Roger and I visited him that night in the psych ward. He was wearing his own clean clothes and looked immaculate: clean-shaven, hair combed neatly. Since he'd been at Tasks and on clozapine, he'd never once felt the need to self-medicate. We played cards and Yahtzee, a game Jim had always liked. We laughed. He thanked us politely for coming.

"I eat as much in two days as I used to eat in one," he said on the third day. No wonder he had gained 150 pounds since he had started clozapine. Jim had gone from an emaciated 170 pounds to his current 320 and counting. "Not being ravenous all the time is a huge relief, and I don't feel so sedated. I wake up naturally at 7 a.m. with racing energy." He sounded like a doctor, reporting symptoms. He looked as if he could be one too. "I'm not even drooling at night anymore." Clozapine increased saliva.

The psychiatrist told me that when a person stopped taking psych meds, the bad side effects go away first, before the good properties also disappear. "We're titrating him onto drugs," the doctor said. "There are nine possibilities. One is bound to work."

A couple of days later when Roger and I were visiting, Jim mused soberly, "People here are talking nonsense. Maybe they use drugs. I wish I hadn't used so many drugs in high school. I think it brought on the trauma I've been through." I could tell Jim's delusions were creeping in, but he was still making sense, trying his best to keep himself together.

"Thankfully you aren't using now," Roger responded.

"Why did I have to be the one in a hundred to get agranulocytosis," Jim moaned, "when I'm already the unlucky person out of a hundred who got schizophrenia?"

"Super unfair," I agreed. "Maybe they'll invent another med with fewer side effects." Who am I kidding? I thought to myself. All the promising new meds coming out had just as many side effects as the older ones. I feared that Jim would return to using drugs again.

"What were you doing when you were my age?" Jim asked, looking at me. His face was glum. I noticed he hadn't shaved. "Teaching, right?"

We all knew what he was getting at. Roger and I were married by the time we were his age and each of us had a strong start in our first profession. We weren't spending time in a psych ward, stalled in life. I felt like weeping. Clozapine had been a miracle drug for Jim, but now all bets were off.

=

The day before Jim was discharged—while he and I were outside on a smoking pass—a cold March wind slashed my cheeks. As I wrapped my arms around my body for warmth, I noticed Jim hadn't shaved for days, his clothes were unkempt, and he was already noticeably thinner. He forcefully spit on the grass. I bristled. The good properties in the meds the doctors had told us about were nearly gone. These were symptoms I had never wanted to see again.

"I can't watch TV," he said when we got back to the ward. "My thoughts are too incomplete. I hate having to sort out what's real again." He was looking at me out of the corner of his eyes. "None of the patients are as special as me. No one is as powerful. Or as violent."

My gut quaked, but I didn't answer. I didn't know what to say.

Jim glanced at the TV—a report on the invasion of Iraq. "If I'd accomplished the things I was supposed to, the world wouldn't be breaking up," he said, concern wrinkling his brow.

My stomach felt queasy, the way it does after someone close dies.

"Jim's no longer getting any benefit from clozapine," a doctor told me.

No shit.

You could have fooled me if any of the new drugs were working yet, but Jim was discharged back to his lodge. It seemed crazy not to keep him at the hospital until he stabilized, but I'd already learned that mothers were listened to far less than insurance companies. With medical permission, Jim dropped his college classes but resumed driving the van. His stopping college was enough to break my heart. Just last semester I'd had a call from Jim's accounting teacher saying what a fine student he was.

"These new meds are causing me to see faces, and some of them have phrases attached," Jim complained when he called. "I think I'm acting okay though."

"I'm glad you are able to talk about it," I said. He was going down fast. We were losing our son again. One night I had a dream that Roger and I lost our infant in shallow water and couldn't find him. Even though we were distraught, we consoled ourselves that this time we weren't alone. We had Tasks.

In another week, Jim was irritable when he came to visit us. He said people at work were calling him names. He had to stop driving the van. Tasks assigned him to janitorial work at a military building instead.

"Most of the name-callers are soldiers," he said sadly. "I should have helped them with the world." His whole body sagged.

"Don't you think those could be voices again?" I suggested. We were sitting in our family room watching late March flurries. Jim's favorite band, the Grateful Dead, was playing "Friend of the Devil." "You had a break with clozapine, but now the voices are back."

"Mom!" he shouted. "There. Is. No. Perfect. Med. I heard these things on clozapine too. And I don't hear voices! You're wrong. People are mean and some are really saying these things." He sat on the edge of his chair and waved his hands, palms down, shooing me away.

"I've been sick and fucked up for so long that I have a stupid look on my face. People see it. They know I'm a loser."

"It's your brain not working."

"I know I need more meds," he said, quieting down and relaxing back in his chair, "because people are responding to my delusions. I get strange looks from them." He looked at me strangely. "You've got a halo around your head and light is shooting from your fingers."

I smiled slightly, glad that I was angel-like and not the Antichrist. Also, it was better that Jim was articulating what was in his head instead of smirking at sights we couldn't see.

"I would go to prison if I could have my mind back," he continued. "At least, I'd be willing to be locked up for a month or so." He smiled. "But even the way I am, I still wouldn't want to be anybody else."

"I wouldn't want you to be anyone else either, Jim," I said, my voice wavering. "No matter what."

17

Jim Is Amazing

August 2003

By fall, when Jim had been off clozapine for more than six months, he stopped taking the meds that weren't doing much good and punched out a window in a lodge neighbor's garage. He was taken back to the psych ward.

"When we let Jim out of restraints today, he tried to strangle someone," a nurse said over the phone.

The hospital had made sure Jim signed a release right away, following my new law, which was tangible progress on that front. Other visible progress involved the Mental Health Caucus. Many legislators had joined, and mental health lobbyists loved coming to our informational meetings to more easily get their bills signed.

If only we could have said Jim was making similar progress.

"When we stopped him," the nurse continued, "your son stabbed himself with a pen."

"Good God!" I keened.

It was the lowest point I could imagine for my son. When Jim started eating his feces and urine, hospital staff moved him to a seclusion room. They placed a urinal in it and stationed a young intern nearby outside his windowed door. Whenever she saw him start to raise the urinal to his lips, she commanded, "Don't do it. Set it down, Jim," her voice successfully overriding the voices in his head. When I came to visit and witnessed this, I went to the bathroom, vomited, and went home.

The next day the nurse reported Jim had been banging his head on the floor, so they had to check him for a concussion. "He's too ill for you to visit," she told me when I called.

The next day the same nurse said he still couldn't have visitors.

"Last night he leaped over the nurses' station," she said. "To touch a bee on the calendar, he said, to keep out of hell." She paused. "He terrified the staff."

"I'm sorry." I pressed shut a plastic bag that contained tomatoes I was freezing. Without Jim to help eat our produce, we had too much. Keeping busy helped some, but mostly I couldn't assimilate all that was happening with Jim, the son who we thought had conquered his schizophrenia with clozapine.

"He can't control it," she said, her voice turning more sympathetic. "He's responding to internal voices."

"What if no med ever replaces clozapine?" I said to Roger after supper. He was reading another old newspaper. Perhaps reading everything in systematic order was his way of having some control over our chaotic lives. But it bugged me. I wanted at least my husband to be healthy, but I held my tongue.

Before he could answer my question about clozapine, I quickly moved on. I couldn't go down a road where without clozapine, Jim had no future.

"At least Tasks is really good at communicating with us," I said.

"And hanging with Jim," Roger answered, reaching for the next paper.

On advice of friends at NAMI–MN, where I was still serving on the board, I called the hospital a few days later to announce, "I'm going to have to see my son today." I gripped the receiver tightly enough to feel the heartbeat in my hand. "If the doctor objects, have him call me." I needed to see for myself how my son was doing. Sue Abderholden, the new NAMI–MN executive director, who was bringing new energy to the organization, had told me that recent research showed that patients with schizophrenia received significantly less care in psych wards than other patients.

The nurse called back. "The doctor says you can come after we bathe him," she said, then added, "Really, very sick people do get better." This was the first time anyone had given me this assurance during this hospitalization. I basked in it.

When I arrived, I was shown to Jim's isolated room. It was dark and reeked of sweat and urine. It felt warm, despite the air-conditioning.

The nurse turned up the light. Jim's oily hair was matted to his skull and he looked thin.

I'd never seen our son in restraints. Leather straps were fastened around his ankles and wrists. The nurse brought in a chair. I sat near his legs, laying a book I had brought on the floor.

"Hello, Jim. I wanted to visit you. You're missing out on some good tomatoes."

He strained to lift his head off the pillow to see me. "I'm glad you came. I can't believe I haven't called you." He sounded hoarse.

"They told us not to visit. Are you feeling any better?"

"No, I feel awful."

I held up the latest *Harry Potter*. "If you want, we can read some." He smiled a little and nodded.

I opened the book and began to read. He stretched his legs as best he could in the restraints and settled in. I had always read to Angela and Jim at bedtime, and Jim had enjoyed reading together long after Angela got too busy.

"Fuck you," Jim moaned quietly, startling me. He flinched and put up shielding arms as best he could in the restraints, as if someone were trying to stab him.

"Voices?" I asked.

"Yes," he whimpered.

"There's no one here but us, honey." I read a couple more chapters—punctuated by the attempted stabbings—until an aide brought in a supper tray: pizza, apple slices, finger food; no silverware. She loosened a strap on one hand enough that Jim could maneuver.

"We can talk while you eat." I rested the book in my lap. "You must be hungry." His stomach had been rumbling like a bathtub drain.

After the nurse departed, Jim stared at the food. "I can't eat, Mom. The last time I did, they made me feel guilty the rest of the night. I promised not to eat again, but they weren't happy, so I made myself vomit." He shrank into his white sheets. "But I'm starving."

I thought of Grandma Teddy's voices forbidding her to eat, telling the rest of us to go ahead.

"Those apples look good," I said, pointing. "Why don't you try a slice?"

"I have to protect Jenny." His Tasks staff person.

"Is she your soul mate now? Last time you were this ill it was Laurie," I said, making conversation. Laurie was a girl Jim had dated once in college.

He chuckled, a small but unmistakable laugh. "I'd forgotten about her."

"Maybe your delusion is weak, if it can't stick to a soul mate from one time to the next." I emitted a sliver of a laugh too.

Jim was grinning broadly. All of a sudden—after all the stress—the ridiculousness of delusions and this whole business of mental illness struck me as hilarious. We looked at each other, like two kids being silly, and broke into laughter.

A young man with a slight mustache poked his head in the door. "Hey, Jim," he said. "Sounds like fun. What's shaking?" Jim looked at him but didn't answer, so the man gave up and ambled away.

"Who was that?"

"My old roommate before they moved me here. He thinks he's Zeus." Jim grinned again. "I have to kill him."

"Does he know that?" I giggled.

"No." Jim chuckled.

The clueless guy peered in again, smiled at Jim, bumbled off.

We caught each other's eyes and dissolved into shaking fits of laughter. This was so different from earlier times. I wasn't the Antichrist. Jim knew I was his real mom. The real Jim was reemerging.

After we calmed down, he said, "Look what I can do." He slipped the unloosened hand out of its restraint.

"How'd you do that?" I asked, somewhat disconcerted.

"I work it around and it stretches. One day I got a foot out too."

"Must be scary hearing voices," I whispered.

"Eight voices told me to go off my meds." He replaced his hand in its strap.

I walked over to his bed and kissed his matted hair. No one asked me to leave, so Jim and I talked and read for six hours. The new meds were taking hold, and hopefully he would soon be able to return to Tasks. Roger and I hoped he would be able to drive the van again, but even if he was a janitor, he would have a nice home, friends, money, and independence. His fate could be different from Grandma Teddy's.

When the nurse walked me out, she said, "Jim has insight into his illness, no matter what shape he's in. That's rare." I beamed at her, my eyes shining. As she unlocked the door, she added, "Mindy, you have an amazing son."

18
The Depths of Delusion

December 2004

The doctors settled on a diagnosis of schizoaffective disorder for Jim. Many consider it the worst mental illness because it is a combination of two dreaded others: bipolar disorder and schizophrenia. After Jim left the hospital for the Anoka treatment center again, Angela planned a trip to Germany for Roger and me so we could get away. Even better than the trip was that soon after we returned, our daughter gave birth to our first grandchild, Taylor. My ever-present, aching tiredness over Jim's illness practically evaporated when I got to hold that precious little bundle.

Jim was at Anoka for eight months. He voluntarily stayed longer than required in order to try for a better drug than Haldol (haloperidol). It was the only antipsychotic that worked for him at this point, though nowhere near as well as clozapine. Every time he was prescribed a newer, supposedly better drug, he started to become psychotic. I admired him greatly for taking charge of his meds. In the end we were all just glad there was one that worked at all.

Jim loved holding Taylor when Angela and Matt brought her to Minnesota. I was worried Angela might be hesitant to let Jim hold her baby, but she smiled and handed him Taylor soon after she was in the door. Jim had a knack for babies. He could easily soothe his niece into slumber.

As the new year approached, Jim resolved to get back into shape. He was adhering more strictly to his raw vegan diet, and he exercised more. In late December, he and I walked around Lake Calhoun in Minneapolis on a cold, blustery day. He had selected this lake because it was twice as large as Como, so he could get in more steps.

I looked out over the barren, frozen lake. We were alone, but I recalled the swimmers splashing in summer waters.

Jim's frame was becoming more evident again. "Mostly because I don't feel so hungry on Haldol," he admitted. "I just hope I don't get TD." Tardive dyskinesia, a side effect of some antipsychotic medicines, including Haldol, causes involuntary movements. Jim had been frightened when he saw an old man with a constantly thrusting tongue in a psych ward a couple of years earlier.

I squinted through the space between my wool hat and the matching scarf wrapped around my face and neck. Jim wore the stocking hat he had knit, the one he saved for really cold days. His hands were bare. He put them in his pockets when they got really cold but otherwise wanted to keep them free for smoking.

"Want to hear my delusion?" he volunteered, his voice muffled in the high winds.

"Sure." My moist breath turned icy behind my scarf. "You've told me some parts, but I'm interested in hearing the whole thing."

He lit a cigarette and we started walking. "In the beginning, there was only one god." He took in a long draw of smoke. "A female. She was supposed to work at rising through the levels of the universe."

"Nice the god is female." When I laughed, my breath made my scarf momentarily wet, until it froze again. It was a luxury to hear about Jim's delusion when he wasn't in the middle of it.

"I thought you'd like that part." He grinned. "It was hard work and increasingly so as she got higher and higher. She could keep rising herself or create a male god to do the work for her. Eventually, though, she would have to kill him, if she wanted to continue rising."

He looked at me searchingly. When I didn't react, he continued. "She did this once and then had to start over." His glasses fogged over, so he tossed away his cigarette, removed them, and wiped the lenses on the shirt he pulled from beneath his jacket. "When she got to the sixty-fifth level the second time and only had ten or twelve levels to go, she couldn't hack it, so she created another male god."

We passed the park building.

"If she'd completed her work, everyone would've been happy in heaven," Jim said, as if he were recounting a folk legend. "But her work up the levels was hellish. She and the male god were in hell and had to always be uncomfortable and do things they didn't want to do."

"Like what?"

"The female had no arms but had to keep swimming," he answered. "That was hard. Then the Big Bang happened and the Milky Way and planets started. I created all that, Mom." He smiled shyly, looking at me. "I'm also the devil."

My core felt numb, like the skin between my hat and scarf that was getting scoured by the wind. He wasn't telling this part in past tense. Did he still believe all this?

"On Earth, nine religions started. There were different levels of people, like the hues, hecks, and hairs. One set was female and the other male. There were three or four genders for each sex." He stopped and tried to light another cigarette, shielding the spark with his hands. The wind extinguished several matches. "Fuck," he said, giving up. We continued on. "I was born to two non-soul-mate parents. Biologically, people are supposed to marry soul mates," he said, slowing down and looking at me. "Dad and you didn't, so I was doomed from the start."

I slowed my pace to match his. "Dad and I are very different people," I said. I thought about Roger's logical nature, his inability to express his emotions. Once when we were strolling while on vacation and I was feeling romantic, I reached over and took my husband's hand, but he reflexively snatched it away, shy of the public display. Of course Jim had noticed Roger's and my differences. And we each had different ways of coping with his illness. I tackled the mental health system and Roger continued to handle the money.

Jim and I walked in silence until he said, "I was happy until I was two or three, but then you decided I should be selected for an awful life."

"Me?"

"You were from a different universe, so you didn't fully appreciate what an awful thing you did. There are dits and dats, but you're a dot—the only one. You're different from other groups," he said, then grinned. "Also, sorry, Mom, but you're a man."

I snorted a laugh but refrained from commenting. I wanted to hear him out.

He blew mucus out of his nostrils onto the dingy snow, where it froze quickly. "From three up until I was twelve, I lived a miserable life. I had no memory, so I couldn't learn and was vulnerable to everyone picking on me. All the head gods of the nine religions did things to me."

"Sounds miserable." The ends of my scarf whipped at my cheeks, and my long black coat furled and unfurled on my legs, like a flag.

"Yeah. When I was around thirteen, it got really bad." He stooped to grab a handful of snow, crushing it into a snowball. "I was bad."

"You were a pretty normal teenager, Jim."

He threw the snowball. "You don't know, Mom." He wiped his cold hands on his jacket and pushed them deep into his pockets and looked at me like I was an idiot. I guess I was for arguing with a delusion.

"I had one chance, after my Alaska trip. I was happy from then until the beginning of college, but I blew it. I used weed again." He frowned. "Otherwise I could have gotten out of all this."

"If you hadn't gotten mental illness, you could have gotten out of all this," I said indignantly. "I'm sure drugs didn't help, but mental illness isn't your fault, Jim." It was hard to hear Jim blaming himself for his illness, for the genes he had received from me. Both Roger and I were still a long way from regarding his drug use as anything but a choice, however.

He ignored me and pressed on. "After that, I had things I had to do to climb the levels. I didn't want to, but I didn't want to be tortured, and also I wanted to get to the fun party and have good sex with my soul mate."

"Like?"

"You know. Breaking windows, Dad's ear, eating piss and shit. I didn't always comply, so the tasks got harder." He looked wretched. Raw winds gusted relentlessly. "When I tried to kill myself, it was because I couldn't do the really hard things after I resisted easier things."

"What things?" I made my hands into fists inside my mittens, expecting to hear the part about having to kill me again.

"Kill a man with my hands, rape a woman, cut off my dick, rip out my heart, and then rip out my throat. In that exact order."

I slowed my steps, letting these words ripple through my brain, then reasoned, "You'd be dead before you got to ripping out your throat."

"Mom!" He said with a smile. "Delusions don't always make sense."

"What else?" I wiggled my fingers inside my mittens to keep them warm. I had been somewhat comforted to hear that it was a man he had to strangle until I remembered I was a man in the delusion.

"There's a lot more. Every time I have a psychotic episode, it picks up where it left off," he said, putting his bare fingers up his coat sleeves, "and it gets worse."

I suddenly felt tired. I thought about future episodes Jim might have to endure, where his chilling delusions would get worse. We passed a porta potty the strong wind had toppled. The turquoise shell lay on its side, like a felled tree. The wind swept through my coat.

"Let's head home," I suggested. "I'm cold." Jim had frost in his eyelashes.

When we reached the car, winter darkness was descending. I had trouble getting my numb fingers to insert the key in the ignition. As we drove home, with the heater on high, Jim added one more thing.

"There are three levels," he said, rubbing his hands. "On the first, I only occasionally hear or see things that aren't there. I can live with that." He paused. "Mom, can I have a cigarette in the car just this once, since I couldn't get my matches to work?"

"Definitely not," I replied automatically. I didn't have to walk on eggshells when he was doing well.

He shrugged and continued. "On the second level, I control other people's thoughts and can tell by their faces what they're thinking. I'm smarter than anybody." He smiled sheepishly. "The last level is when I'm totally gone—into the other world."

"What level are you now?" I figured I knew, but I wanted to hear him say it. I was grateful he wasn't at that last level, where we'd spent so much time recently.

"Definitely the first level. Only 1 percent of me believes it's true."

"Good ratio." It was dark as I pulled into our driveway beside Jim's big car.

"But it could be true," he said, as if that might be a good thing. He got out of the car and came in the house for a cup of coffee to warm up before he went home to his lodge.

After he departed, I continued sitting in the family room, sipping my coffee. Roger and I were glad Tasks Unlimited helped Jim handle his paperwork and mental health needs and that we could sit back and enjoy him as our son. He had more paperwork now that in addition to Medicaid, which paid most of his medical bills, he was also receiving disability payments to augment his Tasks salary. Roger and I had resisted Social Security Disability Insurance for years, but we finally hired an attorney to help Jim receive these benefits when he wasn't always able to work full-time. We were elated that he had a healthy rhythm to his life and good friends at Tasks, but I felt sorry that he had to contend with all this. More than anything, I wished his new psych meds could relieve him of as much suffering as clozapine had.

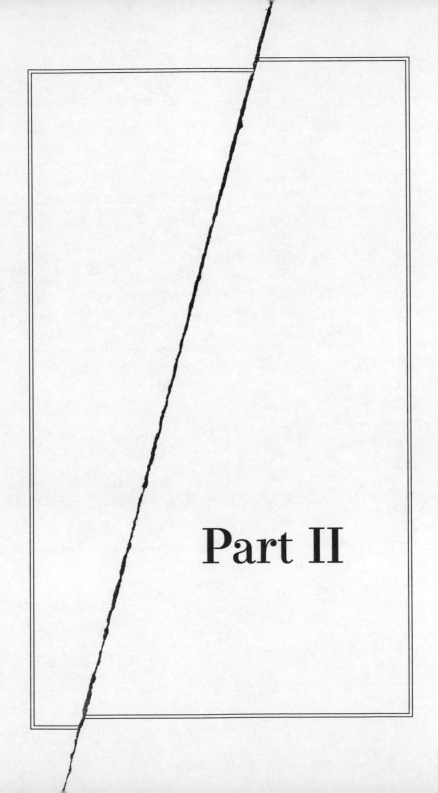

Part II

19
Vulnerable Adult

June 2006–2007

Colorful artwork adorned the walls in the Ecopolitan, Jim's favorite restaurant in a trendy neighborhood of Minneapolis. Strains of Indian and Nepalese music permeated the air. Angela and Taylor had come here with us on their last visit. Taylor, who brings joy to all our lives, was to turn two the next month. An attractive young waitress walked up to take our order.

"I'll start off with a shot of wheatgrass. Then I'll have carrot juice." Jim turned the page of the menu. It had been nearly two years since he told me about his delusion while we walked around Lake Calhoun, years when Jim had taken his healthy eating to new heights. He now only eats raw vegan. "What salad do you recommend?" He knew most of the entrées by heart but liked to hear descriptions.

"My favorite is the vegetable," the young woman said. "Every vegetable is sliced so thin you can practically see through it."

"Okay, and the radish and beet dish for my main course."

"Good choice." Her pen flew over her pad. "I love how that dish is held together by figs and pureed almonds."

I ordered the same salad and main course, and Roger went for a small salad, saving room for a finish of frozen prunes and bananas that approximates ice cream, one of the few raw vegan dishes he liked. I was glad he was a good sport about coming.

I stared at the candle flickering in a glass container, conscious of my son's hands drumming on the table. Jim had been studying hard at Metro State, taking difficult accounting classes. He had recently started doing some basic office accounting for Tasks besides his regular janitorial work. Tasks held out the possibility that he could eventually move up to higher-level work. Roger and I were beyond pleased.

"It's nice to be here." I took a sip of my organic juice.

"Healthy eating will heal me," Jim declared, leaning his elbows on the linen tablecloth. "What food I put into my body is more important than all the meds you want me to take."

"Meds are good for you too." Roger folded his arms.

"I'm glad you're working on being healthy." I refolded my napkin and set it on my lap. "But . . ."

"Animal products probably made me sick in the first place," Jim interrupted. "The awful food you fed me all my life." He looked accusingly at me. "I also need to get rid of the toxins I already have in my body," he lectured. "Dr. T is helping me do that."

As if on cue, the restaurant owner ran into the dining room. A boyishly handsome Peter Pan full of energy, Dr. T always seemed to be on the run. He moved from table to table like a politician working a room—touching shoulders, shaking hands, training his dazzling white smile on each person in turn.

"There he is now," Jim crowed with delight, as if he were one of the Lost Boys. Jim beamed at him when he reached our table.

"Good afternoon," the energetic man effused. Jim had told us he was also a chiropractor. Dr. T was diminutive; his short black hair was neatly cut. He placed a hand on Jim's shoulder. "How're you doing, Jim?"

"Great," Jim responded happily, exchanging a conspiratorial look with the puckish man. Jim had been attending Dr. T's weekly lectures, held in a room above the restaurant.

"I'm glad he's taking your advice and smoking less," I said to Dr. T.

"We're glad you have Jim's attention about drugs not being healthy too," Roger added. Since Jim had had to go off clozapine, he talked a lot about the virtues of marijuana. We worried that he might turn to self-medication again.

"How do you think Jim's doing overall?" Dr. T turned his body toward me, his beady black eyes glinting. Behind him, someone dropped a plate, and I jumped a little at the sound, then gathered myself again. Dr. T didn't even turn around.

"He's getting straight As in some pretty difficult accounting classes."

"Wonderful to hear." He glowed at Jim.

"Once he graduates," I continued, "his company might hire him to work as an accountant."

I caught another look shooting between Jim and Dr. T. This one sent a shiver up my spine. It looked diabolical. It somehow reminded me of the looks Jim had exchanged with high school friends as they sat politely in our living room, planning to get high as soon as they departed.

I didn't eat much. Instead, I watched Jim devour his raw vegetable salad, the beets and radishes, and the vegan ice cream concoction for dessert. We were mostly silent, listening to his stories about Dr. T's lectures, what he was learning, how it was changing his life.

After dropping Jim off, I asked Roger, "What do you think is going on between them?"

"I didn't notice anything." Sometimes it infuriated me that Roger was so unobservant.

The next week, as I was preparing supper, Heather Erickson from Tasks called. She had replaced Jenny as lodge coordinator. She said Jim wasn't doing well. "He may have stopped taking meds. He keeps going to his room for water or making other excuses to leave the table, where he's supposed to be swallowing his meds in front of his lodge mates." Daily med witnessing was one of the few hard-and-fast requirements of being at Tasks.

"Oh no," I murmured weakly. I wiped my hands with a towel and sat down on a kitchen chair. "Do you think it could have anything to do with that chiropractor?"

"He idolizes him," Heather replied. "When I commented on how sunburned he was, Jim said, 'I can't get skin cancer, because Dr. T's diet will protect me from all diseases.'"

"What can we do?" I asked. I had already learned that much of a person's social intelligence goes out the window with schizophrenia, and Jim had always been easily led. "Jim says he's told Dr. T he has schizophrenia."

"I'll send a vulnerable adult form telling him of Jim's legal status and the possible repercussions for him if he doesn't take that into consideration," she replied.

I asked Jim about his meds when he came over a couple days later to make a raw vegan supper.

"They're killing me! Dr. T says they're terrible for my health." Blood vessels swelled in his neck. He slammed a bowl onto the counter and glared at me. "I'm working with him to phase off my meds."

I set down the vegetables and stared back. "You know you can't do that." I wanted to shake him. "Think of how you were all those months after clozapine, before the doctors settled on Haldol, the only drug that works for you anymore. What if even that stops working after you play around with it, like the other drugs did?"

"I know better than to go off it cold turkey, and so does Dr. T." Jim's mood changed in a flash. He smiled confidently. "Dr. T says I should phase off slowly and can be off all my meds in three months. Instead, I'm taking the supplements he's recommending." His words ran together now and his hands moved in the air. "And I can buy them right at Ecopolitan."

I remembered the lines of bottles and rows of supplements I'd seen in a small room off the restaurant dining room.

Angela, Matt, and Taylor came to visit that weekend. In a quiet moment before she saw her brother, I told Angela about what had happened. She was upset. After she had taken the NAMI family class and saw how distraught many parents in her class had been, one of her takeaways had been concern for Roger and me. Like all of us, she had been relieved when Jim became stable again, but now her fear was revived.

After Jim arrived, I could hear her talking with him in the living room about his accounting classes and Taylor. I turned back to my work in the kitchen preparing supper, but after a few minutes, I heard Jim's voice rise to a shout. "Mind your own fucking business."

I rushed into the room and saw Angela's white face screwed into tight lines. "You know how you get when you aren't medicated," she shouted back, her neck turning red. "Do you want to hurt Mom?"

"You don't know shit," Jim yelled, spewing spittle. "You stupid, ignorant bitch." He turned and headed for the door, looking like he was going to cry.

Angela stood in the living room beside the couch and sobbed as I had never heard her sob since she was a little child.

I wanted to hold both my children.

Jim's car was still in our driveway, so I went to him first, before he drove off. He was sobbing behind the wheel, the car not yet started. I reached in and hugged him. "I love you so much. Angela was trying to help. She wants you to be healthy just like Dad and I do."

He quieted. "Thanks for coming out, Mom. It means so much." Tears continued streaming down his face as he started his car and drove off.

In the house, I embraced Angela, but she couldn't be comforted.

=

We didn't see Jim for a full week after Angela and her family left. Then we got the call. He was back in the hospital. Following Dr. T's advice, he'd gone too low on his meds and was in serious relapse. According to Heather, Jim had become grandiose and rude, wasn't sleeping, thought bad smells were seeping through the walls, and was barely eating. Tasks furloughed him from his lodge and office work. He had to drop his accounting classes. He was back to square one. So were we.

I decided to file a malpractice complaint.

"Can it be legal for a chiropractor to advise our son to abandon all his meds?" I asked the attorney taking my deposition for the attorney general.

"Chiropractors aren't licensed to prescribe medicine," the knowledgeable young man replied, "so he shouldn't be able to unprescribe either."

"Dr. T asked Jim exactly how much money he had before recommending what he needed."

"He does sound like a charlatan."

"The next week, Jim said he was going to quit accounting classes and become an alternative medicine doctor like Dr. T. He wanted to help people, like Dr. T was helping him." I stopped talking and blew my nose. "By the way, why are we calling him *doctor*? No real doctor would ruin my son's life like this."

The attorney nodded.

"Jim's no longer a promising college student or a budding accountant. He doesn't even have his janitorial job—or a place to live when he gets out of the hospital." I gasped a breath. "When Jim's not taking his meds, I'd like to send him to live with that chiropractor instead of us and see how he likes it."

I was glad for a break when I flew to Washington a couple of months later for a national NAMI board meeting. I had been elected to the national board two years earlier, shortly after Taylor was born. Angela had brought her to a reception to help me campaign. As usual, on this trip I stayed an extra day to see my granddaughter and her parents. We'd had many phone calls to smooth things over since the argument between Angela and Jim, but we only fully relaxed after Jim had been hospitalized without incident. Angela didn't tell me until years later how much she had feared for my life during that time.

After Taylor's nap, Angela and I took her for a walk to the park in her stroller. Runners and bicyclists were out in force.

"It's sad that Taylor will never know her uncle as he would have been," I said. "Soon she'll be old enough to notice when he isn't doing well."

"She likes him," Angela added noncommittally, pulling a flower from a tree hanging over the sidewalk. She handed it to Taylor, who was humming "Old MacDonald Had a Farm." I remembered when Taylor had sat in Uncle Jim's lap at Christmas, learning to tap a beat on his drum.

I surveyed Angela's expression. "Dad and I know it's hard for you."

"I wish I could have an adult conversation with him," she admitted as we neared the neighborhood park. "I get tired of his proselytizing about the benefits of weed every time we go to coffee houses." Angela and Jim had always marched to different drummers. In high school, her friends had been the good students, the athletes. His had been the druggies. Both said their friends disdained the other's. I was happy when they were both out of high school and Jim had visited Angela during her D.C. internship. I had hoped that they would become better friends. Afterward, both said it had gone "fine," but Jim had already been sick. He was diagnosed shortly afterward.

"I'm sure that gets awfully tiresome," I agreed. "But he doesn't have enough to talk about. Especially compared to you."

"Less all the time," she said, pulling her daughter from the stroller and setting her down in the grass. Taylor, who still had a skip in her run, headed for the jungle gym and began to climb. There was plenty of sand under the structure, but the metal bars looked as if they could hurt if a child landed wrong. I wished I could protect my granddaughter from all harm in her life, including mental illness, but knew that wasn't possible.

After I returned to Minnesota, I felt vindicated when the restaurant owner lost his chiropractor's license because of what he had done to Jim. I knew the change wouldn't help Jim, but maybe it would help other vulnerable people who were mesmerized by this man. I didn't feel as good about it as I thought I would, however, because when Jim was allowed to return to Tasks, he didn't resume accounting.

20
Mother's Day Turmoil

May 2011

It was May, the time of year when we exchanged our winter coats for jackets and when I typically felt more hopeful. Over the past five years, the Mental Health Caucus had thrived. We hosted great speakers and toured places like Anoka-Metro Regional Treatment Center and Tasks Unlimited. The preceding session, we had passed historic funding for the mental health system. I was pleased the topic of mental health had been in nearly every caucus memo since my fuss.

Jim hadn't resumed seeing the so-called Dr. T and had been doing pretty well at Tasks. He had had a small relapse three years earlier after he met a woman named Colleen, with whom he started using drugs. They broke up after only a couple of months. He hadn't seen her since, but the way he looked the last time we saw him reminded me of his time with her. Recently he had started working full-time as a janitor, so we hoped that was the only reason he looked so tired.

I had made only a few entries in my journal since the relapse. I write to ease my stress and grieving, but when Jim does better, I slack off. Roger and I loved the fact that Tasks and Jim handled everything. They acted quickly to nip his relapse in the bud. Jim did a stint in a chemical dependency program and now had regular drug tests to make sure he stayed clean, a requirement in order for him to remain at Tasks.

Despite being exhausted from jammed-up end-of-session work at the legislature, I drove with Roger to meet Jim at a nearby Asian restaurant for a quick Mother's Day dinner. I noticed immediately that he was thinner. His fingernails were dirty and his eyes watery.

"How's work going?" I asked as we ordered our pot sticker appetizers.

He took a long time to respond, as if he were sorting out his thoughts. "Okay."

"Is working full-time too much for you? You look tired." I had worried when Jim informed us that Tasks was doubling his hours just when they had enrolled him in a peer-helper training program. The staff members assigned to help him were new—none would remember his relapses or how quickly they could develop. We hadn't met the last two workers and didn't know the current person's name.

"It's fine, Mom," he said impatiently.

I let it drop.

Jim spoke little during the rest of the meal; he sat slumped over his plate, looking down, eating only half his food. As the waitress cleared the dishes, Jim excused himself to use the restroom. He'd already been there twice during the meal.

I took the opportunity to compare notes with Roger. He was the only one who really understood, with whom I could commiserate and share my anxious feelings. Many of our friends used to ask about Jim, but the questions had petered out. I didn't blame them. Roger and I didn't discuss him as much either, but we hadn't returned to talking as much about things like our futures either. Jim's illness had changed all that.

"Do you think he's using?" I asked, using my fork to trace a row in my rice. "He looks terrible and he's going to the bathroom so many times."

"They still test his urine for drugs, don't they?" Roger asked. "Wouldn't they know?"

"I wish Heather were still his contact person." Heather had been promoted within Tasks, with good reason.

Roger sighed, rattling the ice in his glass. "Someday, I want to just enjoy something, without having to worry about Jim."

I ignored that comment. "I hope they're monitoring him more closely with all his recent changes."

Roger didn't answer because Jim returned. As he slipped into his seat, I noticed his nose was running. Roger laid his credit card on the bill.

When I hugged Jim goodbye, he blew air at me and grimaced as if I had bad vapors. This was old behavior, his paranoia kicking in, something we hadn't seen for years. I felt a chill and my stomach constricted.

"Honey, you don't seem too good," I said warily. "Do you think we should go with you to the hospital?"

"No way," he replied, softly. He shrugged on his light jacket and wiped his nose on the sleeve. "Let's go."

I gave up with relief. His caseworkers would see him tomorrow. I knew we could sit for hours in the emergency room and then still be sent home if he didn't meet their strict criteria for admission. One of the main reasons I'd fought so hard for changes in mental health care was for early intervention in urgent cases. Since we passed the civil commitment reform bill, however, families had begun telling me that hospitals were using a different standard for admissions, one that was harder to meet.

Later, as I lay in the dark of our bedroom unable to sleep, I replayed the conversation at the restaurant. I knew I should have insisted Jim go to the hospital. I had a sense of impending doom, as if a violent storm were heading our way. My skin prickled with panicked electricity.

It had been sixteen years since my father had died and one since my mother had died. My sister Joan and her husband had died unexpectedly seven years earlier because of heart issues. With all of them, I could eventually put my raw grief behind me. Only the dull ache of missing them remained. It never totally went away, just moved to the background. They only died once.

My grief about Jim zoomed in and out constantly.

Spring and fall were the times of year when he was prone to relapse, when the seasons changed. Spring was also when my work at the legislature increased. It took so much effort, and I couldn't juggle both needs. For the first time in nearly twenty years, I thought seriously about not seeking reelection.

The next morning, my thoughts were jumbled and I felt out of sorts. A harshly ringing phone roused Roger and me, contrasting abrasively with the peaceful spring morning.

"It was a bondsman, offering his services," Roger said bewilderedly, after hanging up. He stared ahead with unfocused eyes. "Jim's in jail."

We barely spoke as we got ready for work. I was shocked but also oddly relieved. Jim was in jail and hadn't tried to overdose again, something I now realized had been hovering in my mind ever since we'd said goodbye the night before. I felt strangely calm as I drove the familiar route to work and trudged to my office.

My legislative assistant, Liz Mandelman, quickly found the county sheriff's jail log. Jim had been booked at 2 a.m., just a few hours after our Mother's Day supper, for criminal vehicle operation, charged with a gross misdemeanor.

My calm dissipated. My heart raced like a stoked engine. I pushed away from Liz's cubicle wall and turned to unlock my office. Before I even opened the door, she handed me the pertinent statute. Penalties ranged from three to ten years. *My God!* It was my worst nightmare: Jim could become like Kyle Zwack, his life rotting away in prison, what I'd been working all this time to avoid. Outside my window, I saw two young men tossing a Frisbee on the green grass of the Capitol grounds, the usual demonstrators on the sidewalk carrying handmade posters. I felt like having a cigarette, but I hadn't smoked for decades, so I settled for a cup of weak coffee.

I stumbled through my day. When it was time for the afternoon floor session, I walked over to the Capitol and sat at my desk in the House chamber. When my friend Representative Alice Hausman arrived, she put her hand on my shoulder. "I've heard about Jim," she said, "and I'm so sorry." News traveled like lightning at the Capitol. She started to give me a hug, but I stiffened, not wanting her to crack my shell. "If you hug me," I said more harshly than I intended, "I'll start bawling."

Alice backed off, nodded. She took her seat, two down from me. The legislator who sat between us took the cue and dove into his computer without looking my way.

Another colleague, who represented the district where Jim's accident took place, softly tapped me on the shoulder. "Here's the number of my city council member. She has a good relationship with the police and can find out what's going on."

My eyes stung at his kindness. I managed a thank you.

Later, I took a break and dialed the number. "Your son was going at a high speed and missed a stop sign, struck two cars and injured one person in the front car," the city council member's staff said. "No word on how badly."

My stomach roiled. I ached for those poor people and for Jim. I didn't speak for the rest of the session.

Jim called the following night from the jail, asking us to pick him up. With whirling minds, we hurried to the car. The spring night was warm and noisy, and there was more traffic than we had expected. Laughing young people were out carousing, calling to one another, their carefree lives so unlike our son's.

Two dark figures were crouched on the curb as we approached the jail, bent into their phones. One was a young man with black hair. The other was Jim. He leaped up with a guilty, relieved smile and hopped into the back seat. I heard the other man urgently ask someone to come get him. I wondered, Did the system just disgorge people from the jail abruptly into the night? Even when it was twenty degrees below zero?

"How'd it happen?" I asked Jim after he buckled his seatbelt. The other young man wasn't having any luck—he was dialing again. I thought about offering him a ride but quickly discarded the idea. We had our hands full. I always hoped that each time would be our last, but maybe we were just like Sisyphus, doomed to never be successful and to know it.

"I had to ram that car to get a deeper understanding of the universe," he replied, as if he was making sense. "I didn't mean to hurt people, just the car. I screwed up. I should have hit the first car instead." He ground his teeth, something he'd been doing a lot lately. "That car was empty." He looked almost indignant.

"It's my fault for not trying harder to get you to the hospital," I said.

"I wouldn't have gone to the hospital," he replied. "I had to save the world before it ended."

In the morning, I took our subdued son to the hospital. We should have taken him the night before, but all of us were exhausted. It took all morning for him to be admitted. I was furious and laden with guilt, berating myself for not doing this on Sunday night after our supper.

In late afternoon after I got home, a Tasks worker called. "I met with Jim on Friday," she told me. That had been two days before the accident. "His room looked like a wild animal had ravaged it. Groceries, trash, dirty clothes, and dishes were strewn all over. I've never seen a room like that at a lodge. And he was dreadfully rude. I didn't suspect he was so near relapse, though . . ."

She was supposed to be the professional, but I'm sure she, too, had been tired on a Friday afternoon, as I had been Sunday. We were both guilty. "Neither did I," I said. "I could plainly see his brain wasn't working, but mine should have been."

"I talked with one of Jim's friends," the case manager continued. None of the other programs I knew would have done this. "The friend said that for the past few weeks, Jim's been snorting bath salts on a daily basis." She cleared her throat. "And he's smoking K-2 about every day as well."

"What's that?"

"A synthetic form of marijuana. It's legal, like bath salts. Jim probably used them because they wouldn't show up in his drug tests."

I stared out the window. My stomach hurt from anger at Jim for being so conniving and from the pain of thinking how bad he must feel to have done this. Once again, it hit home that addiction and mental illness went hand in hand. I knew the numbers weren't good. Fifty percent of people with mental illness used drugs, and vice versa.

"Where could he have gotten this stuff?"

"At any head shop. It can cause hallucinations, even in people who don't have mental illness, so imagine what it does to Jim."

"A bill to curtail synthetic drugs passed the Senate yesterday," I said, remembering the talk at the Capitol this week. "I haven't been paying much attention to it, but now I will. Please keep us posted if you know anything more about Jim." I knew by now that parents were often the last to be told something.

The next day, I looked up the House author of the synthetic drug bill. I might not be able to save Jim, but maybe I could help somebody else. Amid noisy legislator chatter and the backdrop of someone ranting at the microphone, the legislator told me that he thought next year would be plenty of time to pass the bill. He was in the majority, so he should have been able to get his bills heard if he really wanted to, but I knew that time was limited at the end of session and legislators had to pick their battles. He must be prioritizing another bill, pushing that one instead.

"If you don't get your leadership to get this bill up on the floor," I threatened, "I'll go to the press, tell my story, and say you don't see any urgency. If you need any help with leadership, let me know." His face tightened. He knew I would. I clomped back to my seat, breathing heavily.

The bill passed the next week. The same week, Jim's social worker called again. Tasks had decided Jim would not be allowed to return to his lodge for the indefinite future.

21
Really Bad News

A sprinkling of overnight snow had freshened the landscape on the day I drove to the Andrew Residence holiday dinner. Jim had been living there since leaving Tasks seven months earlier. We still didn't know the outcome of his gross misdemeanor charge for the accident he had caused or how the people had fared. Thinking about them tore at my soul, but as time went by I concluded no one had died or the charge would have been raised. After Jim's case manager had checked last summer, she said there were no pending charges. I began to think no one had even been seriously hurt.

Maybe Jim's civil commitment was enough punishment. He had temporarily lost his rights, as well as his housing and job. He had been sent to chemical dependency treatment and community care—similar to a halfway house—and then to Andrew. All this had also forced him to drop out of college again.

My name was on a plaque inside the door. I had received the Andrew Award four years earlier for my mental health legislative work. At that time, I had been glad Jim wasn't impaired enough to have to live at Andrew. He had been solo camping in Montana—a trip Tasks hadn't wanted him to take—but Roger and I took a risk and helped him swing it.

Now we felt like cocooning our son.

Even Taylor felt protective. Since she was four, she had visited Minnesota for a week or two each summer. The last summer, she had read a book about Dorothea Dix and learned how people with mental illness used to be treated. When she arrived for her visit, she went straight to her Uncle Jim and sat in his lap, gently hugging him with her head on his chest. They stayed that way for a long while.

We knew Jim was capable of more independence, but for now Roger and I liked Andrew Residence. Jim didn't. He spent every minute he could at our home. While he was there, he spent a lot of time dehydrating food. He made kale chips, mock cheese, "meat," and dried seeds, sprouts, and vegetables, all things he used to buy at Eco-politan. His dehydrator was a fixture on our counter, often plugged in for days at a time. He also liked to be at our home for a bit of privacy. Faced with limited resources, Andrew packed three people into each room of its large high-rise. Jim couldn't wait to leave.

I met Jim and his friend Matt just inside the dining room. Matt was filling in at the dinner for Roger, who had a conflict. Andrew's executive director, a serene man with a kind smile, was carving ham for each person coming through the buffet line. When we joined the line, Matt held out his plate for a slice. He was a gentle young man with straight brown hair and the ubiquitous medication belly. He had been studying to become a doctor, like his father and brother, before his mental illness struck. Now he worked in a mailroom for Tasks Unlimited.

We carried our plates to a window table to savor the scant December sunlight. After we were settled, Matt reached into his pocket and pulled out a wrinkled legal-size envelope. He handed it to Jim.

"This came to the lodge for you." Jim and Matt had lived at the same lodge before Jim had to leave. Good friends were the one vestige of Tasks from which our son could still benefit.

Jim set down his forkful of steaming ham and took the envelope. He was breaking his vegan diet today. "Probably bad news," he said, without optimism.

"Open it so we can enjoy our food," I encouraged. It looked like more of the voluminous paperwork he constantly received, asking him to document that he still had schizophrenia and was still poor, to make sure he wasn't cheating the government. I wondered how much money was saved by weeding out those unfortunates who couldn't keep up.

Jim ripped open the envelope, tearing the letter inside. He read it, holding the two pieces together, his head turning, line by line. "Really bad news," he moaned, batting it across the table to me as if it were scalding his fingers.

I scanned the page. My holiday cheer bled out. "You're right," I said, softly laying the letter on the table. Jim's charge had been increased from a gross misdemeanor to a felony: felony assault with a deadly weapon, his car.

"Sorry," Matt muttered, as if he were at fault, his eyes trained on his napkin.

A family sat down at the table next to ours, laughing—as I had hoped we would be.

We had heard nothing about Jim's car crash, and tendrils of hope had sprouted. But apparently all that had happened in the past seven months wasn't enough. The letter said Jim would be arraigned in two weeks, three days before Christmas—when Angela, Matt, and Taylor would be visiting. Only Jim's friend Matt finished his meal.

The next week, I scrambled to find an attorney before Taylor and her parents arrived. Normally holidays were a time when I grounded myself in family traditions: baking cookies, decorating, cooking favorite dishes, and making the house sparkle. This year I had to rush through everything, weighted down by constant anxiety.

The magic of Christmas in seven-year-old Taylor's eyes helped fortify us for a time. Our whole family, including Jim, saw *The Wizard of Oz* at the Children's Theater Company. One evening, after Taylor was tucked in bed, Angela and I found time to talk over cookies and hot chocolate.

"Jim seems good," Angela began, blowing on her cup. "Anything new?"

"He got a letter shortly before you arrived charging him with a felony for the accident he caused," I said. I twisted a strand of hair. "Needless to say, it threw us all for a loop. The letter didn't say anything about the other people. We thought all those things he had to do were his consequences." I nibbled on a sugar cookie.

"Seems that would have been appropriate," she agreed, one eyebrow raised. She took a sip from her cup. "What now?"

"I guess we'll find out more about the criminalization of mental illness." I stuffed the rest of the cookie in my mouth.

In January Jim's attorney informed us the occupants of the other car were fine. Like Jim, they had been released immediately from the emergency room. I wasn't aware how heavy my worry about them had been all these months until it was lifted. My steps felt lighter. We should have hired an attorney sooner, but we had thought we could save the money. I'd thought a lot about having been too tired at the end of session to pay attention to my son, to maybe prevent the accident. It was high on my list of reasons I decided to announce at the end of the year that I wouldn't seek reelection.

=

My last months in office went by quickly. On the final day, in the first week of May, I took my last votes in the early morning hours. They were relaxing hours, not like the hours before I had driven to Montana to get Jim out of jail. That night I had skipped the retirement speeches, but tonight I would give one. Traditionally, just after we adjourned, retiring legislators gave farewell speeches. Occasionally, members would surprise us by announcing on the spot that they wouldn't return, but most legislators, like me, had given our districts warning months before.

I was exhausted. I fingered my petrified-wood power ring, waiting to give my speech. They were given in order of seniority, so I would be near the end. I had served twenty years, fourteen of them after Jim got sick.

One of my favorite mental health bills had addressed postpartum depression. A father had sought me out after his wife had become seriously depressed after the birth of their baby. The bill we wrote required hospitals to provide new parents with information about this illness before they took their babies home. After it passed, NAMI held an educational program on postpartum depression. They host this program annually to this day. The Mental Health Caucus was a roaring success: active and with almost as many members as the Early Childhood Caucus. I had handed my leadership spot to another legislator four years before when we gained the majority and I became chair of the Education Finance Committee, a major committee that would require a lot of my time. In that session there had even been a House subcommittee, on which I'd served, that dealt solely with mental health.

The speaker called my name. I stood, took my microphone. "I'm proud we passed a visionary mental health bill last session, with the most funding in the history of our state." I smiled. "Do right by people with mental illness," I admonished my colleagues. "Or my ghost will roam these halls, haunting you."

When they smiled broadly back, I almost lost my vow not to cry during my speech, as many legislators did. I was proud that during the next legislative session, they heeded my words and upped the amount of funding to a second historic level.

Soon after we adjourned, my friend Mary McLeod arranged a tour for me. It had been fifteen years since Roger and I had met her at the NAMI class. She had worked hard to help raise funds for a state-of-the-art psych building at Regions, a prominent St. Paul hospital. The old building had been dismal when her son Matt had been treated there for his schizophrenia. The building was nearly finished as she and a hospital administrator showed me around. I was impressed by the private rooms, the many patient phones in a large, colorful dayroom, the gym, and the sunporch. I hoped Jim wouldn't have to be in a psych ward any time soon, but if he did, I hoped it would be at Regions.

A week after I gave my last speech on the House floor, Roger and I drove Jim to court. Like me, Roger had been tense about Jim's accident, even though he hadn't said much. Today the lines on his pale face were clearly drawn.

Kathleen Gearin, a respected judge nearing the end of her career, presided. Courtroom procedures reminded me of the legislature. The judge said she was chagrined it took Jim a year to get to court. She rebuked the prosecutor for the harsh charge and on the spot reduced the felony charge to a gross misdemeanor—music to all our ears. Roger started to say something, but I shushed him. He never remembered not to talk in court.

Jim was sentenced to mental health court for two years, where he would be required to refrain from drugs, do community service, pay a fine, and work. If he completed his two years successfully, his charge would become a misdemeanor. Hearing the judge's words turned up the volume of the music in our ears. These things were not punishment. They were productive things that could help turn his life around.

22
ACT

For the next five months, Jim received services from an Assertive Community Treatment (ACT) team that overlapped with his stay at Andrew Residence. Roger and I were glad he was still civilly committed and required to accept Andrew's intensive level of care, supplemented by help from his ACT team in making future plans. An ACT team provides wraparound services to help people with serious mental illness live successfully in the community. After Jim found an apartment, he was given permission to leave the residence.

"It feels good to be out of Andrew," Jim said, squinting at the February afternoon sun. "I didn't belong there."

"You needed the apartment to leave," I said, as we drove to his ACT team meeting. "I agree it took longer than it should have."

Jim's ACT team case manager's initial method of finding an apartment had been for the two of them to simply cruise around in his car looking for vacancy signs. Jim was to copy down phone numbers to call on his own later to see if they accepted rental vouchers. None did. I snapped down the visor to shield my eyes. "Good thing Ted finally told you about the county list." After I had asked him about it, I thought.

"Yeah." He didn't pick up on my snarkiness.

"What's the status of your voucher?" Jim's voucher was his rent subsidy. It was exceedingly hard to get one of the federal Section 8 vouchers, which assist very low income families and elderly or disabled people in affording housing in the private market. Minnesota also provided rental assistance to low-income people with serious mental illnesses through the Bridges Rental Assistance Program, in the form of Bridges vouchers. Those were also hard to obtain, but

Jim had told me his ACT team's company provided another form of rental voucher.

"I'm fourth on the list," Jim smiled with excitement as I parked the car.

Ted was sitting at a computer in a corner of the conference room. A thin, middle-aged man with curly blond hair, he rose to greet us with a confident smile. I had met him five months earlier when Jim began transitioning from Andrew.

"Jim only told me about this meeting yesterday," I said, taking off my coat. "I hope it's okay I'm here. He hasn't gotten his license back since the accident, so he asked for a ride."

"Of course," Ted said, without much conviction, sitting back down at the computer and continuing to type.

I was glad to be here, welcome or not.

More people entered the small room and shook my hand before joining us at the table. The psychiatrist, a serious-looking bearded young man, gave me a lingering look of deep sympathy. It startled me. While I might have welcomed this at a first-diagnosis meeting, now it felt odd.

I was glad to see the nurse. She was about Angela's age and had come to our house once to give Jim his regular shot of Haldol. She lifted a hand in recognition. The supervisor came in last, filling out the roster.

"Jim and I have gone over his goals," Ted began, authoritatively. "He's accomplished some big ones already, getting his apartment and fulfilling almost all of his mental health court requirements."

Only because Roger and I had been driving him to all of those, I thought to myself. No one looked at me. I felt as if I were the principal observing a classroom, making them nervous. I was known in the mental health community for my legislative work, so that may have contributed. *Or was one mother making them uneasy?*

"Jim's signed up for SNAP," Ted continued. SNAP is the Supplemental Nutrition Assistance Program, help that used to be provided via food stamps. Today's version is a plastic card, indistinguishable from a credit card. Jim had never been on food stamps before. I felt a brief flash of shame. Both my parents came from rural communities where it was common to refuse government help until you were starving.

The room was hot; a vent blew air on my neck. I watched my son, but he seemed relaxed, at ease with these people. Finally, at the end of the meeting, the supervisor asked if I wanted to say anything.

"What about his voucher?" I asked, grateful I was getting a turn. "Rent will take up almost all of his disability check, and he doesn't have a job yet."

"There are a lot of people looking for those subsidies," Ted said, almost lecturing.

"I know how hard it is to get a voucher," I said in a low voice. "But Jim says you have some and he's fourth on that list."

The nurse piped up. "The time for him to have gotten a subsidy was when he left Andrew."

The team turned toward her as one. She straightened her back and continued, directing her words at me. "People who are homeless or leaving large institutions have preference for vouchers."

"He missed his chance?" I asked numbly, unfolding my hands and sitting forward. I looked directly at Ted. "What can be done now?"

"Nothing. Those are the rules," he said. He crossed his arms, stared at me.

The nurse looked as unhappy as I felt but stayed silent.

These people held all the cards for Jim's services, and for communication with his family—or lack thereof.

"Well," I said, as levelly as I could, "then Jim needs a job. I hope you'll help him."

"Oh yes," Ted chirped. "That's one of your goals, right Jim?"

Jim nodded and grinned. He seemed oblivious to the fact that he hadn't gotten what we had come for, that the ACT team should have made sure he had a voucher before he had left Andrew. We all stood up. The meeting was over.

"Christ," I groused to Roger that evening. "If I'd known Jim wasn't getting a voucher, we would have looked harder for a better apartment. Half the mailbox doors in his ratty building don't work, and his carpet is nothing but cigarette holes." I slammed down the mail I was opening. "We could have gotten a much better place."

Roger looked up from his newspaper and nodded.

"And if Ted helps Jim with a job like he helped him get an apartment . . ." I trailed off.

When Roger turned a page, I noticed the issue he was reading was eight months old. I thought about pointing it out, but the look on his face stopped me. His countenance was at once guilty and defiant. Even though he tried to maintain an equilibrium, I could tell he, too, was deeply disturbed by what had happened. I stacked the mail neatly and headed to the kitchen to start supper.

It was summer before Jim had a job.

=

I turned over and looked at the glowing digits on the bedside clock. 2 a.m. Could only half an hour have passed since I last looked? Roger was lying on his stomach, snoring like a small engine, with one long leg dangling off his side of the bed. Yesterday when I had cleaned our backyard shed, I was shocked to find his stash of months-old newspapers, the ones he read instead of current ones. I guess this was what stress looked like for him. The newspapers reminded me of a scene in *A Beautiful Mind* when John Nash's wife discovered newspapers and other papers he had pinned up on the walls in a shed. Nash had schizophrenia.

Lightning punctuated the pouring rain outside, and I could smell the fecund earth in our garden. I was thankful the July night was warm because Jim was out in this mess, helping clean the stadium after the baseball game. He'd been under the gun to get a job in order to graduate from mental health court, so he had taken the first one he could get. I never thought at age sixty-five I'd be worrying about my thirty-five-year-old child on his first night of work.

I twisted and turned in bed, like a ferret preparing a nest. Another flash of lightning revealed our cat crouched uneasily at the foot of the bed.

I envisioned Jim's tall, lean form at the Twins baseball field, stooping over an industrial broom, his graceful fingers curled around its handle, the bristles gummed with soggy paper cups and napkins that clung to the bleacher steps like mollusks.

In the morning when I opened my eyes, it was quiet and light. Jim called before I finished the newspaper.

"Are you up already?" I exclaimed, setting down my coffee cup.

"I haven't been to bed," he burbled. "We got done at 7 a.m. Good timing, because the bus was there." Jim knew city buses. We suburban parents with cars didn't. "Buses don't run in the middle of the night."

"Did you talk with any of the other workers?" I always hoped he would make connections.

"I didn't talk to anyone. I had my symptoms," he said with disgust. Jim's bouts with anxiety shut him down, making him feel suicidal at times.

"Sorry," I said, sympathetically. I took a sip of coffee. "Did you get wet?"

"What do you think? Of course. Everyone was drenched."

That night, Jim called to say he still hadn't slept, possibly because he had waited to take his meds in the morning, the ones he usually took at bedtime. He'd met a new friend at a coffee house, cleaned his apartment, and made lists of books he wanted to read and of possible camping trips.

"Go to bed, Jim," I pleaded. He sounded manic. I was glad his ACT team was checking in with him.

A week later, he came over for supper. After we ate, Roger went to a meeting at church and Jim and I headed for the deck. The Twins were out of town, so Jim wasn't working. I braved his cigarette smoke because he was more talkative then.

"I feel terrific after a good night's work," he said, taking a long drag. "I had to walk home the last couple of times because work ended before the first bus came."

"Did you feel safe?" I asked, waving away smoke. Jim's apartment was in South Minneapolis, so he had to walk through downtown and then several more blocks.

"No one bothers me," he said, then grinned broadly. "But I get offered a lot of cocaine."

Hearing this made me glad his urine was still being monitored for mental health court. "Not what you need," I said. "Plus you have better uses for your money."

At the end of the week, I drove him to pick up his paycheck.

"I haven't had a check for over two years," he said, jiggling his leg with anticipation. "Since I left Tasks."

As soon as the car came to a halt, he bounced out to join the crowd of young people milling around the warehouse-like building, smoking and talking. Jim melted easily into the crowd and smoked a cigarette before going in.

His check would be small. He earned $8.50 per hour, minimum wage. And he had had to buy two lime-green T-shirts with "Industrial Staffing" emblazoned on the front, shirts he would never wear anywhere else. I guessed this was one of those "good jobs" the promoters of government stadium subsidies had boasted about when they were trying to convince legislators to cough up funding. I was glad I hadn't fallen for it.

On the way home, Jim's cell phone rang. He looked at the number and announced, "My friend from the coffee shop." It must be the friend he had met on his manic day after the first night of work. Jim smiled as he listened, then proudly said into the phone, "I can get together any night but Friday. I have to work that day."

I loved that Jim was proud of having this job, but I wished his ACT team would help him find something better. As soon as the baseball season was over, he would be out of work again. It was something to put on his résumé, which had been blank for too long, but he would need more than this to satisfy the court.

23
Celebrating in Mental Health Court

February 18, 2014

It was a mild day as Roger, Jim, and I entered the art deco county courthouse. Today was Jim's last appearance in mental health court, ending the two-year relationship. He'd cobbled together two cleaning jobs: a church and his condominium building.

After the rent on his shoddy apartment had been raised last fall, Roger and I took out a loan and purchased a condo. We rented it to our son at an affordable rate, as if he had gotten a voucher. We felt privileged to be able to do that, but I ached for the other people with mental illness who didn't have the support we could provide for Jim. Roger and I were not wealthy. We wouldn't have been able to help at all if we had also had to cover Jim's other bills that were paid for with public assistance.

The courtroom was plain, with uncomfortable wooden benches. Jim checked in with the staff at the front. They congratulated him effusively, making him fidget and look down. He smiled with closed lips when he rejoined Roger and me at the back of the room.

"Why're you sitting way back here on a ceremonial day?" our friend Mary laughed, when she arrived with her son Matt. He and Jim had gotten together with us parents a few times since I toured the new hospital with his mother. She was an attorney, comfortable in courtrooms, and hustled us to seats near the front. This was a day of celebration, of sorts.

People filed in and took seats on the benches. The air was stuffy, everyone a little hot in their heavy winter coats. This was a regular day in mental health court for everyone except Jim. He twitched his leg, and his thumbs in his folded hands circled each other at a fast clip. When it was his turn to approach the bench, he stood quietly in his usual slouch, hands folded in front.

"Congratulations, Mr. Greiling," the judge said from her high chair. "You've been very successful here, and I'm proud to award you this certificate." Roger and I smiled at each other; praise for our son was something we rarely heard. It was deserved. Besides the two jobs, Jim had resumed college classes (this time majoring in psychology), had completed hours of community service at two nonprofits, had paid his fine, and had never failed a urine test or missed a court appearance or chemical dependency class.

Mary led our small group in a burst of applause. The whole room joined in heartily, and Jim's fellow court clients looked happy for him. One of their own had made it.

Afterward, we walked to an upscale restaurant to celebrate with dessert. After our sundaes arrived, Matt handed Jim a card. "It's from both my mom and me." Matt was on clozapine, which made him seem steady, even peaceful. How I wished Jim still was. We wouldn't have been here if he hadn't gotten agranulocytosis. After they finished their dessert, the young men went outside for a smoke.

"I wish Jim and Matt were friends," I said to Roger on the way home, after we dropped Jim off. "But I can't arrange playdates anymore."

Roger agreed, keeping his eyes on the road.

People like us had many chances for friends. Recently I had reconnected with Jill, a woman who lived near us whom I'd met years ago in a class. She reached out because her son Steven now had schizophrenia too. She had no one else to talk with who really knew what she was going through. Our longtime friends Stephanie and Jim DeBenedet also knew about living with serious illness from their experience with Stephanie's multiple sclerosis and with her dad's bipolar disorder. Roger and I also shared meals regularly with friends from our church. We needed the relaxation and laughs these good friends provided, and we wished the same for Jim. Being alone was achingly the saddest part of his schizophrenia.

Lack of initiative was part of the fallout of the disease as well. Mary had told us that Matt mostly hung out with two fellows in his apartment building, easily within reach. Jim met people at coffee houses, but the people he connected with had time on their hands, as he did, and usually some type of mental illness.

Roger knew all this; I didn't press him with it, as we'd been over it so many times. He knew my history too—Grandma Teddy being my first encounter with serious mental illness at a time when I hadn't been equipped to understand it. We pulled into our driveway and got out together, but I felt alone with my worries. Our house was warm and welcoming, but I was at a loss about the future. People needed people to survive. What would happen to Jim if he stayed so isolated?

24
The Risk of Hospitality

March 26–April 1, 2014

Five weeks later, as I was backing out of Jim's condominium parking lot to take him to his psychologist's appointment, he announced, "I can tell what a person is like inside just by looking into their eyes." He was talking louder than usual. "I'm a good judge of character. I've found a roommate."

My hackles went up.

"He's a friend of Amy," Jim continued. Jim had met Amy the year before through a coffee house friend. He said she'd had a hard life.

"Where'd you meet him?"

"At a bar," he said nonchalantly. "Nick—that's his name—didn't have a place to stay because his girlfriend kicked him out. We hit it off, so he came home with me. Yesterday we talked all day, until late at night. We just really connected, you know?" Jim changed the radio channel to rock. Most of the buttons on my car radio were his stations.

"Does Nick have a job?"

"He's in a tight spot. He's out of work." Jim looked at me, pleading, knowing I wasn't impressed. "He's looking for a job. We got along so well, Mom. He loved the condo and really wants to be my roommate."

I thought of Jim's longing for a good friend, not just a person he talked to casually at a coffee house. But after the fiasco with the Eco-politan owner, I knew Jim could easily be taken advantage of. "Does Nick have a mental illness?"

"Maybe some PTSD," Jim replied. "He'd like to get on disability, like Amy and me."

Nick knew Jim had money coming in. "Where's Nick now?"

"At my condo."

"You just met this guy and now he's by himself in your condo?

151

What if he robs you blind and isn't even there when you get back?" The angst that had been rising in me boiled over.

"Mommmmm! It's not your decision! Stop doing this!" he wailed, holding his hands over his ears. "I'm thirty-six years old and haven't had any fun since I was a teenager. My life's been robbed. Just when I'm starting to be happy again, you're acting like this."

"Dad and I own the condo, so it is our business," I huffed, still playing the parent card. But maybe Jim had a point.

Jim hummed and wagged his head back and forth in time to the music while peppering the air with drum tapping. I noticed he had a self-satisfied smirk on his face. I realized he was high, probably thanks to Nick. It was useless to argue.

Jim slid out of the car the instant we arrived and disappeared through the psychologist's door. I'd never met this man, but I hoped he could help Jim think more carefully about inviting a person he had just met in a bar to live with him. I waited in the car but was too worked up to read my magazine.

Jim sauntered back half an hour later. "My psychologist agrees with me," he said with satisfaction. "You need to butt out."

I seethed. Either the psychologist had really said that or he wasn't clear enough with Jim to be of any help. "Could I come in and meet Nick when I drop you off?" I heard myself saying. "You could register for summer classes while I'm there."

"Sure," Jim said, smiling elatedly, as if he thought I was coming around.

After we parked, Jim rang the doorbell.

"Why're you ringing your bell?"

"Nick suggested I leave him the key, in case he needs to go out."

I counted to ten, my stomach boiling.

Nick was there and buzzed us in. He was sitting on Jim's blue easy chair, one we had given him from our previous set of furniture. Nick rose and walked swiftly toward me, all smiles, extending his hand, happy as a puppy to see me.

"So, this is Mom. Glad to meet you," he smarmed. "Your son's a great guy, and I'd really like to be his roommate. With your agreement, of course." Charm oozed from every pore. "Jim and I've just been flying the last couple days, we've connected so well."

Swirls of dust circled in the March sunlight coming through the living room windows. I felt unsettled.

Nick was a thin young man, a bit shorter than I. He was deathly pale and had red-rimmed eyes. He resembled a homeless child who didn't get enough sleep or fruit and vegetables. He sat down again in the chair and started typing on Jim's computer.

"I need to register," Jim said to him. "I forgot to do it yesterday, when we were talking." He beamed at Nick, as if he were a liberator.

"I'm working on my résumé," Nick said, in a slightly irritated tone. Then he looked at me, stopped, smiled graciously, and purred, "but if Jim needs to use his computer, it's his computer." He emphasized each *his* and extended his hands, palms up, as if he were a waiter in a restaurant, ushering Jim to his own chair so he could use his own computer. My unease increased.

As Jim logged in, Nick ostentatiously removed a piece of lint from the floor and industriously placed it in the wastebasket. "We need to keep the place tidy," he said, glancing at me, as he sat down next to Jim. He had a military haircut, clean but rumpled clothes, and nice teeth and was handsome in a boyish way.

"I'll tell you straight up—the way I like to do—I dropped out of high school when I was fifteen," he embarked, rightly assuming I wanted to hear about him.

"How old are you?" I was sitting across from him. Something about him made me want to order him out, but I knew Jim and the mental health system would view my doing that as interfering with his independence.

"Twenty-four. My grandparents raised me. My dad was an alcoholic and my mom left." He talked easily—a virtue Jim always appreciated in others because of his social anxiety. "I went back to high school and then an arts college, but I didn't graduate. I've been working."

"Where?"

"A pizza place—but they cut my hours, so I quit." He ran his hand over his short hair. "I'll say honestly, I don't have the rent money. Too big a stretch right now, but I can get it. I can always get a job. Or borrow from my grandmother. I haven't borrowed from her in a while. My grandpa would hire me if I need him to. He has a small carpet-laying operation. Nothing like Carpet King, real small-scale.

I've worked for him before. I'll pay Jim $150 up front and the full rent when I get my job. All right?" All this with smiles to melt icebergs. He sounded manic like Jim.

"By Tuesday," I said, thinking fast. I didn't believe he'd be able to pay, but I sensed that fighting both young men, especially when Jim was high, would be futile, maybe dangerous.

When I got home, I googled Nick. Thinking of him there in Jim's condo made my skin crawl. I found a mug shot and multiple arrest records, approximately two per year for the preceding four years. Based on his fast releases, I guessed small-time drug infractions. In the photos, Nick stared peacefully at the camera; he had shoulder-length hair, a mustache, and a small goatee.

I called Jim, tapping my pen against the counter.

"I'm not perfect either, Mom," he said, rebutting my suspicions. "I have mug shots too."

"You were very ill," I said sternly. "What if he steals your stereo or computer?"

"Everybody needs a chance," he said stubbornly.

I knew his case manager Ted wouldn't want to get involved in this, so I left it until Jim called the next day, even though it never left my mind. That's the thing about having a child with a serious mental illness who isn't stable or is high: they rarely leave your mind.

"We've lost the keys. I need your set."

"What do you mean *we* lost the keys?" I demanded. "Do you mean Nick?"

"No, Mom. It was my fault," Jim pleaded. I could hear him making something in his kitchen, probably coffee. "When he gave me back the keys, I didn't put them on my chain. They must be here somewhere, but we can't find them."

"I bet he knows where they are," I said, banging breakfast plates into the dishwasher.

"No, Mom, he's put out about it too."

"Keep looking," I said crabbily, slamming the dishwasher door shut. I hadn't slept well and was tired. "You can't have my keys."

Roger and I took a walk around Como Lake that afternoon. We'd been walking together more lately, now that Jim was doing more things with other people. Walking gave us both a chance to talk and to have the other's undivided attention, a rare opportunity. It was a gusty, overcast day.

"I'm trying to live by the serenity prayer," I said as we rounded a bend. "Especially accepting things I can't change." Various people had recommended we go to Al-Anon, but we hadn't made the time.

"Not much else we can do," he agreed.

"Do you ever wonder what our lives would have been like if Jim hadn't gotten sick?"

Roger walked slower, touching his belt buckle, a habit of his. "We'd sure have other things to talk about." He smiled. "But you shine—with all you've learned about the mental health system and have done for Jim and others."

I smiled at his praise, something I didn't hear often, Roger being Roger. "I hate it that he's so dependent on us since Tasks gave up on him." I wrapped my scarf one more time around my neck. "Think there's something in us that likes this dynamic?"

"What do you mean?"

"Maybe we think it keeps us younger to continue parenting him. Maybe we should just let Nick rob him. Might be a good lesson for him." I grabbed my scarf again. "What if the psychologist is right that we should butt out? Angela gets on me for enabling him too. We do always swoop in when things go wrong."

"We need to keep a better eye on him," Roger replied. "More of an eye than the mental health system does."

"Maybe if he were an addict who didn't also have schizophrenia . . ." I said. "It was so much easier when he got more help. Plus, at Tasks, we were part of the team. Andrew Residence wasn't bad about involving us either. But this ACT team ices us out."

Three days later, Jim called to say the keys had surfaced. Plenty of time for Nick to have copied them.

=

"Nick stole forty dollars from my wallet when I was sleeping," Jim whispered urgently when he next called. He sounded upset and possibly frightened. "And I think he copied the keys."

"Is he there now?" I asked, my spirits lifting to hear his words. He was speaking in such a hushed voice that I guessed Nick must be nearby.

"No, I'm at a coffee house with Paul. We're sitting outside." Paul was another of Jim's friends from Tasks. It was a glorious fifty-degree day, incredible for March.

"I got to thinking," Jim continued, still whispering, "when I found my keys, they were in their usual place. I'm positive I would have seen them there if they'd been there all along."

I heard loud talking in the background. I imagined the sidewalk tables were packed today, with this weather—the reason Jim was whispering.

"Do you want Dad and me to help?" My muscles relaxed as if I, too, were sitting outside in the sunshine. Jim was safe with Paul and catching on to Nick.

"Yes." I heard him take a slurp of coffee.

"Do you feel safe with him another night?"

"Uhh, not sure."

"Do you want us to come over tonight to help get rid of him?"

"Yes," he breathed with emphatic relief.

"Ask Paul to stay with you. At 8:30?" I responded with the same relief. Paul was a big, strapping young man, slightly younger than Jim.

When Roger and I arrived that evening, Paul opened the door. "This is a shitty situation," he said, looking slightly exhilarated. I always found him genuinely likable and personable, not fake like Nick.

"It sure is," I concurred. Roger nodded at Paul and thanked him for helping.

"Nick and his girlfriend cleaned and rearranged the place," Paul supplied. "There're out now. Looks like she's planning to move in too. They had sex here once." I noticed there were no tobacco crumbs on the kitchen counter, where Jim rolled his cigarettes, and the kitchen spotlight was newly trained on a vase of flowers on the kitchen table.

Jim came in from the bedroom. "This proves he copied the keys," he said triumphantly, gesturing at the living room and kitchen. "He was gone when I left with Paul, so he had to have keys to get back in and clean."

I smiled. Now was not the time to say I told you so.

"We should bag up his things," Paul offered.

"Great idea," Roger agreed enthusiastically, handing him a grocery bag from the kitchen.

"Angela wondered about calling the police," I said. "I'll have my phone at the ready, just in case." Angela faithfully called us every week, usually asking about her brother and serving as a sounding board. I especially appreciated her adult role after my parents and only sibling had died.

After the scurrying around to collect Nick's things, we stationed ourselves in the living room and Jim turned on his stereo. A soft Grateful Dead song soothed us. Nick's stuff was piled by the door—quite a cache: a laundry basket full of clothes, the bag he arrived with, and two grocery bags full of things, even his toothbrush.

"We should pull the blinds," Paul suggested, rising to do so. He was really into this. "My heart is beating fast, you guys," he said, sitting again.

"Mine too," I said. "I hope Nick goes quietly, but if not, we have him outnumbered." I looked at the three big men, each nearly twice Nick's size.

Finally, the doorbell rang. Wisely, Nick chose not to use the key. We heard his voice joined by a feminine one yukking it up outside. Only Nick came in, warily, like a stalking cat. He looked surprised to see Roger and me, smiled weakly, but quickly recovered.

"This must be Dad."

He started toward Roger, but I stood and cut him off. "You're being kicked out," I said, pointing at his things by the door. "You stole money from Jim's wallet and copied the keys."

Nick's eyes hardened and narrowed into angry slits, but a placid face emerged so quickly it was hard to imagine the anger had been there. "I didn't steal his money. I have my own," he said, pouting and gathering up his things. "And I don't have keys."

"Yes, you do!" Roger shouted, standing up too. "You copied Jim's."

"He's just mad because I had a girl here this weekend," he said, softening his tone. He turned to face Jim. "Let's keep in touch, Jim."

I had to admire his aplomb.

"Yeah, see you around, man," Jim replied amiably.

Paul grabbed the remaining bags and followed Nick out. When they were gone, I told Jim that we were going to have to change his locks and that until they were changed, he was going to have to stay put in the apartment. He didn't argue.

After Paul returned, he and Jim went outside to smoke. Roger and I stayed awhile longer to decompress and to make sure Nick stayed gone. I gave the condo one last look. In the bedroom Nick had taken, I found two glasses behind the curtain, one with a cigarette butt in it. I also found a plastic kit that looked as if it were for first aid, containing a hypodermic needle and several tubes of Red Cross numbing agents.

"Pathetic," I said to Roger after I put the glasses in the sink and held up the container. "Nick must be hard-pressed. Look what he's been shooting up." On the way out, Roger tossed everything in the outside garbage bin.

We laughed like fools on the way home. Sometimes I worried we were losing our sense of humor, but not tonight. "Fifteen years ago, we would've been unlikely suspects in a drama like this," I said. "Now even this seems normal."

"Throwing Nick out felt pretty darn good," Roger allowed. "If only we could get rid of all Jim's problems this easily."

=

I poured out the story the next day to my beautician. Kathy Tempesta is a personable woman whom I'd been going to since Angela and Jim had been young enough to color at her table when I couldn't get a sitter. She was an empathetic ear. Her brother, who had died a few years earlier, had had schizophrenia.

I wiped a stray hair off my nose. "And then I found a needle and some Red Cross numbing stuff he was reduced to using," I concluded, chuckling.

Kathy turned off the hair dryer. "Mindy!" she said, looking at me incredulously. "That's a kit. For heroin!"

I saw my surprised face in her mirror, a gray streak on one side of my bangs. I looked older than I'd thought. "I didn't see any heroin."

"He wouldn't keep his stash in the kit! That would never leave his person." She turned the hair dryer back on. "He must've been using for a long time, because those numbing agents are for when you're having trouble finding a vein."

I didn't ask how she knew.

After she finished drying, she set the hair dryer aside and sat in the empty chair beside me. I had cried in just such a chair when I told her about Jim's first civil commitment, fifteen years before, when I had had to testify against him as if he were a criminal.

"And that pale, pasty face you describe is a hallmark of a heroin user, Mindy. They're the charmers of the world, so tell Jim not to feel bad he was taken in."

Roger was as shocked as I was when I relayed this information. We had both led such sheltered lives. "Good thing we got Nick out when we did," he said. "I hope Jim's learned something from this about choosing better friends."

"I wouldn't count on it," I said sadly. "He wants friends so badly. He believed everything both Nick and that so-called doctor at Ecopolitan said. I fear he's vulnerable to any person who tries to take advantage of him."

25
Colleen

As I was waiting to check out a book at the library, a tall, lithe woman walked up to me. Brown-rimmed glasses rested on her upturned nose. It was Colleen, the woman Jim had used drugs with six years before. Neither he nor we had seen her since the drugs had caused Jim to relapse. Her hair was shorter and grayer, but otherwise she looked about the same. "Hi, Mindy, how're you?" she asked, her eyes dancing. Her hair was parted in the middle, exposing a high forehead.

"Fine." I didn't want to engage.

"Good book?" she asked conversationally, pointing at the novel under my arm. Her smile widened, and she interrupted herself. "How's Jim? Is he still living in the group home?" She dragged out "group home" to emphasize her disdain for that living arrangement.

"Doing well. He's got a condo."

Her face lit up like a jack-o'-lantern. "Maybe I should call him then," she said with a mischievous laugh. "But nooo, I'm just kidding."

A shadow crossed my heart. I feared she wasn't kidding. When I got home, I set my book aside. Reading usually grounded me, but not today. I told Roger I'd made a mistake. I had an uneasy feeling Colleen was going to contact Jim. Roger frowned too. Their crack use had caused Jim's hospitalization and long recovery, and we attributed his subsequent drug use that had gotten him kicked out of Tasks to the opening of that door. Colleen was eleven years older than Jim—which felt like a big difference to me, especially considering how many years he had lost to mental illness. She had gotten ill when she was twenty-seven, already on her own. Her parents, people I knew from local politics and liked, had helped her obtain the rent-subsidized housing she lived in after she became ill. Two of her siblings also had mental illnesses. Unlike Jim, Colleen didn't work and hadn't made any new friends after her old ones fled.

A week later, while we were driving back from a weekend trip to Chicago, Jim called. He was cat sitting at our home, a service he enjoyed and we appreciated.

"I have a surprise for you when you get home," he said.

"What?" I asked.

"If I told you, it wouldn't be a surprise," he answered playfully. The cat meowed in the background.

After I hung up, I told Roger I feared Colleen would be the surprise. He said that he doubted it, that I was too paranoid, but I was unable to concentrate on my book the rest of the way home.

This was one time I didn't want to be right. But, sure enough, when we carried our suitcases in the front door, Colleen was perched at our dining room table beside our exultant son.

"Here's trouble," she said with a smirking laugh.

"Hello," Roger gruffed and then quickly retreated to the basement. He didn't emerge until after she left.

I talked to Colleen briefly. Jim was quiet but got up to refill her cup. I saw the coffeepot was two-thirds empty: they'd been there for a while. After they headed to the deck to smoke, I unpacked. My limbs felt leaden. Any relief I'd felt from our getaway in Chicago vanished.

The next day, I googled her. No mug shots. No web presence at all. Perhaps I was building up the hazards of Colleen too much. Maybe she could be a perfectly okay girlfriend for Jim, I tried to reason—the one he'd been missing from his slim life, one who understood and accepted mental illness. I could only hope she had stopped using crack.

The next week Jim came over to use our computer, explaining that his was a "piece of shit." (Only later did we learn he and Colleen had sold it for drugs.) For his homework, I happily surmised, since he had started his summer class the week before. Colleen tagged along. They went downstairs to the computer where I heard them conferring in quiet voices. It sounded as if she was helping him type. She'd said she used to do office work. When they came upstairs, Jim's guilty-looking face dashed away my good mood. Almost defiantly, he said, "Don't be mad, Mom, but I dropped my class."

"What?" I asked, my lifeblood seeping from my heart. Why had I let Colleen know Jim was no longer under the protection of Tasks? I had put so much pride in his doing well before this fall.

"It was a capstone class—meant to be taken just before graduation." Colleen was standing close to Jim, smiling confidently. "I accidentally registered for it."

"Why didn't you just switch to another class?"

"The deadline has passed." Colleen took his arm, and he smiled lovingly at her. "Also, I need a leisurely summer," he wheedled. "We haven't seen each other in so long."

"He's longed for a girlfriend," I said to Roger over supper that night. "It's painful for me to go to weddings and see his friends and relatives get married, start families, and pass him by." I took a sip of wine. "Think what it must be like for him."

"But he's been doing so well," Roger said, laying down his fork.

I stopped eating too. "I know. I don't think I could take her dragging him down again." The thought of another roll of the boulder up the mountain and the inevitable fallout made me feel exhausted. When I tried to read before bed, I fell asleep after one page.

Two weeks later, while I was walking on a local trail to ease my stress, Angela called. "I thought you'd like to know why Jim called me today."

Our children don't talk much these days, but Angela's tone told me I wouldn't be glad about this call.

"Why?" I asked, cupping my hands over the phone to shield it from the wind.

"To borrow money."

I stopped beside an arch of roses next to the asphalt path, feeling a sudden weakness.

"He said he has debts," she said with disdain. "I might have thought about it if he'd asked for, say, fifty or a hundred dollars." She gave a mirthless laugh. "But he said that amount wouldn't help."

"What'd he ask for?"

"Fifteen or twenty *thousand!*"

"Fifteen or twenty *thousand!*?" I repeated, sitting on a bench next to the roses. "What kind of debt?"

"He wouldn't say," she fumed, "but unless it's a mortgage, Matt and Taylor and I combined couldn't run up that kind of debt. I hope you're not going to help him pay it. You and Dad are always enabling him."

I paused before answering faintly, "I'll talk to him. One of these days we'll try Al-Anon." After we hung up, I crushed a rose between my fingers, releasing a strong fragrance. It reminded me of a funeral.

=

"Angela says you tried to borrow money from her." It was pouring rain the next day, and I was in no mood to make this conversation easy for Jim. He'd crossed a serious line. "A lot of money."

"It sucks being poor, Mom." His voice over the phone sounded unrepentant. He was at Colleen's apartment, as usual. "Angela's got plenty of money. Colleen has a rich brother who helps her out. I'd like to see Angela or you and Dad get by on what we do. None of you have a clue." It all sounded rehearsed. Not like Jim's voice: more like he was parroting Colleen. I could hear her voice in the background above the blaring television.

"I'm sure we don't," I replied, "but it doesn't sound like you do either, if you're spending all that." I was pacing now, in time to the rain drumming on the roof.

"Colleen and I've been kind of bad," he said, slowly, in that same false voice. "But neither of us has had a good life. We just need a good summer, to have some fun. Like other people."

"What do you mean—bad?"

"A little coke, Mom. Just a little coke."

"Cocaine!"

"I admit it kind of got out of hand."

"Cocaine, Jim!"

"We've stopped."

"Stopped? Because you're out of money?" I shouted. "Is that what you called Angela about? More money for coke?"

"For my credit card."

"What the fuck, Jim!" I took deep breaths and got my calm back. It wasn't easy. We agreed that they needed to come over so we could talk.

I watched them drive in and stop in the driveway to lean on her car and smoke cigarettes, then they slid in the front door.

"Hi, Mom," Jim said, tentatively. He looked worn. I gestured to stools at the kitchen counter and they sat. Colleen was quiet for once. Usually she talked incessantly. I noticed for the first time Jim had vertical lines in front of each ear, like older men.

"How much, Jim?"

He hung his head and spoke into his chest. "$50,000."

"Oh my God! You spent all that on cocaine!"

"We went out to eat some," Jim said, "but coke is expensive."

Colleen covered her mouth with both hands, stifling a giggle. Jim laughed too, but nervously, without smiling.

"This isn't one bit funny," I roared. "There's no way Angela or Dad and I or anyone else is going to bail you out of this."

They exchanged looks. Jim's face was sober and scared. Colleen's somehow bordered on exhilaration.

"Come on, Jim," she said, pulling him up. "Nothing for us here."

"Yes, you go," I screamed after them. "You aren't getting any money for crack here."

When I told Roger, his eyes shrank into his skull. He set his papers down on the counter. His dad had owned a collection agency, and he equated unpaid debt with shiftlessness. He had coached his kids to do the same.

Sitting beside him on the couch after he got settled, I was calmer, but I was in despair too. Jim's future had been promising less than a month before, compared to years prior. He'd finally gotten on decent meds, he was back in college and had a place to live and a job. All before Colleen.

We'd risked taking out a loan to buy Jim's condo, which now sat empty. He was missing some rent payments to us.

"He got that card in college, before they regulated student debt," Roger said. "We'll have to look at our home equity line to pay this off."

"You've got to be kidding." I stood up, remembering Angela's words. This was Roger's way of enabling. I tended toward offering too many rides or providing food. "We're not going to pay this. They'll just keep buying more crack!"

Roger just shook his head. He buried himself in newspapers and watched TV until I went to bed.

I called Jim's case manager in the morning and asked in a rattle-snake sort of way how it was going with Jim's finances. Ted had recently started working with Jim on his money matters, taking over from Roger and me. Before, I had gone over Jim's credit statement with him every month; Roger had assisted with bank statements and taxes.

"Jim's declined my help with his finances. It's his right."

"If you were going to abdicate all responsibility for our vulnerable son's finances," I struck, "why for God's sake didn't you at least tell us? I suggest you and Jim march down to Legal Aid or somewhere and find out how he can declare bankruptcy."

"As long as Jim's on food stamps, no credit company can touch him."

"That's nowhere near good enough," I spewed, my pulse pounding. "This is on you. How about that good job you keep promising? Get him out of that apartment and away from Colleen, and he might have a life after all." I slammed down the phone.

26
A Better Job

I was skeptical that the ACT team would find a better job for Jim, but I knew he needed one. Employment improves self-esteem, and regular activity staves off mental distress. Jim had always done best when he was working at Tasks. Grandma Teddy was happiest at the state hospital when she eventually got to work in the kitchen. She worked every day with the paid kitchen help and the other women patients who were deemed healthy enough to be there. Her letters to me at college were full of news of the kitchen work and menus. She bragged about all the tomatoes she prepared, potatoes she peeled, and cakes and pies she baked.

I searched online and found a NAMI class on employment. After the class—which was aimed at people younger than Jim, as many recent improvements to the system seemed to be—the teachers advised me to contact the Department of Human Services (DHS). They said to ask if Jim could use other employment services instead of the ACT team. I was grateful they reminded me to advocate for Jim. When I was in the legislature, I had helped many people do exactly that, but I had been forgetting to be as aggressive for my own son.

When I called, someone at the department said no. The ACT team received Jim's employment funding and it couldn't be transferred. But I was on an advocating roll, so I contacted my state legislators. I asked them to fix this through legislation allowing clients to take their employment dollars elsewhere. Soon after, DHS set up a meeting with the ACT team, Jim, and me. The goal was to make sure Jim found a job. They said ACT teams needed employment dollars in order to have enough overall funding. For the time being—whether it was due to my anger or just to his credit card being maxed out so that he had no money for drugs—Jim was more sober and motivated to work.

Afterward, Jim's job search with Ted accelerated.

I recommend advocacy like this for every family dealing with mental illness and addiction. The system isn't always forthcoming with information about the benefits people could receive or diligent about ensuring funding goals are accomplished. Yes, I definitely have a leg up, having been a legislator, but everyone should know that it should be part of every legislator's and county commissioner's job to assist constituents who need help with things like this.

Soon Jim and his case manager scheduled an interview for him to work in a group home. I was surprised, given his history, that the company immediately hired him, but Jim said he had checked the disability box on his application. Surely they had done a background check.

I whooped for joy when he told me. "This could be your big break. You like to help people. Remember when you helped that guy in college with calculus?"

"I'd rather work with people with mental illness," he said, "but they only had developmental disability openings. Once I get established, hopefully I can switch. I know more about mental illness."

Jim was a star trainee as an aide, acing quizzes and reveling in the practical trainings, such as learning how to operate a van lift. He fit right in with the other employees. I drove him to work on his first day on the job.

"Taylor made the honor roll," I said, making conversation to go with my happy feelings, "and she also received a big citizenship award."

"Cool." Jim loved his niece, now in fifth grade, and he was excited about this job too.

"I'm so proud of you too, Jim," I said.

"I'm going to try hard to grow up now," he declared, warming my heart.

There was no bus service, so Roger drove Jim home after each shift, and I continued to take him. Fifty miles each round trip. Case manager Ted said the ACT team couldn't be expected to help with transportation, even though they had found him this job.

I worried to Roger that night. "He's going from barely working to back-to-back fifteen-hour weekend shifts."

"And is responsible for vulnerable people," Roger agreed, stacking the papers he needed for work tomorrow. "At least there's other staff."

Our minds eased when, after a couple of weeks, Jim's supervisor, Bonnie, told him he was doing a great job. What could be better? The holidays were approaching and both our children were excelling.

After concluding her term as president of the National Press Club, during which we often heard her on the radio and saw her on TV, Angela had scored the White House beat. Her office was in the White House basement, and she'd be traveling around the world with President Barack Obama on Air Force One. I felt like pinching myself every time I thought about her exciting life, so different from her brother's.

Jim's job went well all fall. We saw him shine with the growing responsibility and success. The whole family celebrated the holidays with more hope than ever in our hearts.

In February, Angela called to say she was flying to St. Paul for an Obama event and had tickets for Roger and me. We picked our way over icy downtown sidewalks and arrived early. Union Depot, a renovated train station in the heart of St. Paul, was the perfect spot for the president's speech on transportation.

I was pushing past people I hadn't seen since I had left the legislature two years earlier when we spied Angela. She was waving amid TV cameras in the press section, smiling her lovely smile. After we hugged, she snagged a fellow journalist to take our photo. Roger managed to get on TV that night, standing next to the president.

I was glad the chasm between Angela's world and her brother's wasn't quite as deep. It meant that Roger's and my balancing act, where we tried to value and honor each child's life in turn, wasn't quite as tough.

One evening a couple of weeks later, Jim called from work. I was in my pajamas ready for bed, but any sleepiness disappeared at the upset in his voice. I'd driven him to work earlier through blinding snow. If Jim didn't love his job so much, I'd be ready to hang it up because of the far-flung location.

"Yesterday my coworker at the home told my supervisor I'm not pulling my weight."

"Where'd she get that idea?" I heard the snowplow going down our street.

"When the coworker got here last night, one man's diapers were dirty." I heard him crying softly. "I work all the time around here, Mom. Except for when clients are asleep, I cook, clean up, change diapers— everything. But I was the only staff person here. The man is fragile."

"You were alone?" I exclaimed. "What about your coworker, the one who claimed you're not pulling your weight?"

"She's not here all the time."

"Is anyone else from the staff with you now?"

"No, that's why I can call." His sobs were loud. "And the clients are asleep."

"Quiet or you'll wake someone up," I cautioned. "They shouldn't have put you in this position." Hot anger ratcheted up in me. Even if company policy was to have only one staff person at night, Jim was too new an employee to be left all alone. And were they taking his disability into account?

"The supervisor Bonnie stops in sometimes," he said. "But she told me not to change the man's diapers by myself. He just got back from the hospital. It takes two people to operate his lift."

"If Bonnie told you that, why'd she listen to that other worker?"

"Maybe to cover her butt, Mom. She's usually here a couple of hours, but yesterday it was only half an hour. Plus, my coworker shouldn't talk." He snorted angrily. "When she was here she spent half her time in her car, talking on the phone."

A couple of weeks later on another freezing day, Jim came over to our house with worse news. He shrugged off his jacket and sank into a dining room chair. "Bonnie's giving me notice. Says this work isn't my spark."

My heart ached at the despair I saw on my son's face. I dried my hands on a dish towel and got two cups out of the cupboard. "Did you remind her she told you not to change the diapers when you were alone?" After I filled the cups with coffee, I accidentally banged them together and coffee sloshed over. I wiped it up.

"I was too flustered," he moaned, gripping the cup I set in front of him.

I knew well how Jim—like so many people with mental illness—is flattened by criticism. He had quit his apartment-cleaning job after receiving a critical letter, even though it had been a blanket letter that applied to another worker. I set the carton of cream on the table, feeling as if I were being fired too. This would never have happened to Angela.

"Now Bonnie has a new thing too," he continued in a bewildered voice, adding cream to his cup. "She asked why I only take one client places."

"I didn't know you took any of them places."

"I took Kent to Minneapolis a couple times for lunch and tea. They let me use the van. The regular weekday worker suggested it. She's great—the kind of person who should work there."

"You're the perfect person to take him out," I said, imagining my son with Kent at a coffee house, where Jim personifies mellowness. "Why only him?"

"Kent's the only high-functioning one. If he were at any other home, he'd get to go out all the time."

I heard the TV go on downstairs and thought of how Roger would take this new development. He'd been down in the basement for hours.

"If they wanted me to take any of the others, I would have," Jim continued. "Why didn't Bonnie just tell me?" His voice rose and then calmed. "I even took Kent to the Minnesota River Bottoms once. I had to bundle him up."

"What did he like best?"

"He was up for anything." He smiled a little. "He never wanted to go back."

"You enriched his life." My coffee was cold, too bitter now, and I got up to pour it out.

"In six days, I would have completed my probation. No one told me anything but good things about my work until now."

I rested one hand on his shoulder, not knowing what to say.

"Just when I was celebrating that he's finally working at something worthy of him," I lamented later to Roger. We were both huddled in the basement now as the winter wind howled outside. "Grandma Teddy was always happier when she was working. After she lost her salesclerk job, she went downhill fast. I hate to think of Jim with nothing to do except be with Colleen at her apartment."

"What if they're still doing drugs?"

"Just what I worry about," I said, "and without this job . . ."

We were silent for a while.

=

I was astounded when Jim called the next day to say his manager had asked him to work his usual thirty-hour weekend. Apparently he wasn't being fired after all. "But I told her," Jim finished, "even if I'm not fired, I quit."

A police detective called Jim a week later—four days after Christmas. Kent, the client Jim had taken on outings, had reported that Jim smoked marijuana on the job and sexually abused him.

"I told the detective nothing of the sort happened," Jim spit out angrily, as we talked. I thought, *Oh my God! This couldn't be happening.* Hasn't Jim suffered enough in this world? Hasn't our family suffered enough? It was late afternoon, already getting dark. The colorful lights on our Christmas tree were switched on. The days between Christmas and New Year's were normally a mellow time of the year. In the kitchen was the dinner I had put together, but I knew nobody would have any appetite for it now. I ached for Jim, standing by the deck door, his arms crossed tightly over his chest, the picture of despair and outrage.

"He kept asking me over and over and I said, 'Listen, buddy, this didn't happen.'"

All of a sudden I felt dizzy so I sat down. Music blared from the radio. The holiday cookies I'd arranged on a plate sat untouched. I had been hoping for a normal visit, but so far this was anything but.

"The detective asked if I smoked marijuana," Jim continued. "I said yes, but never with clients. I told him any intelligent person who spent any amount of time with Kent would know he only talks a little and never says anything new. All he ever really says is, 'Let's go to Disney World.'"

I could just imagine. Jim's clients had severe developmental and physical disabilities. He did his best, but he never should have been left alone with them. I tried to muster up some words of encouragement. "It sounds like you handled this really well," I began, but he interrupted me.

"It's hard for me to believe he came up with this on his own, Mom." He picked up a cloth elf from the end table and squeezed it like a therapy ball. I watched the knuckles on his slender hand tighten and relax, over and over. "I bet my supervisor Bonnie put him up to it. She was mad I wouldn't work that weekend, when she didn't have anyone else. I wouldn't put it past her to have coached him."

I felt cold, as if I were outside in the freezing snow. "It does smell like it could be retaliation."

"I suggested they give Kent a drug test for secondhand weed smoke. That would prove he's lying."

Jim was thinking more clearly than I felt.

"When we had our training, they said abuse charges from clients are common."

A rush of comfort flooded over me. Of course it was common. This was a medically complex community. I didn't doubt my son on this for a moment, but I also thought he'd have a hard time defending himself. "I always thought people with developmental disabilities were innocents." It was naive of me, I realized as I said it, and Jim shook his head.

"They have mental illnesses too. Some of their meds are the same ones I take."

We planned out a strategy of sorts over dinner, with Roger's help. To be on the safe side, we hired an attorney. This would cost several more thousands of dollars. I wondered how much we had spent on attorneys for Jim alone. She said since the officer had interviewed Jim by phone instead of in person, they must not have evidence. She also said he'd be interviewed as a matter of course by Health and Human Services. And so he was.

"How do you think it went?" I asked Jim as we walked around Lake Calhoun a few days later.

"No idea." I could see his breath clouding the air as he smiled. "But I rate myself a ten."

"You must have done a wonderful job," I said, "because I know you're a hard grader." I was hoping for more of those smiles; they had been few and far between these past months. But Jim just nodded, shoved his hands in his pockets and plodded on. "Your attorney says Kent's sister is pressing the case aggressively. She believes her brother because he's fixating on you longer than anyone else."

Jim scowled. "I don't know why he's saying that shit."

"Who could blame him?" I said. "It shows what a good job you did. You took him all those places he never got to go. Maybe this is his way of trying to get you back. Also, it sounds as if he's made these charges before. Maybe Bonnie wasn't involved."

"People are stupid and evil," Jim snapped. His mood had completely changed and I thought carefully about what to say next. He deserved his pessimistic view after all that had happened, but he could accelerate surprisingly fast.

"I agree the company handled your employment poorly. Do you want to file a complaint?"

"No." He kicked a clod of snow in the path. Hard.

Later that afternoon, I looked into discrimination anyway. I made a few calls, but my inquiries went nowhere, except to uncover the fact that Jim shouldn't have been hired in the first place. Evidently, he hadn't passed the background check.

"They hired him and put him to work with vulnerable adults before they checked him out?" Roger asked at dinner, in disbelief.

I pushed my plate aside. I hadn't been able to eat much for a few days; my stomach was constantly upset. "If anything had actually happened, especially when Jim was the only one there, they would have been in a world of hurt."

"What do you think really happened?" Roger asked.

"I think they took a hasty look at Jim and snatched him up. He couldn't be the only person they hired without a background check. They probably gambled, knowing they could get the background report before probation was up. They had plenty of time to get rid of him."

Roger nodded, chewing. "Sounds plausible."

I reminded myself that I needed to eat and pulled my plate back. Grief had been a constant companion this past week. I agonized over how sad it was that Jim had lost a job that was meaningful for him, even more than over his buzz-saw experience. It was a lost opportunity for the people in the home too. They deserved enthusiastic, empathetic workers like Jim.

Roger had cleaned his plate. He wiped his mouth and pushed back his chair. "You look tired," he said kindly. "Maybe you should go to bed early."

I nodded. But getting to sleep wasn't easy. My mind raced. Would Jim be charged, go to jail, lose the few positive things left in his life?

I shouldn't have been surprised when, after two months, Jim received an official letter that summed up their investigation as "inconclusive."

"A common result," our attorney said.

"I wonder how Jim even copes." Roger said.

=

We tried again in early summer. Jim took classes to become a peer specialist, a person with a mental illness who is paid to help others with similar illnesses. The teachers, professional, impressive people who also had serious mental illnesses, amazed and inspired him. Jim was thrilled with the classes and aced the homework. As I drove Jim back and forth for the classes, he told me they were the best he'd ever taken, that they were giving him a new perspective on the mental health system and how it treated people with mental illnesses. His eyes were opened for the first time, he said.

Colleen and I had attended his graduation. Jim wanted her to come. Each graduate made a small speech, and he received an A in the class. I was choked up with pride, but afterward Colleen scorned the teachers and students, saying their language was too flowery. I was infuriated and wished I hadn't brought her. She probably didn't want Jim to better himself and move on from his life with her. After that, Jim's enthusiasm waned. I knew she was a negative influence on him, but I also knew how much he loved her.

Jim called one of the resource people from the class about doing an internship as a peer specialist, but he never heard back. It wasn't long after that that Jim started believing his condo was cursed and moved in with Colleen. Roger and I didn't like the arrangement but had no power to change it. We knew he was using again.

27

One Very Lucky Young Man

August 31–September 13, 2015

I hurriedly slipped on my silk kaftan, crumpled beside the bed where I'd thrown it the night before. It was 4 a.m. Through the screen windows I heard a dog bark in the distance, competing with the ringing phone. I didn't make it in time.

The phone's caller ID read *Colleen Kelly*. I'd told her to call any time, day or night, if Jim needed help. Despite starting to work a few hours at NAMI–MN entering data, he wasn't coping well and had little else to do. He rarely talked about his future anymore. His case manager had said people with mental illness tended to stay in unhealthy relationships longer than other people because they had so few other relationships.

I took time to pee before I called back, knowing I had to take care of personal needs before surrendering to a crisis. Despite the sultry night, cold seeped into my heart, making my hands and bare feet like ice.

"Sorry to call you at this hour," Colleen said, tentatively but rather calmly. "There's been a little trouble with Jim." A large-sounding bug hit the screen.

"Trouble?"

"He jumped off my balcony," she poured out, in a conspirator's tone. "You know I'm on the third floor."

"My god." My heart began racing, touching a familiar painful spot in my chest.

"A police officer wants to talk to you. Here he is."

"This is Mindy Greiling." I sounded surprisingly calm.

"Your son's going to Regions Hospital," the officer said. "You could follow the ambulance, but I wouldn't recommend it." I heard bleating police-radio static. "You won't be able to see him for at least an hour. Take your time."

"Thank you," I mumbled. Blood pounded in my ears. I could see my son, writhing in pain, paralyzed, below Colleen's window. I'd noticed that third-floor balcony when I'd dropped him off. It was a very long way up. In the background, I heard Colleen saying something.

"The girlfriend here says she doesn't have any gas in her car," the officer added. He put her back on. Jim had said they only put ten dollars' worth of gas in her car at a time.

"I feel so stupid about the gas, Mindy," Colleen gushed. "Could you pick me up?"

"Okay . . ."

She talked over me. "I asked the cop if Jim was ever going to walk again, but he said, 'Lady, I'm not a doctor. How do I know?' Jim was just lying on the ground when I got down there, he couldn't get up or move his legs. The downstairs neighbors heard him yelling outside their patio door and called 911."

I hoped that the police had arrived quickly. The station was close, and they weren't strangers to her public housing complex.

"I was asleep when he jumped. I didn't even hear him. I only woke up when the cop was at my door. He told me to get on some clothes and come down." She giggled. "I just had on a short nightie."

"I'll be by in a half hour," I said, cutting her off. "I'm going to shower. I'll call when I'm there." I felt impatient with her prattling at a time like this.

Roger had gotten up and was hovering near me in a T-shirt and boxers. His hair was standing up in places, his stubby beard whiter than his hair. He rubbed his eyes, looking as tired and bedraggled as I felt. I told him what had happened, that Jim was going to Regions. I advised him to go to work and said that I would keep in touch, that there was nothing he could do yet. We knew from long experience that we needed to split up to save energy. I claimed the short straw because I needed to know.

I mechanically ran through my morning routine: cat, toast, teeth, shower, clothes, makeup, hair. I omitted my precious newspaper and didn't take it with me. I knew the words wouldn't make sense.

With more time to think, I questioned my quick agreement to take Colleen, but when we reached the hospital I was glad that she was with me, at least at first. Her chattering made our visit seem less surreal. I bought us vending machine coffee.

In his curtained stall, Jim lay stiffly on his back beneath sheets and a light blanket. He was unshaven, gaunt, wild-eyed. He'd done it this time, I realized.

He gave us a fearful look, as if we'd come to eat him, then zeroed in on Colleen. She smiled at him serenely and walked to his bed.

"Colleen, you have to kill me," he pleaded, reaching out his thin arms. She emitted a little laugh and rolled her eyes at me.

"I fucked up and now you have to finish me off." He began crying as if his heart would break. I shouldn't have brought her.

"You're going to be all right, Jim," she comforted, taking his hand. "You're at the hospital now."

He wasn't calmed. A nurse came in and intervened. "We'll do imaging tests," she informed us looking over her shoulder at Colleen and me, as she wheeled Jim off.

"He's really deep in his delusion," Colleen said as we waited. I heard staff people rushing about and talking urgently outside the curtain.

"Probably why he 'needed' to jump off your balcony," I said.

"He tried other things yesterday," she whispered, touching my arm. "I should have called you, Mindy. I know I should have. I feel so guilty."

Before we got any further, Roger came in—a welcome, calming face—and a nurse brought him a chair. I felt a rush of love for my reliable husband. Despite his inability to show his feelings, he had shown up when I didn't expect him. His presence calmed my churning stomach. Colleen stopped telling her story, and I told Roger what little we knew.

After Jim returned—in a somewhat calmer state—a man wearing a suit and a stethoscope stepped softly in, radiating empathetic energy.

He introduced himself as the surgeon. I instinctively trusted him.

"Several vertebrae are fractured, and he has a bulging disc." Concern saturated the doctor's voice, but he smiled encouragingly and looked from Roger to me. "Those may heal naturally with time, but there's no question he needs immediate surgery. Two of his vertebrae are cracked almost all the way through."

My heart hammered against my chest, but my words failed me. Roger was also silent, but Colleen groaned audibly.

"The cracked vertebrae are compressing his spinal cord into 20 percent of its usual cavity."

"Will he walk?" Colleen blurted.

"He's one very lucky young man," replied the doctor. "We have too many conferences like this one where we don't have such good news after accidents like this."

"Accident?" I thought.

The physician spread images of Jim's wrecked spine onto his sheets as if he were laying down a hand of cards. Jim didn't even glance at them.

"We're going to fuse four vertebrae, which we don't like to do if we can help it, especially with someone so young, but we have no choice."

"Will he be able to walk?" Colleen repeated.

"Yes, but don't expect him to be able to do any fancy yoga moves." He smiled at Jim. "He'll probably have old-man back issues before his time. But the good news is that he's not an old man like most folks who have this surgery, so he should have a decent recovery. The surgery will be tomorrow."

After the surgeon left, we were all hustled out with Jim, as he was moved to a hallway to make room for an incoming accident victim. No one had said a word about Jim's schizophrenia.

He became increasingly agitated and again implored, "Kiss me goodbye, Colleen, and then kill me." He sobbed loud enough to wake the dead. She kissed him on the lips. I saw people looking at us judgmentally, as if we had disruptive toddlers.

"Can't you give him something?" I implored a nurse hurrying past. "He's psychotic, and I'm afraid he'll rear up or lurch off the bed and break his vertebrae completely."

"The doctor didn't order anything."

"Please call a psychiatrist then."

An hour later, Jim was more agitated and we were still in the hall-way. I barked at another nurse, "No one seems to be factoring in my son's extreme mental illness crisis. I really won't be happy if he's par-alyzed because he severed his spine. No one at this hospital is doing anything about that."

A psychiatrist showed up fast after that. She and I made eye con-tact, and her look told me we were on the same wavelength about the delay in consulting her.

At home that night, Roger emailed close relatives, suggesting they send cards. He'd never done that before. We in Jim's immediate family sent him cards when he was in the psych ward or treatment programs, but except for our sister-in-law, whose brother had had schizophrenia and committed suicide, few other people did. It was true: the silence of mental illness was deafening.

"Everyone knows what to do when it's physical," I said to Roger, as we lay in bed, sleepless. The dog was back at it, barking in the dis-tance. "If Jim had to be in a wheelchair, maybe he could get housing."

"Certainly more sympathy."

"I wish Colleen had called us sooner," I said, turning over. "She started to tell me how Jim was acting the day before he jumped, but then you came in. For better or worse, I agreed to take her to the hos-pital with me tomorrow, so I'll find out."

=

"You know how Jim loves his phone?" Colleen asked. She and I were holding vigil in his room in intensive care, but her presence brought me no relief. Instead she reminded me that he wouldn't be in this situation had he not used drugs with her. Nurses bustled in and out, taking his vitals and checking machines. He hadn't woken since his surgery.

"His pride and joy," I responded. Jim's phone kept him organized, in sync with the world.

"The ads were right," she chuckled, "about that phone case you bought him."

"What do you mean?" We had gotten Jim a rugged case after Verizon wouldn't insure his phone anymore because he had lost or broken so many.

"Supposed to protect his phone—even if it dropped sixty feet, right?"

"Yes?"

"Yesterday, he threw it off my balcony," she said with glee. "As hard as he could. He wasn't going to get it afterward either, but I made him." She sounded proud of herself. "And it still works. Without that unbreakable case, no way."

"Not something he would do in his right mind," I said, wishing again she had called someone then.

"That night he got a knife from my kitchen drawer." I felt as if I were at camp listening to ghost stories. "He tried to cut himself, said he was trying to kill himself. I hid the knives and told him to come back to bed."

"Next time call 911." Colleen was usually more mature than Jim, having gotten ill later in life, but something I couldn't put my finger on seemed to be missing in her.

"I should have. He responds to commands when he's delusional. Did you know he doesn't have any nipples?"

I was horrified, but then thought she must be making this up. "Are you sure?"

"When he was at Anoka, a long time ago, he snipped them off," she said with a laugh. "No one found out, including you, right?" Her wide smile unsettled me.

I winced. Now I thought I believed her. I wondered what else Jim had told Colleen that no one else knew. "It's good he has you to confide in."

Soon after Jim was moved to acute care, Colleen and I began visiting separately, ostensibly so he would have more visitors but also because Colleen was becoming more than I could take.

The stress of all this was causing Roger and me to be short with each other. We visited Jim separately as well, partly because we didn't want to argue in front of him. When I arrived on one of my days, sun was spilling into Jim's room. He had more cards piled on his bedside table than he had ever received: fruits of Roger's prompting. There was also a card from Jim's new coworkers at NAMI. Lovely flowers from Angela's family graced his nightstand, next to cardboard flowers and a Mylar balloon Colleen had bought.

I asked Jim about his nipples.

"I used a nail clipper," he owned up. "Hurt like hell."

"I wish you didn't have these terrible thoughts," I said with sympathy. I guessed this had happened when his breasts were swollen from a side effect of his psych meds. Mental illness can be so humiliating. "It's always you who gets hurt."

"You have to pay my guy," he said forcefully, suddenly changing the subject. He struggled to sit up in his back brace.

Jim called his drug dealer his "guy," and he had told us he owed him nearly $2,000. The crack purchased with the $50,000 charged to the credit card had long since been consumed. I had asked a social worker what we could do about this guy.

"Nothing," she said. "You and Roger aren't guardians."

Also, unlike Dr. T, a drug dealer didn't have a license to revoke because he was ruining a vulnerable adult.

"Don't think about him. Focus on getting well," I said to Jim, wishing his meds were working better. The doctor had temporarily taken him off Haldol for the surgery, and he still wasn't fully readjusted.

"Dad and you are loaded. You wouldn't miss it," he scolded, suddenly looking regal, like Grandma Teddy issuing orders. Roger and I had led a middle-class existence, rising to that after years on one income. Jim sounded as if Colleen had been coaching him again. Jim had said his dealer had called that morning.

"Tell him you're in the hospital," I said wearily. "Or better yet, don't talk to him."

A nurse arrived and took Jim's blood pressure. Her face didn't reveal anything, but I guessed it was high.

"You don't get it," Jim continued after she left. "Want me to lose my knees? Colleen's car to get keyed? My guy knows where she lives." He stared at me angrily. "He knows where you live too."

"Oh?"

"He was there."

"You had a drug dealer in our house?" I felt my own blood pressure rise.

"He wanted his money. You were out of town." Jim smiled. "It's business." He seemed proud he had business.

"He must be a stupid dealer to give you drugs before you pay." I knew I shouldn't rile him up but couldn't help myself. "I'd better leave. Dad will come tomorrow." I got up.

When I reached the door, I glanced back and Jim bellowed, "*Fuck you, bitch!*" His face was red and contorted.

An attendant rushed in. I locked shocked eyes with her before I disappeared down the hall to the elevator.

"Have a nice evening," the parking attendant intoned as I exited the ramp.

"You too," I replied automatically. Driving home in the privacy of the car, tears didn't come as they had on many drives home, especially in the early days. I was too much in shock. But for the first time in years, I wanted to call my mother.

The next morning, I sat on a park bench alongside a forested walking path. I gazed up at a swath of tall white pines, my neck tilted fully back. Even though it didn't seem like a windy day, the tops of the trees, where balls of soft needles and pine cones resided, swayed back and forth in wide arcs. When I lowered my eyes to street level, the bare, sturdy telephone-pole tree trunks were immobile. I tried to tell where the rocking ended and the stillness began, but I couldn't.

To the young, fit runner who scooted by with a nod of her head, I must have seemed like the tree trunks—placid and still, but my brain was rocking violently like the treetops.

"Fuck you, bitch!" still thundered in my ears from a few hours ago. I knew Jim was terribly ill, but that didn't make it easier to hear those words from my usually loving son. Psychotic barbs are an ugly part of mental illness and addiction that people without personal experience don't see. How deeply hurtful those psychotic barbs can be.

Even when Jim was out of his mind and wouldn't remember all he said, he still looked normal. I envied people whose children were dying but still had kind minds even as they died—people whose children only died once, whose suffering could wane. When the wounds of our grief finally scabbed over, a crisis like this tore them open, and we were thrown back onto the pyre of bloody, raw grief.

A thought crept into my head. What if Colleen had lived on a higher floor? Jim would be out of his misery, and so would we. We'd be done with all this.

The next time I weighed myself, I found I'd lost ten pounds in the two weeks since Jim had been hospitalized.

28
Care-Meeting Chaos

September–December 2015

Jim was calmer on my next visit. He invited me to his care meeting the next day. "So you'll know what medical supplies to buy," he said, "before I come home."

I felt panicky about the meeting the rest of the day. Although the whiteboard in his room had listed his release date as two days later, no one had talked to Roger or me about how that would work or the medical supplies Jim said I should buy. He needed gait-belt assistance to get out of bed or into his wheelchair, and he was still a little psychotic. His leaving in two days seemed like magical thinking or insurance company dictum.

When I arrived the next day for the meeting, Jim commanded impatiently, "Wheel me outside. I need a smoke." I wheeled him into the hallway. It had been two weeks since he had broken his back. When he had arrived at this ward the week before, I had protested about having to take my son outside onto a smoke-free campus to smoke, but a nurse had overruled me, saying, "It'll be good for him."

Today a different nurse blocked our way. "You'll have to smoke afterward, Jim."

"It should be a short meeting," he consoled himself, "and then we can go outside."

I pushed my son into the conference room, where five or six people were already seated. I pulled up a chair and Jim wheeled himself to an open spot half a table away. He had on blue scrubs and a burgundy Montana T-shirt. I admired his ability to look self-confident but remembered how many meetings he had endured, meetings where everyone discussed his mental health.

"Jim, how do you feel you're doing?" a doctor asked smoothly, beginning the meeting. "We've heard good things from physical therapy."

Jim grinned. "My therapist says I'm ready to go home." His hands were folded on his lap, thumbs slowly circling each other.

"You're doing well with your physical recovery," she said, pausing as if thinking how to phrase her next comment. "You're here to get help with your mental recovery as well."

The room stopped breathing.

"I guess?" Jim said tentatively, his voice rising to a question.

"So we're sending you to the psych ward."

Jim unfolded his hands and put them on the table. "I don't want to, but I guess I have no choice," he said with resignation. "So okay."

The room breathed.

"How long?"

I held my breath. I'd felt huge relief when Jim agreed to go so easily but now felt that slipping away.

"Depends, maybe a couple weeks." She smiled briefly and hurried on. "After that, we want you to get more help in the community." Jim and I both knew that meant another stay in a three-month program, a sort of halfway house.

"I'm not okay with that." His hands tightened into fists. "I won't do that."

"We're recommending you be committed." Jim would have to go where the hospital said.

"I'm really not okay with that," he said, outwardly calm at first. Then I saw the set of his mouth tighten. I ducked my head. "Fuck that," he shouted suddenly, pounding the table. "That sucks, and you're all a bunch of niggers and bitches. Fuck you all."

He fluidly picked up a computer in front of the woman next to him and flung it venomously at the wall. I heard a heavy thunk and looked up to see a large dent in the plasterboard.

Staff on both sides of Jim dissolved into the corners of the room. I sat glued to my chair, immobilized. I felt physically ill.

Jim wheeled his chair over to survey the dent and noticed the wall phone. He seized it, pulled it off its holder, and sent it flying across the room. He began hurling objects right and left, everything he could reach. Missiles of pens, notebooks, and drinking glasses crashed about.

He looked satisfied with the havoc he was causing.

"Jim, you'll hurt your back," the doctor in charge of the meeting implored softly.

He paused momentarily.

Before he could move on to a framed picture he was eyeing, four burly young men arrived.

"Hold it right there," one said. "We can't allow you to do that." He pulled down Jim's arm, and the men wheeled him off.

I noticed Jim's projectiles had been hitting walls and tables but not people. Except for causing the car wreck—when he had been aiming at the vehicle and not the occupants—Jim hadn't ever hurt other people, including me, even when his delusion had demanded it.

If he had still had his fulfilling job taking Kent to coffee houses and the Minnesota River Bottoms, if he hadn't just hung around with Colleen with nothing else to do, maybe he wouldn't have a broken back and wouldn't be committed to the psych ward.

This meeting hadn't been fair to Jim. The hospital had given him mixed messages. I was surprised he'd been as cooperative as he had at first, before he learned more. Even not getting his last cigarette probably contributed to his anger. He knew the psych ward was locked and didn't allow smoking.

When I had worked on civil commitment reforms in the legislature, I saw the process as a way to help Jim and others like him. I still knew it meant he could finally receive support—ending the long summer at Colleen's that Roger and I had known would not end well—but by now I knew civil commitment wasn't a panacea. And even though Jim's illness could make him as vulnerable as a child, I could see how humiliating it was for him.

Soon after Jim and the men departed, the staff filed out of the conference room. None of them looked at me except for the doctor.

"I'm sorry. Are you okay?" she asked after they left. Freed from being in charge of the meeting, she slid her chair nearer mine. "I have a son too. Is there anything I can do?" By her tone and look, I knew she meant a son with mental illness.

"If you have a son, you know there isn't anything anyone can do for me now," I said through tear-filled eyes.

=

In December I went to another hospital meeting. The patient representative, a stout woman with salt-and-pepper hair, met me at the hospital door. I glanced down at my power ring as she shepherded me through a catacomb of hallways to the North Shore conference room. I thought of evergreen trees and frigid Lake Superior waters.

Advocacy was supposedly the last stage of grief, and here I was advocating again. It felt as if our family were running in circles. However, I hoped today was more of a beginning. I had triggered this meeting by sending a letter to the hospital after Jim had been discharged. I had praised his terrific hospital social worker before giving my suggestions for improvement. Shortly after we were seated, two hospital executives entered. They offered me coffee. I declined.

"I gave you the tour of our psych building," one of the women then said, "when it was brand new."

"My last tour as a state legislator." I smiled, recognizing her now. "I hoped then that Jim would never be in a psych ward again, but if he was I hoped it would be here."

Our conversation stopped when the doctor entered, with apologies for being late. He shook my hand and sat down across from me. I took the opportunity to thank him and the others for the meeting.

"You gave us a chance to look ourselves in the mirror with your eloquent letter," the patient rep began. "Not pretty, but it initiated rich discussion." I wondered how many meetings she started this way.

I had three complaints: (1) The nurse wheeled Jim outside to smoke, near the campus No Smoking sign, and expected Roger and me to do the same. (2) Communication with the family was poor. Even though we had supplied the hospital with a copy of Jim's advance directive, a psychiatrist had said she couldn't discuss our son. The directive should have trumped his not signing releases of information when he was still psychotic. (3) Jim was whipsawed by the system of rotating psychiatrists who each had unchecked autonomy but conflicting philosophies about his care.

The executive briskly dispatched the first item. "Staff's already been educated. If a voluntary patient could get outside on his own to smoke, we couldn't stop him," she cautioned. "But in the future, staff won't assist anyone. I'm surprised this happened in the first place."

Next, family communication. Jim's advance directive said he wanted us to be communicated with, despite his tendency to malign us when he was psychotic. No one remembered it even existed, even though it had been the hospital that had requested it the day of Jim's surgery, and the psychiatrist didn't ask him to sign a release because he was so hostile toward us.

I thought of Jim's hurtful words and took a deep breath.

"We'll flag directives in patients' charts from now on," the soft-spoken doctor said with assurance. "Staff will be educated, including psychiatrists."

This seemed almost too good to be true. The North Shore conference room felt anything but frigid. The patient rep winked at me. She'd been doing that throughout the meeting. Probably her way of encouraging supplicants like me, but I was surprised each time.

The last issue was the two psychiatrists who rotated duty every other week. Twice, one was ready to release Jim, but the next week the other had recommended more care. This caused Roger and me extreme anxiety and did the same to Jim—for opposite reasons. We had thought he needed more help, while he had been hoping to leave. Either way, it hadn't been helpful.

"We're working on that too," the doctor said. "All staff should help make decisions, not just the psychiatrist on duty. As your letter said, social workers and nurses see more of patients and know them better."

I sat back in my chair, palms up, and smiled at everyone. I couldn't believe it. I had arrived girded for battle and instead these good people had come to the meeting prepared and open to making changes. I hadn't needed my ring after all. Successful advocacy wouldn't fix Jim any more than legislative changes had, but it helped. It makes the system better for everyone, including him should he return. That alone felt good.

29
Deny, Enable, Repeat

January–February 2016

As the hospital psychiatrist had laid out for Jim, after his stay in the psych ward he was transferred to step-down housing. Roger and I put his condo up for sale. His case manager, Amy, recommended we do this as a consequence for his drug use. She was his only staff person now because Jim had asked to leave his ACT team. I hadn't been able to summon the energy to protest—even though he was still civilly committed and shouldn't have been able to make that decision. I was frustrated by how little they had accomplished for him and by their poor communication. Like Angela, Amy thought Roger and I did too much enabling of our son, cushioning him from his actions. When the condo sold, we lost $20,000, counting the improvements we had made.

When Jim's community care funding ended after three months, amazingly he was released to live with Colleen. Her apartment was where they used drugs and where he had so recently jumped off the balcony. No one had consulted us. As usual, this arrangement was supposed to be temporary, only to last until Jim obtained an apartment. He had applied for a housing voucher with Amy, but nothing had come of it. Jim said Colleen was still using, but he just watched. I was amazed at his strength. He had been with her for four months.

Roger and I were on sharper tenterhooks when Jim said Amy wasn't going to schedule any more urinalysis (UA) tests, which reveal any drug use. His commitment would soon expire. We wondered how long he could refrain from joining Colleen now. I felt weak and tired after our endless battles. My intense anger at the mental health system was watered down by the fact that Roger and I felt like enablers. We'd sold Jim's condo and remained silent after the plan for

Colleen's apartment had been hatched. We weren't willing to have him live with us, where we would be enablers and the mental health system would check him off as no longer a priority.

One morning I was startled when the phone rang. "I got a Bridges voucher!" Jim's elated voice sang. This was the first good news we had had since before he broke his back the summer before.

"Fantastic!" I shouted, high-fiving him on my end of the phone.

Jim came over to use our computer to immediately start his housing search. We sat side by side searching an affordable-housing website. I had learned about the site through a League of Women Voters housing study I had been spending a lot of time cochairing. We League members were interviewing housing experts, hosting community meetings, and monitoring the five cities within our chapter borders. At this time, metropolitan cities were required by the Metropolitan Council, Minnesota's multicounty Twin Cities governing body, to update their comprehensive plans to meet affordable-housing goals.

Jim and I found a few places that took vouchers in North Minneapolis and the East Side of St. Paul, both high-poverty areas. There was exactly one other place: in our town of Roseville. Jim copied down the information and called. I had campaigned in this building many times. I remembered musty hallways with red, textured wallpaper and velvet sashes. It had reminded me of a bordello. A young man once answered my knock with a joint between his fingers, and emergency sirens were often heard heading there. Jim made an appointment and we went the next day.

I was happy to see the building had undergone a transformation. Musty hallways now smelled fresh, and tan paint replaced the bordello red. Jim was impressed with the workout room and swimming pool. He loved the fact that each apartment had a balcony or patio. I saw dirty February snow where he saw a place to smoke.

The office manager showed us a demonstration apartment. It was smaller than his condo, one bedroom. A galley kitchen with the usual laminate countertops announced affordability. The tiny bathroom was clean. Jim liked it and so did I.

My spirits soared as we walked back to the office, until he muttered under his breath, "Never going to happen. Would've been nice."

I gave him a quizzical look, but he just shook his head.

Jim filled out an application when we got back to the office; then, between tight lips, he told the manager, "My credit's bad."

"Everybody thinks that," she replied airily, putting his application in a folder and writing his name on it. "All you need is a C rating. Not as hard as most people think."

I was baffled by Jim's pessimism. Yes, he had that huge credit card debt he and Colleen had run up, but—after hundreds of phone calls and scores of letters—the company had finally retired the debt, and Roger had been in charge of his finances since.

"I'm not going to pass. The apartment is toast," Jim said again, as he stepped over a dingy snowbank to open the car door. "Colleen and I were bad again." After he buckled his seatbelt, he covered his face with his hands. "Lots of checks are going to bounce."

My heart sank, then was forced back into place by raging anger. I wanted to yell at Jim that he could no longer see Colleen, that she was no good for him, but I knew that would never work. Jim was an adult, and there was no way for us parents to enforce such an edict. Roger and I had noticed that compared to the Tasks Unlimited staff, who had high expectations for their clients, Jim's mental health workers since then were more deferential. It was his right to make bad choices, even when he was committed, even when those choices endangered his life.

"I worried this would happen," I said, more sympathetically than I expected. Jim was so vulnerable and defenseless when it came to Colleen, as he had been with Dr. T and then Nick. I started the car but kept it in park. "Dealers take checks for crack?"

"Of course not. I wrote checks to Colleen and she cashed them." He didn't change the radio to one of his stations.

"The bank allows that?"

"Her credit union does," he said. "They aren't fussy."

I turned the radio down. Usually I was a fan of credit unions, but not today. Yes, Jim and Colleen were ultimately responsible, but it shouldn't be this easy.

"Every time we drove to the dealer's, we told ourselves it would be the last," he sobbed. "But we went crazy. I didn't even enjoy it, I felt so bad. I couldn't sleep. I've been miserable ever since."

"You never wrote bad checks before Colleen. I'm so sick and tired of her getting you into trouble. Why can't you stand up to her when she comes up with these schemes?"

"I'm just as much at fault, but I'm almost glad we're busted."

I was astounded. Jim clearly believed what he was saying, that he was as much to blame as Colleen. "You never did anything remotely like this before."

"As soon as I found out I got the voucher, I stopped."

"Too late," I snapped. "And I bet she didn't."

His ignoring that statement confirmed it. "If I end up being homeless, I'll jump off a freeway bridge," Jim said in a low voice with such conviction I believed him.

"I'm furious the system sent Jim to live with a crack addict, where he'd broken his back just two months before," I seethed to Roger that night over dinner. I'd made homemade bread to go with it, taking some of my frustration out on the dough. "He was civilly committed. They were legally charged with looking out for his best interests." I slapped butter on the bread. "At least Amy's scheduled another UA."

"Little late for a drug test, isn't it?" Roger asked through a forkful of salad.

"No shit. The system doesn't really want parents of adult children around." I took a bite of the bread but hardly tasted it. "I know he's a grown man, but it's agony when he's so vulnerable and they don't exercise good sense. Maybe Grandma Teddy's being in the state hospital wasn't so bad after all. At least she wasn't using drugs and writing bad checks."

The next day I woke up early, with my insides quaking. I skipped breakfast, except for coffee. I had hoped the worst was behind us, that Jim's getting an apartment would be a game changer. If only he could get away from Colleen.

That night Roger announced he had gone to the bank and paid Jim's overdraft. He had bailed Jim and Colleen out.

"What the fuck, Roger?" I spewed, picking up one of his newspapers from the couch and roughly throwing it at him. He caught it with both hands. "This consequence would have hit both of them for a change."

"I thought it was for the best," he said.

"What're you going to do? Pay off every bad check they write? Drain our accounts?" I stood before him, yelling at the top of my lungs, my chest heaving. "You know this won't be the last."

"I thought it was for the best," he said again, quietly but firmly. It was all he could say.

I thought of his dad's collection agency and the shame Roger still felt about anyone defaulting on a financial agreement, much less his own son. Plus we knew some of the people at Jim's bank.

In the end, since Roger had already done it and I also desperately wanted Jim to have a chance, I finally shut up. "I guess if Jim gets the apartment, it'll be worth it," I conceded, all the steam pouring out of me, "but we both need Al-Anon. Angela and others have harped on us for years about our enabling."

This wasn't our first vicious argument. More and more, Roger and I argued over Jim's problems. We hadn't always been like this. In the early days, we had grasped at every shred of information and divided up the workload to care for our son as best we could. But the years of handling so many crises had worn on us. Now we were fractured. I knew married couples divorced over tribulations like this, and I was determined not to let that happen.

Amy called midmorning the next day. I was still reading the newspaper. I had slept poorly and gotten up late. "Jim's declined the UA. He knows it'll be dirty." She cleared her throat. "I've put him on the detox list."

A detox facility was like a jail for alcoholics and addicts, a place where they could sober up. I'd heard they were hellholes.

"Sheriff's deputies will pick him up in a few days," Amy finished. "Don't inform Jim, so he won't run."

I was startled when the phone rang right after I hung up with Amy. It was Jim. Mentally, I already had him in detox.

"I got turned down."

"What?" My exhausted mind wasn't changing gears fast enough. I was further disoriented when I saw three deer in our backyard.

"I didn't get the apartment." He sounded crushed. "No surprise, but . . ."

"Your credit can't be the reason," I butted in. The deer startled and bolted. I walked to the front window but couldn't see them from there either. "Your good dad went to the bank and paid off those checks. There must be some other reason."

"I wasn't denied because of my credit," Jim said. "They checked criminal background."

"Criminal background!"

"There's a link to the background check, but I can't open it on my phone."

"Come over," I commanded. "We'll look at it together."

When he arrived, we printed out the background check. I scanned the first page. A shock wave burned through my body. No wonder he had been denied. I pushed away the cat, purring loudly and rubbing against my leg, and squinted harder at the page.

Gross misdemeanor was listed for the car crash. It was supposed to have been changed to a misdemeanor after mental health court. And a warrant was out for his arrest. It was for another gross misdemeanor charge—property damage.

My stomach cratered. No landlord in their right mind would rent to a known criminal accused of property damage, not to mention one with multiple serious crimes.

I pointed to the property damage charge. "What the fuck is that about?"

"I don't know, Mom," he howled.

The date of the warrant was the preceding September. That was when Jim had been in Regions Hospital. When he had thrown the computer and pulled the phone off the wall. They had charged him with a crime! They had charged our very ill son with a crime and didn't do us the courtesy of even telling us. When I had met with that contingent last December, they hadn't said a word about this. That would have been three months after the hospital had filed this charge.

Jim said no one had told him anything about it either. He left in a cloud of despair.

I fed the cat and then called Regions Hospital. My rage actually calmed me, turning everything into slow motion. The sweet patient representative was curt today. "Our staff is harmed by patients every day, so we routinely file charges."

"Jim didn't hurt anybody and you know it." I kept my tone curt too, holding in my fury. "And you know—because you were at the meeting where none of this was ever mentioned—that the hospital has plenty of blame in how your staff handled events leading up to that incident. This isn't ethical or right. I want this dismissed."

"We'll look at our policies and procedures. I'll let everyone know what you're looking for."

"You do that. Be sure to let them know I'm looking for you to fix what your hospital botched up. You're mangling my son's chance at a life when you're supposed to be a health care institution. Not a place where you turn very sick people into criminals so they have to be homeless and can't get work to pay for housing even if they could get it." I forced myself to take a breath. "You make a lot of noise about being great for people with mental illness, but here we have another example that you have a very long way to go."

"I can't make any promises."

"You'll be getting a formal complaint from me today."

I stomped to the computer and put my outrage into action. I pounded out the complaint and emailed it to everyone who had been at the meeting.

While I was still high on adrenalin, I called Ramsey County Attorney John Choi. He explained that counties dealt with felonies. It was cities that handled misdemeanors. In my wrath, I had forgotten that. His staff gave me a name at the St. Paul City Attorney's Office.

"I can't offer legal advice," the attorney I was referred to said, "but I can say that, in general, if a person voluntarily turns himself in and spends the night in jail, he or she can go to court the next morning and get a court date. Otherwise it could take a very long time.

I hung up and thought about this before I called Jim with the news. Going to jail would give him a certain freedom he couldn't get otherwise, but my rage turned to sadness as I imagined his reaction. His life had sunk to new depths.

Not for the first time, I also thought about those who would not have the instinct to fight, people from cultures where either esteem for doctors and hospitals or past oppression meant no challenging of authority. I thought also of those who wanted to fight but didn't have the contacts and advocacy network I did. I could help Jim in ways that would be far beyond the reach of many people, especially those who were poor. The universal misery of mental illness and addiction made privilege blow away like smoke, except when it came to advocacy.

My son sounded whipped when he answered, resigned to anything. I hoped I could get him to jail tomorrow, before the sheriff's deputies came to take him to detox.

30
Jail instead of the Caucus

March 2016

Jim came over in the morning so we could fatalistically kill the day together before I took him to jail. We were going at night, as the attorney had advised, in order for my son to spend less time in a cell. Jim chain-smoked as we walked around Como Lake.

After we'd exhausted several subjects, I asked, "How it's going now, living with Colleen?"

"I'd give it a seven. It's all her stuff and not my place," he replied. "I hope I get my own place soon."

"Remember when you called and Dad and I were at the library fundraiser? You wanted us to come get you?" I brushed away smoke. "You said Colleen was being mean."

"Yeah."

"What was that all about?"

He lit another cigarette, looked down, and shook his head.

It infuriated me that he was so secretive about most things about Colleen. I admired his loyalty, but she didn't deserve it. I tried another angle. "What do you look forward to these days?"

"Death."

It broke my heart to hear this. Jim often claimed he was happy living what he called a quiet life with Colleen, often not seeing anyone else. He had given up on finishing college, even though he had been nearly ready to graduate. He only worked a few hours at NAMI entering data, work that wasn't challenging, but he couldn't get himself to look for a better job. I often mourned the son we used to have, but I knew that even with schizophrenia he was capable of so much more.

We walked the rest of the way back to the car in silence.

We had lunch at home and grabbed subs with Roger for supper.

Jim and I were as nervous as middle schoolers giving speeches. I'd forgotten it was precinct caucus night until Roger mentioned it. This local Minnesota election year kickoff had been a big night for me in past years. I reminded Jim of when he had driven me from precinct to precinct when he had been in high school. Who would have ever thought that some twenty years later I'd be driving him to jail? I had thought after I retired from the legislature Roger would stop caucusing, but he'd surprised me and kept going. If anyone asked him where I was tonight, he wouldn't say much. He could talk freely about Jim's mental illness, but Jim's drug use silenced him.

Jim and I drove through heavy traffic near the high school, where the Democratic caucuses were taking place. It looked like good attendance for endorsing a candidate to follow Obama. The sun was low in the sky. Melancholy overtook me. I thought again of teenage Jim smiling and laughing as he drove me from school to school as I campaigned for my first reelection. He had asked how my speech had gone each time I returned to the car. He was so encouraging.

Nearing the jail, I felt as if I were delivering my son to a slaughterhouse. The large parking lot was practically empty. I stood protectively near Jim while he smoked two last cigarettes before we walked slowly to the door marked Night Admittance.

"Go with me as far as you can," he requested with yearning.

"I wish I could stay and talk with you the whole night."

"Me too."

We entered the door together and walked down a short hallway. A clean-cut young man in a police uniform greeted us, and a uniformed woman smiled from behind a counter.

"I'm here to turn myself in," Jim said, as we had practiced that afternoon. I felt as if we were in some Western.

Jim waved briefly from his hip when I left, squeezing out a small smile. "You'll be in court?"

"Of course."

The next morning, I told Roger there was no sense in him missing work for the perfunctory court appearance. This time he took my advice and didn't show up, as he had in the emergency room. I arrived early and took a seat near the front where Jim would be able to see me.

He entered the courtroom with his head down, shuffling along in an orange jumpsuit. At least he didn't have leg shackles as he'd had in Montana. He seemed disoriented. He stood in the wrong place but adjusted compliantly after the accompanying officer nudged him. After just one night Jim wasn't himself.

Jail is no place for people with serious mental illness.

I barely wrote down the court date before my son was escorted back to the jail. He never noticed I was there.

A kind deputy grabbed my elbow as I exited the courtroom. "Go home and rest while he's processed," he advised. "Come back in two or three hours." I was often struck by the fact that most law enforcement people were kinder than many of the mental health staff I had met.

I went home and tried to take a catnap, but I was too tightly wound. Instead, I decided to look at one of the photo albums I had made when Jim was first ill. Scrapbooking had been a way of processing my grief. My supportive friend Kathy had brought over her photos and worked beside me for days.

I took the album with pictures taken when Angela and Jim were children to our bedroom. As I nestled against the backrest pillow, the cat jumped up and lay beside me, pressing into my leg. I focused on a picture of Jim, Angela, and some cousins. Angela was in the center, lying on her stomach on the floor, arms propping up her chin. The gap in her smile hadn't yet been fixed. Cousins were piled on her back, mugging for the camera. Jim, the sweetest of little boys, who always liked to hold my hand, was leaning into the picture from the side but smiling like everyone else. Everyone else was now married, owned a house, and had a good job, and most had children. No wonder Jim clung to his imperfect relationship with Colleen.

I stroked the cat as I turned the album pages. I noticed a photo of Angela and Jim with Grandma Teddy at her nursing home. Angela, blond hair tightly braided, was standing confidently beside Grandma's wheelchair, Grandma's mottled arm around her. Jim was snuggled in my lap, both of us smiling contentedly. That was back when I kept my children healthy and was a "good mother," as my college textbook instructed, so they wouldn't end up like Grandma.

When I returned to the jail, I was told to wait on a bench near the door. An hour later, Jim appeared, looking more exhausted than I felt. I didn't see any vestige of little-boy sweetness in his unshaven, scowling face. He was grouchy and hell-bent on getting outside to have a cigarette.

"I couldn't sleep, no coffee, and the food was awful," he complained. "I only drank the Kool-Aid. Why'd the hospital charge me with a gross misdemeanor anyway, when I was there because I'm sick?"

=

Three days later, the friend who lived nearby whose son also had schizophrenia invited me out for pizza. Her son Steven was newer to mental illness than Jim, but Jill was a social worker, so we had a lot of helpful information to share with each other. We enjoyed the luxury of being able to cut to the chase. We could talk honestly using mutual shorthand and felt an immense release from being instantly understood. Through us, our sons had become friends. A couple of months earlier we had added two more moms to our sporadic nights out, but tonight Jill asked to meet with just me.

I was looking forward to this meeting to catch Jill up on all that was going on. We hung up our coats and slid into a booth. Beer wasn't my usual choice, but tonight it felt right. We exchanged pleasantries before Jill launched into her reason for the meeting.

"Mindy, I hate to tell you this," she said sorrowfully, tenting her fingers in front of her lips and pausing to gather her words. "Jim sold morphine pills to Steven. The ones he had for his broken back. When we couldn't wake Steven, we took him to Regions."

There would be no release tonight. My endorphins drained away in a torrent, replaced by intense anger at my son. He knew how fragile Steven's mental health was, knew that his parents watched him closely to make sure he didn't disrupt his body's delicate balance with drugs. Steven always had an attendant when they couldn't be with him.

"He's fine now," Jill assured me quickly, her social worker side at play. "At first, we weren't sure. He was unresponsive for quite a while and could have died if he'd taken all the pills."

"Oh, Jill, I don't know what to say," I murmured. The beer curdled in my stomach.

She placed her hand on mine. "We know Jim's very ill too. We'd never press charges but just think you should know." Our pizza arrived and we ignored it.

"Honestly, Jill, if Jim's ever found dead," I said, gripping my mug tightly, "of course I'll grieve, but I think I'll be glad this is finally over."

"You don't mean that, Mindy." Her earnest, freckled face and kind eyes brought tears to my eyes.

"It'd be better than this unrelenting agony." I felt better for having said this out loud, but I also felt guilty that she was comforting me. Steven was the one who could have died.

"Steven said when Jim called about the pills, he could hear Colleen yelling in the background. Like she was desperate for drugs." She took a drink of her beer. "Are you sure she's good for Jim?"

"She's not," I retorted, taking a gulp of mine. "This isn't the Jim we used to know."

"Steven's going to be okay." She held my hand.

Roger and I confronted Jim that weekend when he came over. He sat on the couch, with his back to our family room window. Over his shoulder, a large crow sat on the railing of the deck, presiding over piles of dirty snow in the yard.

"Steven wanted them," Jim said angrily. I was amazed he was defending his actions. "I told him not to take them all at once."

"Blaming Steven for you selling him pills?" Roger asked incredulously. "Did you know he could have died? Just so you could buy crack?"

"I haven't used anything since Amy pulled my discharge." I'd almost forgotten about his case manager who had put him on the detox list. She was our only remaining shred of the mental health system and was totally inadequate to help us. We were alone with our very ill son.

"You practically killed Steven for drugs for Colleen?" I asked with astonishment. Was there no end to Jim's acquiescence to Colleen's schemes?

He hung his head. The crow flew from the railing.

After Jim left, Roger made himself a sandwich. "We should stop seeing Colleen," he suggested angrily, banging the peanut butter jar down on the counter.

"At least unless she gets treatment and stops using," I agreed.

"She's company for him," Roger said, adding a thick slice of cheese to his sandwich. "But at what cost?"

"Even if it doesn't help Jim," I considered, "taking a break from her will help us. We need to think of ourselves for a change." I got up and turned on the radio. We could never truly get away from our worry. Even on vacations or when we were with family or friends, the possibility of our son's intruding hovered. When we'd been in Alaska three years earlier, Jim had called to say he'd had an accident with our car. Even when he was safe, we fretted. The heavy burden of ambiguous loss over our son had taken a huge toll. Jim hadn't died, but he would never be well. All the bad things that had happened earlier had been peanuts, however, compared to what was now going on with Colleen.

The next time Jim came over, I waited until after he'd made coffee before I broached the subject of Colleen. "Treatment won't do you much good if Colleen doesn't get some too. Dad and I have decided we won't see her until she gets professional help and addresses her addiction." I admitted to thinking she might be too damaged to turn her life around. She'd been using heavily for more than twenty years, compared to Jim's four.

"She should," he agreed, surprising me. "But it's cold you won't let her stay in your lives."

"We can barely deal with you, Jim." I shielded my eyes from the afternoon sun. "She has a perfectly good family, and they will have to deal with her."

When he finished his coffee, I drove him back to Colleen's apartment. What choice did I have? The sun was sinking fast, like the darkness descending on his life. I hinted that since he had skipped out on his drug test, I worried there might be consequences. I wished I could give him more warning about the sheriff's deputies, but I had told Amy I wouldn't.

I was getting more and more nervous about Jim, especially since I was leaving soon for Mexico. My friend Mary McLeod, who had taken

204/ Jail instead of the Caucus

the NAMI class with Roger and me years before, had recently asked if I wanted to take a spontaneous vacation with her. I had leaped at the chance.

Angela called right after supper. "I'm glad you're getting away," she said. I could hear her computer keys clicking; she was multitasking, a necessity in her busy life. "When did you say you were leaving?"

"In one week," I said. "I considered not going, but Mary and I always have fun. She's the perfect person to go with. Her son Matt also has schizophrenia." I took a long sip of my wine. "I'm so tired of this. Mexico, here I come."

"Dad can handle it this time," Angela assured me.

"I hope so. There are so many balls in the air. We don't know when the deputies will pick Jim up."

31
Escape to Puerto Vallarta

March 2016

After he placed my bags on the curb at the airport, Roger gave me a brief hug and kiss. Travel departures were the one time Roger displayed public affection.

"Promise me you'll report in every day, even if nothing happens?"

"Of course," he said with a chuckle. "But you'll only be gone a week."

As soon as Mary and I were settled in our room at Puerto Vallarta, we donned shorts, T-shirts, and sandals and headed for the beach. Under an azure sky, we strolled just beyond the reach of large breakers depositing foam on the white sand. Signs posted near the water warned us not to swim today.

"Why not a hospital?" Mary asked when I got around to telling her about the deputies who would soon take Jim to detox.

"I know," I replied. "Only the chemical dependency part of his commitment is being revoked. He can't get mental health care at a hospital until he meets their high admission standard."

Mary smiled sagely. She understood that conundrum.

"I feel guilty about leaving Roger with all this," I said. "But it's time he shared more responsibility."

"Don't feel guilty for a minute." She emitted a rich laugh. "He needs a turn at all the fun."

I joined in the long laugh, my rigid muscles relaxing. Mary and I often indulged in gallows humor, allowing us to laugh uproariously over our painful lives. Purging our souls laughing was better than crying.

She enjoyed hearing about my tangle with the hospital, and because of her heavy involvement there, she knew all the players. I had pointed out her name to Jim on a plaque in the hallway of the psych building recognizing her role in making the place happen.

Mary and I rinsed our feet at the beach faucets and sprawled on lounge chairs near the pool. As I opened my book, I felt my equilibrium righting. We ate dinner at a restaurant beside the ocean, slowly savoring each bite. We sipped margaritas as we watched the sun go down in orange brilliance. When we returned to our room, we sipped more margaritas on our balcony overlooking the ocean. The warm moist air soaked into our parched Minnesota skin.

"Why haven't I left Roger to deal with Jim's problems before?" I sighed contentedly to Mary, licking salt off the rim of my glass. There were so many times I'd told Roger to just go to work, I'd handle Jim's issues. I'd take the short straw because I needed to know. I'd brought it on myself, but Roger had been content with that arrangement too.

"I wish Jim didn't use drugs."

"Makes a huge difference," she agreed. Her Matt never had. "And Colleen doesn't help."

"Maybe the two of them could manage if they were sober," I said. "But I just don't see that ever happening."

"Jim's so nice. I hope she doesn't keep ruining him," Mary said. "Maybe we should put out a hit."

We delighted in laughing even longer and harder. After we settled down, I decided to check my emails before I hit the Jacuzzi, to see how Roger was doing. I had emailed him earlier about our relaxing day.

Roger's reply read, "I took Jim to the hospital for his postsurgery appointment for his back. Afterward, when he went to have a cigarette, I thought he was out of earshot so I returned a call from Amy. He overheard us talking about the deputies taking him to detox. He went semi off the deep end."

I smiled as I wondered what "semi" meant. It warmed my heart to read such a Roger statement. He was notorious for understating things. I read on.

"Nothing physical, but lots of cursing and noncontact body movement. I told Amy I wasn't comfortable driving home with him in that state so she called the police."

My muscles tightened again.

"St. Paul police and hospital security showed up at the same time. That set him off again, so they put him in the car. I asked if they could take him to detox, but they said that was the deputy's job. After he calmed down, they released him back to me. We went to Jimmy John's for lunch. The sheriff deputies still haven't picked him up, but now he knows they're coming. Glad you're having a good time."

I wished I hadn't heard this on our first relaxing night, but I was the one who had asked him to check in. I immediately responded, "Thanks for handling everything so well. XXOO." I let go to Roger for the first time, good for both of us.

After I sat there a minute centering myself, I told Mary. She was still on the balcony listening to the rhythm of waves lapping at the shore. We looked at each other for a long, understanding moment, feeling sympathy for Jim and Roger. Then we burst into laughter. We hooted and hollered for long minutes.

We lifted our glasses with a flourish: "To Roger."

32
Relapse and Roses

March–July 2016

Jim lasted one night in detox. He became suicidal and had to be sent to a hospital. Thankfully the hospital transferred him to a secure chemical dependency facility instead of Colleen's. While he was there, Roger and I finally decided to give Al-Anon a try. We lasted three meetings.

Roger didn't like the sharing. It went against his nature, and I couldn't get into it either. It all seemed too formulaic. Families had told me they found release in Al-Anon because they could anonymously share secrets with kindred spirits who understood. Roger and I had already done that long ago in the NAMI classes, and we continued to attend NAMI events. I had been speaking openly about Jim's mental illness almost from the beginning, when NAMI had given my name to the press. I regularly networked and commiserated with parents going through similar struggles.

We tried Al-Anon to learn how we were enabling Jim's addiction, but the group we joined seemed inured to the problems of chemical dependency. No one cried or even displayed open distress. They were kind to newcomers, but many people seemed more interested in connecting with established friends.

But the biggest reason Al-Anon wasn't a good fit for us was that there was no mention of mental illness. The reverse was often the case in the mental health world, which often ignored chemical dependency. Our family seemed to be misfits in both places, even though I knew how common co-occurrence was. I came away not at all sure that Al-Anon's advice to detach from a loved one who used drugs heavily was a good idea for a family member who also had a serious mental illness. Jim's sick mind didn't allow him to make needed connections when he hit bottom, just as he could only see that Kyle Zwack should have taken his meds, but not him. There was no way I could detach from Jim, even if I thought I should.

I kept telling myself that Jim wasn't a real addict. He didn't steal from us or commit other crimes to obtain drug money, as other participants described. At least I could report to Angela that we had tried.

=

After three months, Jim was released from the secure chemical dependency facility to try another community care program. He was also working with a new ACT team. Amy had handed his case off to them, acknowledging that he needed more care than she could provide. While Jim was getting all this help, Roger and I accepted Angela's offer to go on a vacation with her, Matt, and Taylor. Angela was ever the helpful daughter, always on the lookout for respites for her parents. We could relax, knowing Jim was safe, and I felt hopeful he was starting on a better path.

We were pumped for this vacation. It was late June, the energetic phase of summer, when plants were verdantly green. Blood-red, dusty-pink, and butter-yellow petals burst forth from the thorny stalks in front of our house. When we returned, lilies and daisies would have joined the roses. I hoped an apartment for Jim would have sprouted as well.

We were heading for upstate New York. One of Roger's lifelong dreams was to visit the National Baseball Hall of Fame in Cooperstown to steep himself in baseball lore, and Angela had arranged a weeklong stay at an Airbnb not far from town.

We flew from Minneapolis to Washington, D.C., then headed north by van with Angela and the family. Roger and I tucked ourselves into the spacious middle seat, where we lounged comfortably and read. Twelve-year-old Taylor and her smartphone claimed the back seat. She was a beauty, freckles splashed across her nose and cheeks like a lioness—a sports fan like her grandfather and parents.

"We're in the mountains now, Mom. Aren't you even going to look?" Angela asked, turning from the front seat to face me. "We're almost there."

"How can I look when the *Lusitania* is sinking?" I glanced at the beautiful low mountains and vast scenery but quickly returned to my book.

Angela shrugged and turned back to gazing at the vista. She was an active outdoorswoman, but she knew that her mother found her deepest pleasure and relaxation in books and theater.

The cozy house that would be ours for the next blissful week was situated in a panoramic valley in the Adirondack Mountains. It had rocking chairs on the porch, soft lounge chairs on the patio, and a large backyard hammock. My muscles softened the minute we unloaded our suitcases.

The Baseball Hall of Fame met Roger's expectations. The first day, we fanned out over three floors of eye-catching displays. Matt, Angela, and I toured a brewery and a Native American museum another day, while Roger and Taylor returned to baseball.

In the evenings, Angela, Taylor, and I prepared salads and vegetables while Matt grilled on the patio and Roger set out deck cushions and opened the umbrella. We dined outside, gazing at the faraway mountains, savoring many bottles of good wine. It never rained.

I almost didn't recognize my life here, even compared to most other vacations, where there was more rushing around, more people to see, intruding on my introverted self. It was so peaceful, no phone calls waking me to send my heart into my throat, no devastating news about my son's next disaster. We played croquet until dusk in the gigantic backyard, surrounded by the low, wooded mountains. We watched movies; I found out my daughter likes depressing ones. We woke up naturally without alarms.

"This is a good time to be here," I said at dinner toward the end of the week. "When Jim is still in the halfway house."

Angela buttered her corn. "Given his recent history, surely they will be vigilant?" Her raised eyebrow told me this was a question. She knew the failings of the system as well as I did.

I raised both my eyebrows back and raised open palms in the warm air. "One would think." I took a healthy drink of wine. "His back is healed, and I pray he gets an apartment soon. He says his hopes are stalled until he has a place to live."

Jim was rarely talking about his future, unlike at this point in earlier recoveries. Before, he had always carried himself and us through those episodes by talking about his hopes: going back to work or school, cooking a new way. It had kept us all going. No more.

"Jim could do fine if he didn't use drugs," Roger inserted, standing up from the table. We all knew that psych meds don't work well when diluted with drugs. "Until he makes up his mind to stop, he's never getting out of this cycle."

"And the mental health system is conflicted about that," I added. "Unlike chemical dependency programs, they often tell clients it's okay to use, so long as they use less." Some programs operated under the harm-reduction model that holds that reducing drug use is a less daunting path for addicts than total abstinence, which may be un-obtainable. I went on, "That may work for some, but not someone as sick as your brother."

Angela nodded her head.

When the rest of the group scattered, Angela and I stayed at the table, listening to crickets and talking. She asked about Colleen. Jim had broken up with her the week before.

"Unfortunately," I said, staring at the dark mountains, "they're back together." During their brief time apart, it was like a dam had burst in Jim. He applied for an honorary society that a college teacher had recommended more than a year before and started registering for fall classes. He recontacted friends he hadn't seen for ages.

My heart had soared, and my grief about Jim zoomed away to its furthest orbit.

"What happened?"

"Colleen called or texted him every few minutes. When he was over, his phone pinged like a xylophone. He kept picking it up, seeing it was her, setting it down. He didn't give her his new address at the half-way house, but she kept bugging his friends until one gave it to her."

"Sounds like a stalker."

"I wonder about her a lot." When I had talked about Colleen's drug use with her brother, I'd been surprised to find that neither he nor anyone in her family was aware she was using. They had a large family, and Colleen was the baby. She wasn't the only member of her family with a mental illness. I didn't want to burden her elderly mother with hers and Jim's problems, even as my worry about her destructive influence on him increased.

Roger or I took turns checking in with Jim most days. He sounded good, balanced, hopeful.

"Have fun," he said. "My next team meeting is my discharge. I want you to come. If I had an apartment, I could leave now."

Hearing Jim sound hopeful made our divine week even more soothing.

The day we departed, Jim texted. "I got a pass and am spending the weekend at your place. Some alone time. I'll have something good ready for you to eat when you get home."

"I'm surprised they let him go to our house without checking with us," I whispered to Roger, showing him the text as we drove back to D.C. Angela and Jim had had keys to our home since they were teenagers.

"Why does he need alone time, when he's already living by himself?" Roger asked. Jim's current facility provided each client with an apartment in their building and helped them learn to maintain it.

"Good question," I said, feeling slightly nervous before pushing the thought aside. "We can ask him tomorrow."

=

When our plane landed in Minneapolis, Roger and I both had voice mails from a neighbor.

"You probably already know this," her calm recorded voice said. "But in case not, Jim left your home today by ambulance. The medical folks couldn't tell us anything, but the ambulance was Allina."

Roger and I exchanged shocked looks before we each retreated, back into our shells. We needed quiet space before facing a new crisis, before grief zoomed in again to sneer at us. We hurried with pounding hearts to baggage claim.

I saw a slack body being carried out our front door on a stretcher. Was the sheet covering his face? Had he taken pills again? Despair over not finding an apartment? Colleen? Why at times like this do I always, in the back of my head, envision Jim dead?

While Roger retrieved our bags from the carousel, I noticed his back was slumped, like an elderly man's.

"Why hello, Representative Greiling."

I turned. A smiling school superintendent was extending his hand. I had enjoyed working with him when I was in the House, back when I had known what I was doing. Now I didn't know how to help my son, much less keep him alive.

"It's great to see you," he exclaimed. "Thank you for your service."

I managed to smile and thank him for his before hurrying off.

Only when we reached the privacy of our car did we allow ourselves a modicum of subdued, abbreviated conversation. Roger would unload the car. I would crank up the phone. Our cheeks were dry, the well of tears held in reserve until we had done our duties.

When we got home, our cul-de-sac was deserted. As kids, Angela and Jim had played safely here, noisy group games with throngs of playmates. As we wheeled our suitcases up the walk, neither the lilies nor the daisies were out yet, but the rose bushes—so hardy and filled with bloom when we had left—were covered with Japanese beetles. The shiny green-and-orange bugs had devoured the blossoms and were eating lacey holes in the leaves.

In the house, Roger looked for bottles. That seemed to have become his job. He found empty bottles of Southern Comfort, cough syrup, aspirin, and various other pills in our wastebaskets. If we didn't regularly dispose of pills, there might have been enough.

The person who answered the phone at the ACT team office said she'd never met Jim and had no idea where he was. So much for their wraparound services. Jim's halfway house knew nothing either, other than that he had checked out to visit us. No, they hadn't known we were out of town. I used the name of the ambulance company to finally track our son down, at a different St. Paul hospital. Regions was full. I was thankful he'd signed a release.

"His aspirin level was twice as high as his body could accommodate," a nurse informed me. "It kept going up most of the night. Now he's on a heart monitor and getting blood tests."

I ached to take back my words saying I'd be relieved if my son died. My throat closed. I felt faint. This wasn't relief. It was eye-popping strangulation.

"Remember that psychiatrist who said Jim doesn't have the type of depression where he'll go to bed and become unresponsive?" I asked Roger, as we sat on the deck that night. I swatted an aggressive mosquito and took a large gulp of wine. "He said if Jim's depression isn't controlled, he'll smile, be high-functioning, and oh, by the way, quietly kill himself and everyone will wonder why."

"Jim's always been a hard case," Roger replied. "You get frustrated with providers, Mindy, but you know as well as I do that working with him isn't easy."

"I know." Jim is a fighter, stubborn like me. I was often proud of him for that, but, yes, it made him a hard case. "Even Jenny at Tasks— who knew him best—couldn't always tell when he was going down," I said. "But at least when he was there we had long periods when we didn't have to worry." I swatted another mosquito and wiped blood off my arm. "That was the best place for him, but they turned out to be like a private school. Great, until they kicked him out. I know they probably gave him more breaks than most clients, me being a legislator and all, but still . . ."

"Clients at Tasks have to be well enough to work," Roger said more charitably. "I was hoping, after all these months, Jim would be getting ready to work again."

"Me too. He does better when he's working." I turned up my glass and drank the last drops. "But every time he has a relapse, he loses ground—and so do we. Do you ever wonder what our lives might be like if we had just had Angela?"

"There's no point in going down that road," my practical husband replied, rattling the ice in his glass.

"I think we'd be enjoying our retirement years a hell of a lot more. You might retire if you didn't want to keep busy and not think. We could have more relaxing times, like our trip to Cooperstown." I drew up my knees on the lounger and hugged them. "But then we wouldn't have our Jim." We were quiet for a while, before I asked, "What would you say is the opposite of enabling?"

Roger smiled at me, close-lipped, but didn't answer.

"Are we just supposed to get out of the way and let Jim die?"

It was dark and the mosquitoes were getting worse, so I went in the house.

33
Treat to Street

After two days, the hospital was ready to release Jim.

Roger and I had talked to him on the phone, but we hadn't visited. Even though he had signed a release, Jim refused to see us. We didn't know if he was embarrassed or psychotic or both. Apparently he and Colleen had been using crack since we left. I doubled my coffee intake.

Jim's case manager said the community facility wouldn't take him back—the place that didn't notice he was using crack and had dished out the pass without checking to see if we were home. But the case manager couldn't place him anywhere else because that facility had his funding for the rest of the month.

"He's physically stable and doesn't meet psych ward criteria," a hospital nurse said. "We have no choice but to release him."

As anger swelled in my breast, I called Jim's ACT team case manager.

"I guess he'll have to be discharged to a shelter," she said. "I can't take him home with me."

"Please tell me you're kidding!" I said, wanting to smack her. I set down my cup of coffee and started pacing. "Jim nearly kills himself and two days later he's supposed to fend for himself on the streets with only a shelter mat at night?"

Roger and I knew if we let our son come home, the system would cross him off their urgent-housing list, but if we didn't, he'd go back to Colleen's. Both were unacceptable options. Not only was Colleen Jim's drug-use trigger, I now suspected she may have had a role in his taking the pills. I even began to wonder if she'd had a similar role when he had jumped off her balcony. I felt like the Greek mythological prophet

Cassandra. I knew what was going on, but no one in the mental health system would listen. Or was it paranoia? Was I going crazy too?

I called my friend Alice Hausman, who, after redistricting, was now my state representative. She had once been a hospital administrator at the very hospital that was now planning to discharge Jim, and she volunteered to call and advocate for him. Alice was careful to acknowledge privacy laws, saying she was just giving input. Still, the hospital floor manager was short with me afterward. "Our patients need privacy," she said in a clipped voice.

"Privacy?" I said, matching her tone. "What your hospital is doing is on my Facebook page, my dear." I made another pot of coffee after I hung up. Apparently she hadn't heard of the Alcoholics Anonymous adage "You're only as sick as your secrets."

Minnesota Public Radio saw my Facebook post, and reporter Cathy Wurzer interviewed me about Jim's suicide attempt and pending abrupt release with nowhere to go. I mentioned in that interview that this is an all-too-common practice in Minnesota, and it actually has a name: treat to street. I said I had called the state ombudswoman, who enlisted the Health and Human Services commissioner. NAMI–MN and county commissioners got involved, and I was invited to speak on a panel of parents before the Governor's Task Force on Mental Health. I could have taken up the entire hour. My adrenaline was pumping so furiously I felt as if I could lift a boulder and throw it through a hospital window. I am always keenly aware that as a white, middle-class, and very politically connected person I have huge privilege. I wish every person with mental illness, and those trying to help them, were listened to in the same way.

The next evening, I hosted a campaign party for Alice. After refreshments, the crowd gathered around her in our family room. She looked meaningfully at me. "Two things I've learned," she remarked, "are that nothing goes well for anyone unless they have housing and that people with mental illness do best when their affordable housing comes with on-site support services." Many guests endorsed her words, and the informed questions and comments from my friends from the League of Women Voters housing study reinforced the need for action.

"I'm grateful for so many good people," I told Roger after everyone left.

"I'm grateful you had a good day," he replied, smiling. "Maybe something will come of your work."

"I try to advocate for everyone," I said. "Not just Jim."

The county had suggested the week before that we pay privately to house him, but even if we made room in our budget to start down that road, it let them off the hook for everyone else. I also noted that the system usually kept Roger and me at arm's length, telling us not to hover or enable. They were handling things, thank you very much. But when they failed, they were all for dropping everything in our laps.

The next day, Jim was transferred to a hospital more than two hours away, where the state controlled admissions. Amazingly, despite long waiting lists for every other facility, half the beds were empty. A nurse grumbled to us that Jim didn't meet their admission criteria either. We visited him there only twice before he was discharged—exactly when his funding kicked back in.

Jim's next halfway house was near our home. When he first came for a visit, he bounded up the stairs to the kitchen where I was preparing vegetables. Fresh organic vegetables reminded me of my son. These had been sitting untouched in our crisper. Jim surprised me by pulling me into a tight embrace in the center of the room.

I'd forgotten how tall my son was until my face was smashed against his chest. I struggled to breathe. When I pulled away, I saw he was wearing jeans and a long-sleeved shirt, despite the hot August day. His hair was long, his teeth were yellow—not things the system seemed to think much about. He hadn't been to the dentist in over a year.

"I'm sorry for all my yelling at you." His voice quavered with emotion. "You're a great mom, possibly the best ever."

Jim's anguished face rekindled my love for this difficult son. "Thank you, Jim. I know you've been having a hard time."

This was Jim without illicit drugs. I wished this stability would last, but I knew his current facility operated under the harm-reduction model and allowed such drugs. Jim's last three places, where he had improved to this point, were chemical dependency programs that had demanded abstinence.

My sober, calm son helped me chop onions, parsnips, carrots, and rutabaga for a stir-fry. I scrubbed beets for the steamer. When the meal was ready, Jim called Roger from the basement.

"This is great, Mom," Jim said, savoring his first bite of beets. His yellow teeth were turning purple. Roger gamely tried some carrots and generously buttered two pieces of bread and added peanut butter. A few vegetables went a long way with him. After a couple more mouthfuls, Jim laid down his fork. "I don't see why you stick with me every time."

"We don't always feel like it," I replied. I put my hand on his arm. "But the real Jim is worth it."

"Like you are now," Roger added, smiling.

"The sober one who isn't high and obnoxious," I clarified. "You really need to stay clean, Jim." I knew our words meant little.

The real Jim smiled and picked up his fork.

After dinner, Roger left for a baseball game with friends, where I suspected he would eat a hot dog. Jim and I cleaned up, and then he asked me to join him on the deck so he could smoke. Sprawled on a chair, he rolled a cigarette. Crumbs of tobacco littered his shirt.

I hated the smoke but indulged my son, happy that he was doing well. I decided he was calm enough to ask a question that had weighed heavily on my mind.

"Did you discuss killing yourself with anyone before you took the pills?"

His eyes filled with tears.

"Did Colleen know?"

"Mom, she loves me," he said, looking anguished. "She wouldn't want me to die." He looked confused and uncertain.

"She knew."

"When I didn't die, she told me to call 911. You should be glad about that."

When it came to Colleen, I wasn't sure what I was glad about anymore. It haunted me to think that she could have prevented this attempt, or worse, that she might have egged him on.

A couple of days later when Jim visited, he asked, "Am I God?" My heart sank. He was high again. He became so agitated I had to take him back to the halfway house early. On the way home, my tears sprouted.

After I returned, I sought out Roger. He was reading his newspaper on the deck, a large mug of pop beside him. I sat down on the edge of a chair near him.

"Do they use this harm-reduction theory on alcoholics?" Roger asked, throwing his week-old newspaper on the deck. "One or two drinks are fine?"

Roger's anger felt more empowering than tears. "A nurse defended it," I replied. "She said clean addicts are the ones who die when they relapse. They lose their tolerance and when they start again it's too much of a shock for their system. But that applies mostly to opioids, not what Jim uses." I sat back farther in my chair and began twisting a lock of hair. I knew that people who used opioids could also take replacement drugs like methadone to stay sober. No such maintenance drugs exist for crack cocaine. "Harm reduction can include abstinence, though, and I wish they'd work on that with someone as sick as Jim."

"And his commitment forbids drugs," Roger rejoined. "These mental health people throw privacy laws in our face but ignore this one."

"Jim says clients can smoke meth and crack at this place, and the staff knows about it," I said. "And Colleen is there constantly, except when they give Jim passes to go to her apartment. They no doubt use there too."

Roger picked up his newspaper and resumed reading. I sighed and went back in the house. The call we were dreading came two weeks later, just after Labor Day. Jim had thrown a coffee mug. It had ricocheted off a windowsill at the halfway house and hit someone in the head. The police had taken Jim to the hospital. The facility didn't want him back.

34

Where Will Jim Live?

October 2016–January 2017

Roger and I squeezed around a table in the hospital's small, airless conference room. I nodded at the contingent seated across from us: two ACT team case managers, a hospital social worker, administrators, and Jim's psychiatrist, a distinguished-looking man accompanied by his secretary, who would take notes.

Jim came in wearing his street clothes, ready for discharge. St. Paul psych wards had been full after he threw the mug, so he had ended up in Minneapolis. Tomorrow was his thirty-ninth birthday. The best present would be an apartment.

This morning I had participated in another interview with an affordable-housing expert for the League of Women Voters study. The more I learned, the more pessimistic I became about Jim's chances. There was just not enough affordable housing, and landlords could be picky about taking rent vouchers.

The most important person at this meeting, Jim' housing specialist, was late. Her job was to help him find an apartment. They searched listings online, and if they found something she took him to apply. I stared out a small window into the ward where patients were lolling about—people like Jim who hadn't gotten to see the bright trees outside. Fall this year was spectacular, almost glorious, compared to what was happening in our lives. Nothing was certain. Jim's finding an apartment was our only ray of hope.

The mental health court had straightened out his record, and the hospital dropped its charges after I raised the roof and Jim spent the night in jail. And Jim's credit was now passable, thanks to Roger. Jim had a chance. For the umpteenth time I wondered how other families who had fewer advantages than we did managed.

The psychiatrist looked at his watch and began without the housing specialist. "Jim is stable and ready for discharge," he said. "What're the plans?" The case managers looked mutely at each other. They were saved by the arrival of the specialist, a pretty young woman with blond hair. When she walked in, Jim snapped to and gave her a small, expectant smile. She returned the smile but gave a slight shake of her head, dashing his hopes. He slumped.

I slumped.

"Jim's application fee was returned today from Renaissance Box, the place he's been waiting on so long," she said in a clear voice. Jim had been excited about this newly renovated apartment building since he had toured it with her weeks ago. The apartment manager had agreed to hold a place for him while his application was processed. "They promised his apartment to more than one person."

Jim's eyes filled with tears. This unnerved me more than any amount of yelling.

We were all so sick and tired of him being shuffled from pillar to post, nobody wanting him, even though everyone agreed he was now healthy enough to move to his own place. I knew the hospital couldn't keep him any longer. They said they would discharge him to the first available place, whether that was an apartment or another care facility. We talked a little more. Everyone was discouraged except the hospital personnel, who seemed relieved.

I thought back on the sad day when we had boxed up Jim's meager belongings at his condo and had them taken to storage. Had we made a mistake following the advice to sell his condo? Like his life, his stuff had no place to land.

I touched Roger's hand with sudden gratitude. At least we were in this together. I didn't expect him to acknowledge me, but he didn't pull his hand away. How did single parents do this?

Jim's discharge only took a few days. Sheriff's deputies arrived at the hospital and transported him to another secure chemical dependency facility, the first place that was available. It was in the same Anoka complex he had started out in twenty years before, the building with the tan tiles. Kyle Zwack had eventually been transferred to Grandma's old state hospital in Rochester after it had been repurposed to a prison, and Jim and I had walked past those tiles again when we visited him. Was the mental health system making any progress at all?

=

"They're strict," I said to Roger on the way to visit Jim. He'd been there two days. We were glad that if Jim had to be confined again, it was in a place where he couldn't use drugs. His brain would have a chance of healing. But we knew he wouldn't be allowed to come home for the holidays. The policy seemed reasonable for most people, but not for Jim, who was just cooling his heels in a holding pattern because he didn't have an apartment.

"That's good they're strict isn't it?" Roger asked.

"Yes, except when the staff wouldn't let Jim's housing specialist take him out to look at apartments," I said. "He can't leave until he has one."

"How's he supposed to get one if they won't let him look?" He changed the radio.

"At least Angela's coming for Christmas," I said. She had recently left her spot as a White House reporter to become an editor at Politico. She and her family could visit Jim even if he couldn't come home. No matter how far apart our children grew, I was thankful Angela was kind to her brother and usually patient with him.

Bare concrete and a chain-link fence surrounded the locked entrance to Jim's building. We buzzed to gain entry. Inside, Jim sat silently at a long table in the visiting room, head down. Per protocol, we visitors sat on the opposite side of the table. Roger and I were prohibited from touching our son. This was more prison-like than Minnesota's highest-security prison, where Jim and I had visited Kyle.

Quiet tears leaked down Jim's cheeks.

Roger and I greeted him. I worked hard to hold back my own tears. We tried to say something encouraging, but the words died in our throats. I couldn't think of any conversation worth starting. Roger mostly sat quietly, and Jim didn't say a word the entire visit.

We left early, something we rarely did.

Jim was happier during subsequent visits. I had straightened out the staff about the housing specialist who had been turned away, but he was still very depressed. He said the nurse had upped his antidepressant. Angela, Matt, and Taylor visited him the day after Christmas. With a kid along, they were allowed to meet in a private room, where everyone could sit casually rather than across an institutional table.

"Jim's never missed Christmas," I said mournfully to Roger after we took down the tree our son never saw. "Think of all his sadness, just because he can't find a place that will take his apartment voucher."

"And all the money being spent needlessly on him because of it," Roger added.

When his allotted three months at Anoka were up at the end of January, Jim, like a hot potato, was batted to "community care"—yet another halfway house.

35
Hope in the Shadows

March 2017

Jim's time was nearly up at the next program, and he still didn't have an apartment. He and a new housing specialist were working harder looking at options. I rushed to the phone when it rang. Jim was usually deep in despair lately, but each time he called I held my breath with fresh hope. It was the end of March, and the sun's slant was kinder.

His voice was filled with wonder. "I've been accepted."

I asked my mind to repeat the sentence. The news settled in drops on my skin. After so many disappointments, I was wary of letting it sink in.

Jim waited silently on his end of the line. He seemed to be having the same reaction. He'd been in ten treatment facilities over the preceding nineteen months: hospitals, chemical dependency lockup centers, short-term halfway houses that the mental health system calls "community care." These were months we never wanted to repeat. I thought of my son sitting at our dining room table calling number after number, each place saying no. I achingly recalled his red-rimmed eyes at the hospital meeting, his tears at Anoka.

"How do you feel?"

"I guess I'm thrilled," he responded slowly. "I'm sure I'll wake up tomorrow feeling even better, but right now I'm just taking it all in. I haven't had time to really process it. It doesn't feel real."

"Not for me either."

"My housing specialist was surprised. He kept saying, 'really?'" Jim chuckled. "Will you go with me to sign my lease, Mom?"

"Of course. We could go to lunch afterward to celebrate." My mind soared.

On the magical day, we toured the beautiful building with a

friendly staff woman. The hallway carpet was new. The office was flooded with natural light and included a communal coffee pot that Jim eyed happily. There were computer and laundry rooms. The location couldn't have been more perfect for Jim, two blocks from a park abutting the Mississippi River.

When the staff woman unlocked the door to Jim's apartment, he and I exchanged joyful looks. The bedroom, modern kitchen, and living room all had high, sun-filled windows and the carpet was pristine, not a cigarette burn in sight. After he penned his name on the lease, he looked soberly at the staff woman. "Since this is a no-smoking building," he asked, "are people allowed to smudge?"

She looked at him quizzically for a moment and then assured him, "Of course."

I also wondered why he was asking about smudging, a spiritual ceremony that most Minnesotans only knew of because of our Native American population. Smudging involves the burning of herbs for cleansing. I didn't give it another thought, however, when the woman gave Jim his key. The reality of my son's being happy and having his own apartment was filtering through my parched body, like the sun had in Mexico.

Maybe now we'd all have peace.

We walked to a trendy café beside the fast-moving river for lunch. The place was bustling, and the waiter sensed our mood.

"A birthday?" he asked.

"I got my own place," Jim bubbled.

I savored the moment and didn't want it to end.

As we left the restaurant, a young man wearing raggedy, dirty clothes loped by. I caught a whiff of strong body odor.

"He looks like you sixteen years ago, Jim," I remarked, nodding at the young man. "I bet you could help him, if you were his peer specialist."

"I guess so." He smiled. "I feel sorry for him. He has so much to learn."

Jim had learned lots over the past eighteen years. One of the most important things was that he acknowledged he needed antipsychotics to be sane. Just to be sure he remembered, he received his main drug through a monthly shot. He was in charge of managing his meds with his psychiatrist. I didn't have to try to keep up any more. I wished he had learned more lessons about his chemical dependency.

We gazed after the young man. Half a block past us, he tossed his backpack down on the sidewalk and flopped beside it, staring into space. Students streamed past him, not looking. Jim and I stopped looking too.

I wondered if the young man's parents knew what had become of their son. He looked nice beneath the grim vacancy. Did they suspect mental illness? Were they in denial as Roger and I had been? Had they tried to get him help but been unable to access the system?

I would have liked to call them. I would have liked to alert a mental health professional and be able to know something would be done. Maybe I should have tried. If the young man passed out on the sidewalk, people might leap into action, but would the mental health system say he was living his choice? Such a long way to go.

When Jim came over the next evening, he called Angela. From the next room, I heard a happy, animated conversation, my children talking like old times. Near the end, I heard Jim say, "I just hope this place doesn't have ghosts, like my last two places."

I stopped reading and perked up my ears. I wondered what Angela was saying.

"I wasn't the only one who saw them," Jim said. "All three of us saw the ghosts. One of my roommates was Native American. He smudged and it helped."

Was Angela smiling? I was. I could see three young men, comrades, earnestly talking about seeing the same ghosts.

=

I arrived early to Jim's discharge meeting. I was wearing a silver ring I had purchased in Mexico. I wouldn't need my power ring today. Maybe I was being foolishly hopeful.

"Your parents love you to a fault," Mark, the program director, said to Jim as he invited us to sit. *Was he saying we enabled Jim?* I had talked with this man over the phone but had never met him face to face. I'd only been in this building once before.

My son settled into his chair, smiling widely at the slight criticism of us. "They won't see Colleen," he said. "She really wants to see them."

"After so many problems involving her, Jim's dad and I had to take a break," I told Mark. "For our own well-being."

"They're . . ." Jim started. His teeth were heavily stained with nicotine.

"Jim, did you hear that?" Mark interrupted. "Your parents need to take care of themselves. Remember how we discussed everyone needs to do that?"

Jim shrugged. He was circling his thumbs rapidly in his folded hands. His brown hair hung shaggily around his worn face, and he badly needed a shave. Jim would turn forty on his next birthday.

Hard life, boiled in.

"You've been a success here," the director said, looking kindly at Jim. "Living alone will be hard, after nineteen months of being surrounded by people." I stared at Mark's pale hands; one wrapped tightly over the other, making his knuckles white.

"I know."

Mark cleared his throat. "Don't wait too long to go back to work after you get settled."

Jim just smiled slightly, making me worry he and Colleen had other plans.

"If you finish your last two classes at Metro State and do the internship, so you could graduate—it'd be good for your soul."

Jim leaned forward excitedly. "Can I do the internship here, as a peer specialist?"

My heart leapt. Jim hadn't given up on that dream.

"If you're doing well. Call me in July," Mark replied, picking up his pen and turning it around. "Even if you don't do well, still keep in touch. We can move the date out."

I was impressed. This wise man knew the score.

"Will I be paid?"

"No."

Jim looked disappointed but hastily recovered. "I'd like to do it anyway," he said enthusiastically, rapidly turning Mark's pencil holder back and forth. "And then I'd like to be hired."

Mark smiled—no promises, but hope.

After the meeting, Jim and I went for coffee. We split a cinnamon roll and sat at a window table. Jim planned to get a haircut and visit the dentist after he was free. He blew on his coffee to cool it, took a long drink, then launched into his latest philosophical thoughts. "It's hard to tell what's really real." He sipped carefully. "And what we're doing here on this planet. You know?"

I wasn't in the mood today. "There are whole books and philosophies trying to figure that out," I said, feeling more like following up about his plans from the meeting. Make them the reality for him now.

But he shook his head at me, then drained his cup in three swallows. "I guess we're here to suffer." He pushed himself to his feet and went to the counter for a refill. He was almost as scruffy today as the young man we had seen the day Jim had signed his lease, but from this distance, who would know that other life inside his head?

When he returned, he was quiet. I took a bite of my roll and licked my fingers. I was surprised when he said, "Colleen isn't my soul mate anymore. In my delusion."

"Your soul mates seem to switch. First Laurie, then Jenny, and after her Colleen."

"And Hestia." He grinned.

"Hestia?"

"When I caused the accident, my soul mate was Hestia."

"Where'd she come from?"

"Percy Jackson books. She was the last Olympian goddess."

"Remember when we walked around Lake Calhoun that day and you told me 1 percent of you believed your delusion was true?" That had been twelve years past.

He nodded.

"How much of you thinks it's true now?"

"Ten percent."

I swirled my coffee in my cup. No wonder he was thinking of smudging. I guessed I should be glad he'd only slid that much, after all his relapses and drug use.

"I wish I had a car."

Jim liked to get off the topic of mental illness. He sometimes said he got tired of me talking about his illness. Roger was more apt to talk about other things, like sports. I knew I should try harder to do that, but my worry forced me to check in.

"Maybe you will someday, if you stay sober. If you find a real job and save money, we could discuss also using some of your trust money." We had set up a trust for Jim so he could receive a small inheritance from my mother. I finished my roll and wadded up my trash, thinking of Jim's expired license, which he had finally gotten back after mental health court but had failed to renew during the previous months of confinement.

He looked at me out of the corners of his eyes. "It hurts me when you won't love Colleen. Don't you love Matt?"

"Matt's a good husband and father for Angela and Taylor."

"Colleen is my Matt."

"Matt's not doing illegal drugs and getting Angela in trouble."

"I'm the one getting Colleen in trouble."

"Dad and I don't see it that way. You never did those things before her."

A loud group of students came in the door and sat at a table near ours. I turned and looked at them for a second as they laughed and jostled each other. I wished Jim were one of them. Suddenly, I was bitter about all he'd missed in his life, all that had gone wrong. "You thought writing bad checks was funny," I said before I could stop myself. "Colleen just laughed when we confronted you two."

He looked down, quiet now. "She's sick too, you know."

"I know," I said with a sigh. I thought of Jim's uncertain future, tried to find an anchor point that didn't include his addicted girlfriend.

"You'd be a great peer specialist, Jim," I said, trying to work his future back into the discussion. "You loved the teachers and passed your training with flying colors."

"Yeah."

"What worries Dad and me about Colleen," I said carefully, "is she doesn't have enough to do besides use drugs. She influences you not to do anything else either."

"It's not the best," Jim admitted. "I try to get her to do things, but she never does."

I was surprised he agreed with me. Maybe this was a start, but I feared it wouldn't be.

We got up, found our coats, and went out into the cold air. I dropped Jim back at the halfway house and headed home to my other life, the sweet cinnamon roll a weight in my stomach.

That night, Roger and I discussed Colleen again. "It's been a year since we've seen her, and she is a big part of his life," I said.

We looked at each other. "Maybe we should see her tomorrow," Roger suggested. Tomorrow was the big day when we would help Jim move into his new apartment. "She could help."

36
Home, for Now

Jim had mapped out exactly where he wanted each piece of furniture to go. When three strong young men arrived from the storage unit in their truck, he confidently directed them. He had them walk his cedar chest in and out of the bedroom, until they situated it abutting the wall, exactly where he wanted it. His nightstand was an old Greiling family piece, beautifully carved. Roger's grandmother's Carriage House maple desk got a central spot in his sunny living room. Our old couch and chairs had held up well, and their blue cloth reflected nicely off the stained-glass lamps on Jim's end tables. His furniture—which represented so much family history and love—had reclaimed its place in his life.

After bringing in the furniture, the movers smoothly stacked boxes in the kitchen and bedroom, boxes Roger and I had marked when we had packed up Jim's condo. Today was a happier occasion. We were all buoyed by elated energy. The whole procedure took only a couple of hours before the young movers scurried off for their Friday nights.

Suddenly Jim's apartment was quiet. The afternoon sun was almost hot for late March, making us sleepy. We sank onto the living room furniture.

"Great job arranging," I said. "Want any help unpacking?"

"No, thanks. I need to know where everything is." His phone pinged, as it had been doing all day, making me wonder each time what was up with his girlfriend.

"Is Colleen coming over?"

"Yes," he hemmed, looking down at his phone. "But she's not ready to see Dad and you." He looked pained. "She wants to come over, but not until you leave."

Roger and I sat on that statement, without commenting. Truthfully, I was relieved. I hadn't unpacked my anger about her negative influence on Jim, and I wasn't sure about her future influence either. After all, tomorrow was April Fool's Day.

But I also knew it couldn't be easy for Jim: having his biggest supporters engaged in a cold war when he had been expecting cooperation.

"Tell her we'll try again when she's ready," I said to my son before I hugged him. Roger shook his hand warmly.

"Thanks for everything," Jim called after us, as we walked to the elevator. I wondered if Grandma Teddy could have succeeded in that apartment if she'd had help like Jim was supposed to be getting here.

For the first time, he was receiving a Community Access for Disability Inclusion (CADI) waiver instead of an ACT team. It could provide things like frozen meals, housekeeping help, and a nurse who would come to his apartment each month to give him his shot of Haldol. Hopefully, his civil commitment would also give him some protection before it expired in August. His life could change, I reminded myself.

We were barely home when Jim and Stephanie DeBenedet called on the spur of the moment, inviting us for a Lenten Friday-night fish fry. We laughed that the restaurant they were going to was just a few blocks from Jim's apartment, where we'd just been. We hopped in our car and headed back to meet them. Roger and I relaxed over the meal, describing Jim's apartment and how well the move had gone. "Been a long haul," I said. "Hopefully now we can just enjoy our son for a while."

It was always a relief to be able to talk about Jim without abbreviating our reports too much so as not to be boring. I sometimes felt lonely when we were with people who no longer brought him up. Luckily, Roger and I had many friends who did and also had some new ones with whom we had mental illness in common.

=

Over the next week, Colleen helped Jim hang his pictures. "We put my Alaska picture at the foot of my bed," he said when he called, "where I can see it every morning. I hope one day I'll return to that innocent time. In this life or the next."

I smiled and silently agreed.

Roger and I spent a quiet week together waiting for the phone to ring, waiting for the next unexpected disaster. None came. I found myself some evenings just staring at the light leaving the sky, thinking about how hard I'd tried to fix the mental health system through my work as a legislator and parent. And how hard we'd tried to fix Jim.

Roger and I could love. We could hope. We could advise. Whether that would be enough, I didn't know. We couldn't do everything, and we were getting older. I knew we needed to step back and let the system try to help Jim stand on his own. The only time that had worked, however, had been when he was at Tasks Unlimited and on clozapine. No other program had come close to doing what Tasks had done, and no other antipsychotic medicine prevented Jim from being vulnerable to illicit drugs or to people who took advantage of him. I hoped that the new mental health staff could help Jim succeed, that they would be more constant than the revolving-door care he had so recently been getting, so they could really get to know him. The real Jim.

Life with a child—or parent or sibling or anyone—with serious mental illness is a life of unpredictability. It had been nineteen years since Jim was diagnosed, since we first entered the world of mental illness—nineteen years of advocating, of fighting the slow-moving health care system, of trying every way possible to find help for my son and others like him.

Maybe the system would help. Maybe things would change. In my heart, however, I knew the truth: Roger and I would always have to stand ready to help Jim when things got bad—when the system threw up its hands, as it had so many times—until we handed off to Angela or died.

When I went outside to take a walk, I noticed my rose bushes outside the front door. Soon they'd need trimming back, before they budded. Spring was a time of possibilities, of hope. We needed that more than ever.

I smiled at the roses as I passed. They reminded me of Jim's life. After all our tending, I hoped he could blossom like the roses and we could enjoy that time together for a long while.

Before the next round of Japanese beetles showed up.

Epilogue

December 2019

I try to resist comparing Jim with my grandmother, but her story proves that the silence and secrecy around mental health care doesn't serve anyone well. When Jim got sick, I resolved to be more open, to avoid feeling ashamed of his illness. It allowed me to advocate for my son and for a better mental health system, something I could never do for Grandma Teddy.

I've wondered many times how her story would have unfolded had she been treated by today's mental health system. Perhaps she wouldn't have lost twenty-three years of her life to commitment, standard treatment for millions at the time. She could have been treated and then returned home, to thrive and to remain in our lives. Unlike today's, the system then could have ensured my grandmother took regular medication and communicated with her family so we could have supported her.

Grandma Teddy never stopped longing to get back home. At first when she would ask about her house, my father lied and said it hadn't been sold. But one day he accidentally drove past it with Grandma in the car.

"Whose clothes are those hanging on my lines?" Grandma demanded.

"The renters," my father said quickly.

"I know better. You've sold my house, Robert. You don't want me to ever come home."

From the back seat, my sister Joan and I saw our father's neck flame red. We rode in silence for the rest of the drive.

A couple of years later, Grandma managed to get home one last time. She walked off the state hospital grounds and caught the bus to our neighborhood. She called from her former next-door neighbor's house, across the street from our home. The neighbor was a conversational woman about Grandma's age who never lost her German accent. Only Joan and I were home.

"Is your dad there?" Grandma asked.

I told her when he would be home from work.

"Okeydokey," she said, as she always did. Joan and I called our mother at work, something we never did, to tell her that Grandma was across the street.

We never saw the sheriff's deputy take our grandmother back to the state hospital, just as we never saw her taken away in the first place.

She just disappeared.

=

I wish I could conclude Jim's story by saying that he is better off than Grandma Teddy ever was. He's had many opportunities that she didn't have. Roger and I have both tried so hard to help him recoup some of the losses in his life. I would like to be able to say that having an apartment solved all Jim's problems, that once and for all he resisted the siren luring him to use drugs with Colleen. I would like to say he found meaningful work as a peer specialist, that he finished his last couple of college requirements and finally graduated. I would like to say that Roger, Angela, and I rest easy about him.

I would like to say those Japanese beetles never showed up.

I can't say any of that.

While Roger and I were in Florida in January 2018, Jim and Colleen burglarized our home for drug money. Despite all we had been through, we were stunned by this new level of addiction. I could no longer protest to Roger, as I had during our brief time in Al-Anon, that Jim would never do such things. I could no longer say he wasn't a true addict.

We pressed charges. We wanted them both to have the opportunity to get help in mental health court. Colleen was offered that option while she was still in jail, but Jim was denied it because he lived in another county. The mental health court in his home county rejected him too. Instead, our son was sent to felony court. Jim's public defender argued that most of her clients should be in mental health or drug court. I was as angry as I've ever been at the mental health system. But this time, my appeals failed. Knowing our very ill son was heading to felony court shattered our souls.

It's a situation that has become all too common, and not just in Minnesota. Instead of providing needed interventions to people with serious mental illness, we let them become so sick that many of them commit crimes, usually lower-level offenses than Jim's and Colleen's burglary. One in two Americans with serious mental illness will be arrested at some point in their lives. According to NAMI, 26 percent of state prison inmates in the United States have a recent history of a mental health condition. The percentage is higher in jails.

The criminal justice system has become our de facto mental health system. Even if inmates were to receive mental health care in jails and prisons, those are anything but therapeutic places for sick and vulnerable people. The past abuses of the state hospital system are too often replicated there. Many attribute the increase in the number of incarcerated people with mental illness to the closing of state hospitals. But while the neglect of community mental health care has certainly contributed, the change is more attributable to other factors—for example, the war on drugs and mandatory sentencing instead of diversion courts. As a former politician, I can attest that it is far easier to increase judiciary budgets than those for health and human services. Even so, only a lucky few make it into mental health court as Colleen did.

Months after the burglary—after Colleen had benefited from having mental health and court staff, treatment, and numerous court check-ins, had performed community service, and had even participated in a summer mental health court picnic—Jim was finally assigned a probation officer. His felony charge had been reduced to a gross misdemeanor. Before he had the chance to meet his probation officer, he intentionally overdosed at Colleen's, trying to end what he termed his "miserable life."

After the new losses for Jim and our family, my energy was in short supply. My mind was blown to pieces and I tired easily. I fell asleep at a party, definitely a first. Most days I was numb about Jim, and when I allowed myself to think too much, tears came. At Regions Hospital, while Jim was unconscious in intensive care, a diligent social worker saw that he had an advance directive and notified us. My meeting with the hospital people had borne fruit.

=

Another positive undertaking, one that has become an important part of my story, was also bearing fruit. Five mothers and I who share the commonality of having sons with schizophrenia as well as substance-abuse issues started meeting regularly a couple of years ago. We find comfort in being together and talking. Those five moms have become my Al-Anon group. We grieve for the adult sons we might have had and acknowledge that we've suffered a tremendous loss. We also know we're the best damn mothers we can be. We applaud each other when we advocate for our children, and we celebrate when they have successes. In addition to me, a former lawmaker, our group includes two social workers (one is also a former psych nurse) and a physician. We bring wide connections and knowledge to our admittedly privileged group. Yet still, like anyone else, we often struggle to know what to do next.

More groups like ours are needed, including multicultural ones. Ethnically and culturally diverse peer groups could help address the stark reality that the mental health system has too few providers of color or services tailored to their experience. There is a deep distrust of the mental health system among African Americans in Minnesota and elsewhere. When I was in the legislature, I carried a bill to create a loan-forgiveness program for culturally specific providers, a program that could still use more funding. At a minimum, cultural competence training should be a priority for everyone.

After Jim's suicide attempt, I couldn't wait until the next Six Moms meeting at a small restaurant in St. Paul. Everyone ordered a drink, and we talked in a leisurely way. As we relished sipping our drinks, I wondered how we could expect total abstinence from our sons. I pulled my chair closer to the table. The dining room was dimly lit. "Jim was naked and comatose when the ambulance came," I said. I fixated on his nakedness. It had become a symbol for me of his vulnerability and suffering. Tears started rolling down my cheeks and my throat constricted, stopping my words. I had never done this at a meeting before. I wanted to stop. I couldn't.

The mother sitting next to me put her hand on my shoulder. "Don't think about his nakedness," she advised gently. I continued to cry softly. I have never sought mental health treatment but am certain that most people who deal with a family member's serious mental illness have some form of post-traumatic stress disorder. This latest episode seemed to be getting to me more than the rest. It was as if my wounds were so full of scars that they could no longer completely heal over between crises.

=

Some time later, when I visited Jim in the hospital, he appeared better. Roger and I were elated when he eventually resumed a low dose of clozapine, the drug that had once allowed him to do so well. A doctor had asked him if he had ever excelled on a different medication. Jim suggested clozapine. According to NAMI, clozapine is the only antipsychotic that reduces the risk of suicide in people with schizophrenia, and it may even reduce their substance use. The doctor acknowledged, however, that this drug is still dangerous for people who, like Jim, have previously developed agranulocytosis. He would be even more susceptible to becoming allergic to it, and if that happened, the reaction would be swift and worse than before.

Given his recent history, it was worth the risk.

On a cool fall day, after he had a good start on clozapine, Jim was sent to the same chemical dependency facility where he had started nineteen years before—one more turn of the mental health system's revolving door. He nixed Roger's and my participation in family programs. I wondered if the staff had encouraged him to include us, but I doubted they had. Despite research showing that people with serious mental illness do better when their families are involved, few professionals put much effort toward facilitating their participation. Some even discourage it, especially with patients Jim's age.

When Jim moved back to his apartment, it had a lot less furniture. The family pieces—the beautiful maple desk that had belonged to Roger's grandmother, the lovely carved nightstand, Jim's lamps and end tables—had been sold for drug money.

Jim broke up with Colleen when he was in treatment, after a great counselor helped him see that their relationship was as addictive as the crack they used, but after he was released they got back together.

They spent most of their time together until the first week in November 2019, when they broke up again. This time Jim says it's forever.

I hope the clozapine will fortify him to better deal with those who exploit his vulnerability.

With help from John Choi's treatment-oriented county attorney's office and from like-minded judge Judith Tilsen, Jim's court order includes having to finish college or work up to full-time. The specter of what his life had wrought made him more inspired and serious for a time, until his probation officer told him she didn't plan to enforce the order. Currently, he's working a few hours at NAMI each week.

=

In time, Roger and I summoned the energy to follow the advice of Jim's mental health workers and seek guardianship for our son. They said having someone be legally responsible would ensure that he accepted help if he needed it. Though it would severely curb his independence, guardianship could better protect Jim from exploitation, something the system's current client-centered philosophy can't do. I strongly believe the system rightly strives for independence and free choice for people with mental illness. I wouldn't want to see us go back to the days of my grandmother. I also believe it is carried too far for seriously ill people like Jim when they aren't making safe choices. At such times, mental health workers should be allowed to be more assertive with clients. Instead, they are trained to live in fear of being sued for not following the laws governing privacy and choice. Even after three recent suicide attempts, Jim's workers prioritized his right to choose not to accept help even when NAMI said no one has ever been sued for such things.

A better option than guardianship would be for the system to recognize that people like Jim need more help than they currently receive. I support the effort to allow judges to order the few most seriously ill people to comply with assisted outpatient treatment if they have a history of multiple arrests, incarceration, or hospitalization. Our family certainly would have preferred the treatment Jim now receives to have been ordered by a judge in a mental health court rather than by one in a felony court.

The criminalization of mental illness is only one area where we need to improve. Our country has a fragmented, sadly deficient mental health system. We have known for some time what is needed to fix it, but the collective will to build and fund a better system is missing. We desperately need increased and stable funding to build a continuum of care so that people with mental illness can gain access to what they need, when they need it. I'm proud to have helped make Minnesota's one of the best mental health systems in the country, but the bar is still very low. We are no different from the rest of the country in being desperately short of mental health professionals and workers, especially those of color. We need more crisis care in hospitals, more community care and support, less discrimination, and more opportunities in housing and employment. While working at Tasks Unlimited, Jim was the healthiest he'd ever been since his illness started. I maintain that it's a lot more stressful to see the world passing you by than to work. When people like Jim have few productive things to do, they can be more prone to using illegal drugs and relapsing. I also strongly support the new national push to reclassify schizophrenia as a brain disease instead of a mental illness. Brain diseases, such as Alzheimer's and Parkinson's, receive significantly more research dollars. NAMI, the Schizophrenia and Related Disorders Alliance of America, health officials, scientists, and doctors all say this reclassification would help find better treatments by producing more research.

Important progress has been made since Jim became ill. In the past twenty years, the public has become more open to talking about mental illness. Much more is being done in the area of early intervention, and schools are beginning to play an important role in teaching about mental illness, recognizing students who are showing early signs and making referrals. But we still need many more people to share their stories—stories that will stick in their elected officials' heads. It is harder to work as a civilian than it was to act in the political ring. Now that I am no longer a legislator, when I want to change something I have to rouse other horses instead of galloping ahead myself. But it can be done. Currently I'm working with my state legislators, judges, and NAMI to provide more opportunities for people to benefit from mental health courts. In the past few years, I've cochaired two League of Women Voters study committees: one on affordable housing and another that called for better training of police officers who deal with mental health crises. We League members shared our recommendations with elected officials, producing positive results in both areas. Recently I reviewed NAMI–MN's legislative proposal to improve the civil commitment process. While I wish it went a bit further to help those who need earlier help, it does propose more assertive intervention for people who are in danger of relapse.

=

Now that the court requires Jim to stay sober, he and the rest of our family are beginning to heal. Because he is doing better, the guardianship proceedings were canceled and replaced by an updated health care directive and power of attorney, contingent on his not relapsing. Mental illness has changed our lives profoundly, but if Jim remains stable and sober, he could give our family much joy again.

In addition to the five moms who help me cope, I have benefited from many understanding friends and family. Roger and I talk with Angela frequently, perhaps more than we would have if she hadn't early gotten in the habit of diligently checking in about her brother. She's mentoring some friends with their college-aged daughter who is new to mental illness; her husband Matt has done the same with a friend at work. Roger and I mentor people in need as well.

Jim's continuing journey includes mentoring too. He's an old hand in treatment groups, where therapists say that when he deigns to talk, other participants look to him. In those settings and elsewhere, he's proud of his sister and brags about her accomplishments. I hold out hope that this time he will do better. Once again the chasm between our children could shrink. Our family's struggle has been dreadful, but I imagine his is even harder.

Granddaughter Taylor, now fifteen and strong in her own right, bears the brunt of everyone's collective advice. Given her genetics, we admonish her not to use drugs. If she were to develop a serious mental illness, we don't want it to be hastened along as Jim's was by his early drug use. Roger finds his emotional outlet by continuing to work part-time, volunteering at church, and going to sporting events with friends.

I know now that our family isn't like Sisyphus, who knew all along there was no hope he would ever succeed in pushing that boulder over the crest of the mountain. We have a shot.

At the same time, the loss we have all felt has been ambiguous, a loss that, to paraphrase the words of Pauline Boss, occurs without closure or understanding. Ambiguous loss is the most difficult loss that people face. It is relentless, indeterminate, and exhausting. We obviously have felt that way about Jim. When he's doing well, we get our hopes up until he sinks into another relapse, when we will again have to pick up the sword and fight for his life. Boss advises that confronting a bad situation as a temporary challenge and trying harder, unfazed by defeat, is healthy. The secret to coping is to avoid helplessness. No one can accuse us of that. I hope our story can inspire others to continue to fight too. As Boss reminds me, "There is no absurdity in perseverance." I take great comfort in her wise words.

I know that I can't fix Jim. I can't go inside his head and flip a magic switch. But I can try to make the mental health system work for him, and for everyone else, more than it ever has. It's the way I cope best. Loss, especially this ambiguous one, has been my constant companion throughout this journey with mental illness. It began with my grandmother, and it continues every day with Jim as we continue to try to navigate our lives together. Ambiguity will cease for our family only if there's a miraculous drug breakthrough or when Jim's story ends. Most days I am at peace knowing I am doing all that I can. Our family is resilient. We persevere. That alone keeps us fighting on.

Resources

My goal in writing this book was to model what I encourage everyone to do: tell our stories. Our collective voices are the best way to shake up the mental health system. It helps to be informed. Here are a few resources you may find helpful.

American Psychiatric Association www.psych.org

Brain & Behavior Research Foundation www.bbrfoundation.org

Mental Health America (MHA; formerly Mental Health Association) www.mhanational.org

Mental Health Minnesota www.mentalhealthmn.org

Minnesota Psychiatric Society www.mnpsychsoc.org

National Alliance on Mental Illness (NAMI; formerly National Alliance for the Mentally Ill) www.nami.org

National Alliance on Mental Illness Minnesota (NAMI–MN) www.namimn.org

National Institute of Mental Health (NIMH) www.nimh.nih.gov

Treatment Advocacy Center www.treatmentadvocacycenter.org

A companion study guide for this book is available at z.umn.edu/mg_guide.

Mindy Greiling served in the Minnesota House of Representatives for twenty years. She was called "the lioness of education at the Capitol" and led the charge to improve the state's mental health system, initiating the nation's first state mental health caucus. She served on the state and national boards of the National Alliance on Mental Illness and is on the University of Minnesota Psychiatry Community Advisory Council. She has received more than eighty awards for her legislative and advocacy work.